Korea
ON THE BRINK
From the "12/12 Incident" to the Kwangju Uprising, 1979–1980

by John A. Wickham

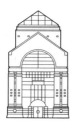

NATIONAL DEFENSE UNIVERSITY PRESS
WASHINGTON, D.C.
1999

The Institute for National Strategic Studies (INSS) is a major component of the National Defense University (NDU), which operates under the supervision of the President of NDU. It conducts strategic studies for the Secretary of Defense, Chairman of the Joint Chiefs of Staff, and unified commanders in chief; supports national strategic components of NDU academic programs; and provides outreach to other governmental agencies and the broader national security community.

The Publication Directorate of INSS publishes books, monographs, reports, and occasional papers on national security strategy, defense policy, and national military strategy through NDU Press that reflects the output of NDU research and academic programs. In addition, it produces the INSS *Strategic Assessment* and other work approved by the President of NDU, as well as *Joint Force Quarterly*, a professional military journal published for the Chairman.

Library of Congress Cataloging-in-Publication Data
Wickham, John Adams, 1928–
    Korea on the Brink: From the "12/12 Incident" to the Kwangju Uprising, 1979–1980 / John A. Wickham, Jr.
    p.cm.
    ISBN 1–57906–023–4
    1. Korea (South)—Politics and Government–1960–1988. 2. United States—Foreign Relations—Korea (South) 3. Korea (South)—Foreign Relations—United States. 4. United States—Foreign Relations–1977–1981. 5. Wickham, John Adams, 1928– I. Title.
DS922.35 .W53 1999
951.9504'3—dc21

                              99–16996
                                  CIP

First Printing, December 1999

NDU Press publications are sold by the U.S. Government Printing Office. For ordering information, call (202) 512–1800 or write to the Superintendent of Documents, U.S. Government Printing Office, Washington, D.C. 20402. For GPO publications on-line access their web site at: http://www.access.gpo.gov/su_docs/sale.html.

For current publications of the Institute for National Strategic Studies, consult the National Defense University web site at: http://www.ndu.edu.

Korea
ON THE BRINK

Contents

This book is dedicated to the memory of

James H. Hausman

Awarded a battlefield commission during World War II, the late Lieutenant Colonel James H. Hausman, USA (Ret.), served in Europe until he was reassigned as one of the first members of the Korean Military Advisory Group (KMAG) in 1946. Long before the Army established the foreign area specialist program, Jim dedicated himself to becoming an expert on Korean affairs. He was the architect of the Republic of Korea army and over the years nurtured enduring friendships and trust with generations of South Korean officers, many of whom rose to senior leadership positions within the armed forces as well as in government and industry. During the Korean War he fought alongside the Korean forces that he had helped to create. Jim later retired to accept an appointment as special assistant for policy and intelligence to the Commander in Chief, United Nations Forces, and ROK–U.S. Combined Forces. His service in Korea spanned more than forty years, longer than any other U.S. military official. Senior American and Korean leaders—including virtually every CINC and ambassador and several South Korean presidents—revered Jim Hausman as a distinguished soldier and civil servant, as well as a valued adviser who dedicated his life to strengthening the bonds of friendship and security between the United States and Korea.

Illustrations

Foreword

by Richard Holbrooke

John Wickham is my friend, the sort of friend with whom an unbreakable bond is forged in a period of extreme testing, when one's true measure is taken. General Colin Powell, who in his autobiography twice refers to General Wickham as "my mentor," describes John as every inch a soldier. But John also brought other great skills to his career as a soldier. *Korea on the Brink* will serve as a valuable politico-military case study for students attending our war colleges, as well as an important resource for serious scholars pursuing research on a particularly eventful period in recent Korean history.

In the fall of 1979, the assassination of South Korea's President Park Chung-hee, and the events that followed, created a difficult dilemma for America. Our overriding policy objective, of course, was to maintain peace and stability on the Korean peninsula, as we had been doing ever since the 1953 armistice. Combined forces of the U.S. and Republic of Korea (ROK) continued to face a hostile and dangerous North Korea. Moreover, our intelligence concluded in 1979 that the North's military forces appeared to be far stronger than previously estimated. These forces, deployed in forward positions along the demilitarized zone (DMZ) just 30 miles from Seoul, could attack with only a few hours of warning. Consequently, the threat of renewed hostilities could not be disregarded. With 40,000 American troops in Korea, their safety and ability to deter had to be our first priority. At the same time another key policy objective of the United States was to foster democracy, economic development, human rights, and the rule of law in South Korea.

With Park's death these goals seemed to be threatened. Internal unrest in the South, renewed tension with the North, and a sudden economic downturn in South Korea combined to confront us with a major crisis. The worst of the popular unrest resulted in a brutal crackdown in

May of 1980 by ROK forces in Kwangju and imposition of strict martial law across the country.

Regrettably, myths still persist over the American role in Kwangju that poison Korean attitudes toward America. These myths are that American officials, particularly General Wickham and Ambassador William Gleysteen, supported use of South Korean army forces in the Kwangju massacre. Drawing on John's notes and personal recollections, this book clarifies circumstances surrounding the Kwangju episode and helps to dispel erroneous myths about the U.S. role.

I first met John Wickham when he visited my office at the Department of State just before leaving to assume command in Korea in June 1979. One of the subjects I urged him to pursue was development of close and harmonious relationships between the U.S. military command and the country team headed by Ambassador Gleysteen. John already enjoyed friendship with senior officials in Washington, including Secretary of Defense Harold Brown, JCS Chairman General David Jones, Mike Armacost at the Pentagon, Nick Platt in the National Security Council, and Army Vice Chief of Staff General Jack Vessey, who preceded Wickham as commander in Korea. John also knew the defense establishment well, having served as Director of the Joint Staff and senior military assistant to Secretaries James Schlesinger and Donald Rumsfeld.

After assuming command, John quickly established close ties with members of the country team, as well as his counterparts in the ROK Ministry of Defense and armed forces. These relationships and effective reporting on developments, combined with comprehensive policy recommendations, served the United States well during the crises that followed the assassination of President Park.

Perhaps one of the most troublesome crises involved manipulation of the media by the Korean military. This occurred just before the ROK presidential election during the summer of 1980 and the American presidential election that November. As this book highlights, Korea's military leaders manipulated an off-the-record interview granted by John in their attempt to bolster the political standing of Chun Doo-hwan by creating the impression that the United States supported him.

The reaction to the interview was dramatic. Officials in Washington panicked and suggested that General Wickham be repudiated, or even replaced. And human rights activists went ballistic. But I knew John Wickham. I knew him as a great commander, a patriot, and a superb public servant. So, fortunately, did his colleagues at the Pentagon. Together, we stabilized the situation after a strange interlude. When the incident began, John was in the United States attending a conference of unified commanders. On his return flight to Korea, General Jones and I diverted him to Hawaii, to demonstrate unequivocally to the South Korean military leadership that the United States was unhappy and clearly disassociated itself from staged media pronouncements of American support for Chun. About 10 days later John told me it was necessary for him to participate in a U.S.–ROK command post exercise. This upcoming military activity enabled me to persuade officials in Washington that John's continued service was important and that he should return to Korea. I was delighted to convey the good news to him. The heartfelt personal message that I sent John at the end of this incident is found in this book. The remainder of his tour was successful and was followed by distinguished service at the highest levels within the Armed Forces, first as Vice Chief and then as Chief of Staff of the United States Army.

Korea on the Brink includes several important conclusions about an eventful incident in Korean history. Of particular significance to me, given my recent diplomatic troubleshooting missions, are insights into the sensitive role that our senior American military commander played during a period of politico-military intrigue and great danger to U.S. security interests. John obviously succeeded in handling the challenges. This is a tribute to his military training and experience, but it also is a tribute, in his words, to the effective relationships he shared with U.S. authorities in Seoul and Washington and with ROK leaders in Korea.

There is no doubt that the multipolar world of today will continue to challenge U.S. security interests, sometimes in hazardous and unpredictable ways. We have seen such challenges in Bosnia, Haiti, Somalia, Panama, and the Middle East. John's book will serve as an especially useful case study for future generations of senior staff officers and commanders. These leaders must be prepared to cope effectively with unforeseen and potentially dangerous politico-military crises—crises that will demand trust and unusually close working relationships between military officers and their political leaders in the field, as well as in Washington in order to achieve U.S. security interests.

Preface

From July 1979 to June 1982 I served as Commander in Chief, United Nations Command (UNC) and United States-Republic of Korea Combined Forces Command (CFC), and Commander, United States Forces, Korea (USFK), and Eighth United States Army. While occupying these positions, I dealt with a series of tragic events including the assassination of Park Chung-hee, a subsequent coup by Korean officers on December 12, 1979 (the so-called "12/12 Incident" which is featured in this book), and the Kwangju uprising when the South Korean military brutally suppressed civilian demonstrators. Any one of these incidents could have sparked a major conflict on the Korean peninsula. I am convinced that war was avoided largely because of resolute actions taken by the governments of the United States and Republic of Korea (ROK) and the combat readiness of both American and Korean forces. That deterrent contributed in no small measure to a politico-economic evolution in South Korea and the peaceful transfer of power, from Chun Doo-hwan to a Korean military academy classmate, Roh Tae-woo, and most significantly, from Roh to Kim Young-sam and to Kim Dae-jung, who was inaugurated president in 1998.

This book focuses on a period that begins with the death of President Park in October 1979 which led to the "12/12 Incident." My account of these events sheds light on how political military policy is formulated within the U.S. Government and, more importantly, on how policy is shaped and executed in the field. For it is the high-level officials in the field who ultimately bear responsibility for the success or failure of American policy. *Korea on the Brink* is written from the perspective of the military commander entrusted to maintain the armistice and defend Korea, should war occur. My objective was not to present a definitive history of this period, a task that others will eventually achieve. Rather, it was to record and reflect on those significant people and events that I observed as commander of allied forces, who numbered almost half-a-million military personnel. Drawing on contemporaneous notes, messages, and memory, I have sought to faithfully relate the facts as I saw them at the time and have analyzed them in the intervening years.

This book must be read in the context of half a century of Cold War confrontation—a situation that continues to this day on the Korean peninsula—a full decade after its celebrated end in Europe and elsewhere. The U.S.–ROK security arrangement within which I operated took shape under the intense pressures of East-West relations, particularly a constant threat of invasion from the North.

At the end of World War II, Communist forces in Korea followed Moscow's universal practice of creating a Marxist-Leninist regime on territory that they controlled, despite UN recognition of independence in 1947 and calls for an election. By late summer 1948 the peninsula was partitioned into the Republic of Korea, led by Syngman Rhee, and the Democratic People's Republic of Korea (DPRK), led by Kim Il-sung. Before dawn on June 25, 1950, not quite one year after American forces had withdrawn, the North attacked the South, and a bitter 3–year conflict ensued as UN forces fought North Korean and Chinese troops to a standstill along lines close to the 38th parallel. Virtually every family on the peninsula suffered from this war. More than four million people fled south, and many families remain divided today.

An armistice in July 1953 ended hostilities and created a demilitarized zone (DMZ), which winds 150 miles between North and South. A month later, Secretary of State John Foster Dulles pledged in a joint statement with President Rhee to negotiate a status of forces agreement that eventually led to the Korean Civil Assistance Command, although the agreement was not signed until 1966. The United States and the ROK did sign a Mutual Security Treaty in 1953 which, together with the status of forces agreement, served as the basis for the U.S.–ROK defense relationship that largely defined my various roles as commander.

Koreans are acutely aware that war could erupt suddenly. The capital, Seoul, which has a population of 12 million (about a quarter of the nation's people) is barely 30 miles south of the DMZ. North Korean fighter bombers could reach Seoul in a matter of minutes. Rockets and long-range artillery could hit targets in the suburbs. The extensive barriers and fortifications that sprawl in depth across farm land to the north and west of Seoul are ominous reminders of dangers that lurk only a few miles away. The DPRK constantly seeks ways to defeat these defenses, for example, by digging tunnels under the DMZ as invasion corridors and by infiltrating special forces to probe the border and the South Korean units arrayed behind it.

Koreans also are attuned to developments in the United States, their principal ally. My tour spanned Democratic and Republican administrations with substantially different policies regarding Korea, as evidenced by the U.S. Government's treatment of Korean officials. The Carter administration was hesitant, almost grudging, in recognizing Chun Doo-hwan who became president in the wake of a coup. In 1977, against the advice of senior military leaders familiar with the situation, Carter ordered an American withdrawal. The Reagan administration, by contrast, canceled further troop cuts and invited Chun to be the first head of state to meet with the newly elected president. Koreans interpret signals from Washington carefully, if not always accurately, and a large part of my job was dealing with the repercussions of those interpretations.

Troop withdrawals unnerved South Koreans, who worried then as now about the ability of a numerically superior North Korea to attack from forward positions with virtually no warning. As commander in chief (CINC), I dealt with the fallout from the Carter withdrawal policy not only in the face of a significantly increased North Korean threat, but also in the midst of ROK political turmoil that both threatened internal security and could have provoked intervention from the North. South Korea was not alone in its concern over the durability of the U.S.–ROK Mutual Security Treaty; other Asian nations also worried about American staying power in the Western Pacific.

On occasion recent administrations have made what I might describe as tactical mistakes in U.S. policy toward Korea. They include impatience with political progress, moralizing attitudes on human rights, threats of troop withdrawals and cuts in military and economic aid, and creating the impression that the United States does not consider South Korea as an equal partner. But, despite tactical mistakes, each administration to its credit has pursued a strategic policy based on national interests. This continuity in strategic policy has enhanced deterrence both during and between times of crisis. The Korean people will never forget this strategic commitment.

I have attempted to provide answers to four questions. First, how did a military commander assure continued deterrence in the face of political and social upheaval that so threatened internal stability in South Korea that intervention by North Korea seemed highly probable? Second, what role did U.S. officials, particularly the CINC, play in the coup led by Major General Chun Doo-hwan and his subsequent rise to president? Third, what connection did the CINC have to the suppression of civilian demonstrators in 1980 that became known as the Kwangju massacre? And fourth, what are the implications for the future, given conviction and sentencing in 1996 of ex-Presidents Chun and Roh and their associates for participation in the coup and corruption?

The events described in *Korea on the Brink* begin with the assassination of President Park, an act that created chaos among the ROK leadership, because Park had prevented the development of a strong political system with effective opposition parties. He did not want any challenge to his rule, which lasted 18 years. His death triggered the December 1979 seizure of control by a cabal of young, able, and ambitious army officers, led by Chun Doo-hwan. These officers were angry with what they saw as rapid political liberalization, widespread corruption, and slow promotions. At the same time, they worried about their careers after the fall of Park, who was a father figure. The coup not only further politicized the officer corps but also fomented lingering opposition to the military establishment within many segments of Korean society.

Disaffection with increased military control over the government and strong-arm policies by coup leaders occasioned the Kwangju uprising. It was brutally crushed by South Korean forces in the belief that rioting would spread to other cities, lead to anarchy, overturn the coup leaders, and even invite an invasion by North Korea.

Such violence against civilians was unprecedented in the Republic of Korea. Hundreds of lives were lost—some claim thousands died. Kwangju remains a deeply painful episode to many, as evidenced by the prosecution and convictions of Chun, who had become president in September 1980, and Roh Tae-woo, another leader of the coup, who succeeded him. Both men and others who supported them were convicted of treason, mutiny, and graft. Chun was sentenced to death, Roh to 22 years in prison, and dozens of others to prison terms of various lengths.

Myths about the American part in the Kwangju episode, particularly my role as Commander in Chief of Combined Forces Command, continue to poison the attitudes of many people in Korea. I trust that this book will provide a more comprehensive understanding of events and help to dispel any ill-will toward the United States resulting from the "12/12 Incident" and the tragic events which occurred in Kwangju.

While I remain solely responsible for this book, I am indebted to the National Defense University and its president, Lieutenant General Richard Chilcoat, USA, a longtime friend, and to the NDU Foundation for its support. That backing would not have been feasible without the generosity of colleagues and former mentors: Secretaries of Defense James Schlesinger, Donald Rumsfeld, Caspar Weinberger, and Frank Carlucci; Tidal McCoy; Jay Khim; William Brehm; and two past chairmen of the Armed Forces Communications and Electronics Association, Ralph Schrader and Gene Murphy.

I am also grateful to several individuals for their assistance: James Hausman, a dear friend and adviser (who died in 1996), offered invaluable counsel based on knowledge of Korea gained over five decades; General Robert Sennewald, USA (Ret.), a friend and my successor as CINC; Steve Bradner and Bruce Grant, solid professionals who served with James Hausman; Brigadier General Douglas Kinnard, USA (Ret.), a superb Chief of Military History; Lieutenant Colonel Brian Haig, USA (Ret.), who edited the original manuscript; and Colonel William Drennan, USAF (Ret.), who reviewed every version of the manuscript along the way. Moreover, I am indebted to Patrick Cronin who as Director of Research encouraged acceptance of this project by the Institute for National Strategic Studies. I am also indebted to the staff of NDU Press—William Bode, George Maerz, and the book's copy editor throughout the project, Jonathan Pierce—who edited the final manuscript under the supervision of Robert Silano, Director of Publications and Editor of *Joint Force Quarterly*. Credit for the design and layout of this book goes to William Rawley and Erika Echols of the Typography and Design Division at the U.S. Government Printing Office.

Finally, I am deeply grateful to my wife, Ann, who encouraged me throughout the course of the project and, as my best friend, shared all of the joys and sacrifices of a long Army career.

Korea
ON THE BRINK

Chapter One

Death of a President

Setting the Stage

The voice on the phone said, "Assassins have just killed Park Chung-hee. We're worried that the North Koreans might capitalize on the confusion by attacks with their agents in South Korea or, worse, by an attack along the demilitarized zone."

It was Dr. Harold Brown, the Secretary of Defense, and although he was normally stolid and unflappable, he sounded alarmed. The date was October 26, 1979, and I had just arrived in Washington, on official business from my post in Korea. My wife, Ann, was with me, and at the moment the phone rang, our suitcases still lay on the floor at Wainwright Hall visitors quarters at Fort Myer, Virginia, a few miles from the Pentagon.

Brown's alarm was the result of a flash message from our embassy in Seoul reporting that Park, the President of the Republic of Korea, had been killed a few hours earlier by unknown assassins.

No one knew whether a coup was underway, although, had that been reported in the cable, we would have been quite surprised—there had been no intelligence reports or indications of coup plotting. In fact, my first thought was that the North Koreans must have been behind the president's death. North Korean terrorists, after all, had tried several times to kill Park, including one very desperate assault in 1968 by a platoon of commandos against the Blue House, the president's official residence in Seoul.

Secretary Brown then said that the situation in Seoul was terribly confused and that nothing was known about North Korea's reaction, or even whether the North Koreans were aware of Park's death. Of course, North Korea's reaction was a matter of imminent concern to us both. Its armed forces were always at a high state of readiness—with armored divisions only 30 miles north of Seoul—making any chance of miscalculation particularly dangerous.

An urgent meeting was scheduled in the White House Situation Room to review the developments and decide how we should react, and Secretary Brown said he would meet me there. He closed by warning me to prepare to return to Seoul immediately after the meeting.

The news left me as shocked as Secretary Brown. We were both well acquainted professionally and personally with President Park, who had come to power through a military coup nearly two decades before. He had since become a permanent, unvarying fixture to anyone who knew Korea. Park was a slight man, but he was also authoritative and certainly charismatic. As a young man, like many other Koreans, he had volunteered to serve with the Japanese Imperial Army. He experienced firsthand the results of military-controlled economic development. The impression was lasting.

After Park seized power in 1961, he and his inner circle began implementing a "Manchurian experiment" in economic development. He immediately formed an Economic Planning Board that he staffed with talented economists, many of whom had been trained in America and Europe. Under his tight control the board was given the task and authority to begin building a new economy. Supported by the country's giant business enterprises, the so-called *chaebol*, and by the nationalized banking institution, Park forged a kind of "guided capitalism" that was to become the foundation for Korea's rapid economic development during the sixties, seventies, and eighties.

Secretary Brown and I had met with Park only a few weeks before at the annual Security Consultative Meeting (SCM) that had been held in Seoul. The SCM normally focused on mutual security issues: defense budgets, modernization programs, joint cooperation projects, and joint force levels. This most recent one had followed the usual pattern. Among the American delegates were General David Jones, USAF, the Chairman of the Joint Chiefs of Staff (JCS), a close personal friend and key figure in my being selected to command in Korea, and Admiral Maurice ("Mickey") Weisner, USN, the Commander in Chief of U.S. Pacific Command (CINCPAC) and, therefore, the senior commander over United States Forces, Korea (USFK). Weisner had been in command for nearly four years and was about to be retired.

Shortly before those meetings, I had been promoted to full general and assumed responsibility for the defense of the ROK, relieving another longtime friend, General John Vessey, USA, an officer held in great respect by the South Korean people and military. Vessey had departed Korea to assume

Greeting President Park at the October 1979 Security Consultative Meeting as Admiral Weisner and General Jones look on.

duties as the Army's vice chief of staff, and he would go on, three years later, to become a superb chairman of the U.S. Joint Chiefs of Staff.

The SCM meeting had been very successful, at least according to my discussions with the senior ROK officers who had been in attendance. Neither I nor any other American attendee had detected any hint of unrest among the ROK military or Park's inner circle.

Thus the tragic news left me not only surprised but also filled with foreboding. Having spent the months since I'd taken command going over intelligence and walking many miles along the demilitarized zone (DMZ), I believed I had a good grasp of the dangerous situation that threatened us. More than one and a half million heavily armed troops glared at each other across the 150–mile-long DMZ. Loudspeakers constantly blared North Korean propaganda. Shootings and ambushes by infiltrating North Korean agents were frequent occurrences. It was perhaps the most tense and easily ignited boundary on earth.

Making the situation more ominous still, our intelligence had recently discovered clandestine increases in North Korean forces near the DMZ, particularly among the frontline combat units, the "shock" troops who were trained to lead the breakthrough of our defenses. That discovery came on the heels of a comprehensive study General Jack Vessey had instituted a few months before I arrived, which had revealed large-scale modernization of their ground forces. With massive Soviet support, Pyongyang's already large inventories of tanks, infantry fighting vehicles, artillery, and rocket launchers were steadily expanding.

Of course, it was well known that North Korea's forces were disposed for attack, not defense. Aerial photographs, visual sightings, and communications intercepts all showed that conclusively. Thousands of artillery tubes were dug into protective caves just north of the DMZ, where they were capable of ranging the outskirts of Seoul and ready to support attacking forces. Tank and mechanized infantry units were kept in positions close to the DMZ, with ammunition stored in protected tunnels. It was an army poised to lunge forward, a powerful juggernaut that leaned in one direction—south.

Any effort to fathom how North Korea would react to this situation was futile. Kim Il-sung and his inner circle were always unpredictable, even baffling, and there was no use trying to speculate how they would respond. Their intentions were as obscure as the thick, early morning fogs that frequently blanketed the mountains and valleys along the DMZ.

I took stock of how well prepared I might be to deal with the situation. I had commanded combat units up through the 101st Airborne Division, served twice in Vietnam, and had been a regimental operations officer for fourteen months along the DMZ. Those experiences provided solid professional training for handling the military threat, but did not equip me particularly well, I thought, for the unexpected political challenges unfolding in Seoul.

Regrettably, no textbook or executive training existed for senior U.S. military leaders to learn how to cope with political-military situations as ominous as this one appeared to be. However, I was not without resources. I had developed an early rapport with a number of ROK military leaders and, fortunately, had arrived in Seoul with very good relations with a number of key officials in Washington, including the Chairman, Assistant Secretary of State for East Asian and Pacific Affairs Richard Holbrooke, and Deputy Assistant Secretary of Defense for International Affairs Michael Armacost. Just prior to the Korea assignment,

I had served as Director of the Joint Staff. A few years before that, as a major general, I had served three years as the senior military assistant to Secretaries of Defense James Schlesinger and Donald Rumsfeld. I was familiar with how the Pentagon operated and knew many of the current players.

Fortunately, I had already developed a very close personal and working relationship with the U.S. Ambassador to Korea, William Gleysteen, and with a number of the other members of his Country Team, particularly the Deputy Chief of Mission (DCM), John Monjo, and the Central Intelligence Agency (CIA) station chief, Bob Brewster. I suspected, when I became CINC, that all these contacts would prove invaluable, but little did I know exactly how important they would actually become.

Initial U.S. Response

Secretary Brown's phone call jarred me out of jet lag. I tried to accomplish what I could before the car arrived to carry me to the White House. About all I had time for was to arrange a return flight to Korea with the Air Force special air mission staff at Andrews Air Force Base and to make one phone call. Because there was no secure phone available in Wainwright Hall, I could not obtain a classified update from my headquarters in Korea or the intelligence center in the Pentagon. However, I spoke on an open line with Lieutenant General Evan Rosencrans, USAF, my USFK deputy commander. Evan reaffirmed everything Brown had told me and alluded, as best he could on an unclassified line, that he suspected the North Koreans might have been behind the president's death. We had only enough time for a brief discussion about the potential for trouble by the North Koreans before the sedan arrived.

I headed for the White House meeting concerned that I still had virtually no knowledge of what was happening in Korea, even as my mind raced with thoughts about the actions needed to cope with the threat of war.

Walking into the White House Situation Room, I met Secretary Brown, General Jones, National Security Adviser Zbigniew Brzezinski, a Department of State representative whose name I cannot recall, and several CIA staff officers. The intelligence officers were unable to provide any additional information beyond what was already known about developments in Seoul. We did learn, however, that ROK military forces had increased their alert status—an entirely understandable development—and that U.S. Pacific Command (PACOM) also had increased the operational ready status of USFK. My very able operations officer in Korea, Major General

Robert Sennewald, USA, was supervising this increase in alert status for the forces assigned to the U.S.–ROK Combined Forces Command (CFC), and I had complete confidence that he would have things well in hand.

The discussion in the Situation Room turned quickly to what concrete military steps the United States should take to deter the North Koreans from exploiting the situation. I recommended that we sustain the heightened alert status that had already been ordered, and deploy additional Air Force fighter aircraft to our bases in South Korea, as well as some airborne warning and control system (AWACS) and Navy P3 (antisubmarine) aircraft. I also recommended moving some selected naval forces, including an aircraft carrier, closer to the peninsula. I was pleased when General Jones strongly endorsed these measures. The AWACS aircraft in particular would be valuable because they could be flown quickly to South Korea, and North Korean radar would detect their presence almost immediately. These aircraft could be kept in orbits that would last many hours each day, and the observation of those orbits would help to deter any hostile action by the North which was well aware of AWACS ability to identify hostile aircraft and vector defensive fighters to engage them.

Some participants were concerned about the potential for provoking the North Koreans and began to argue that if we were to reinforce, we should do so slowly and with lighter forces. I replied that deterrence should be our most important consideration, and that the prompt deployment of substantial combat forces would be absolutely essential in order to minimize any possibility of miscalculation about our resolve.

I noted that historically there had always been debate about the balance between deterrent actions and provocation when it came to the North Koreans. The same debate had been played out over how to respond to the "tree-ax incident" in 1976. Two U.S. officers had led a small detail into the DMZ Joint Security Area in Panmunjom to trim branches from a large tree that was blocking the observation of a UN-manned guard post. In an ambush that clearly had been well planned, the two officers were jumped and killed by a group of about 30 North Korean soldiers.

One of my predecessors, General Richard Stilwell, USA, recommended a strong, demonstrative response—cutting down the tree to make it a symbol—but he first had to override objections about the possibility of provoking the North. As it turned out, Stilwell's logic won out and a strong demonstration was arranged. Confronted by an ominous display of force, the North Koreans backed down completely, and a detail of American and South Korean soldiers pared the tree down to a stump.

Before the meeting concluded, decisions were made to execute my recommendations on reinforcement and to take prompt diplomatic actions to warn the North Koreans against military intervention. Of course, condolence messages would be sent to the ROK authorities. Secretary of State Cyrus Vance would attend the state funeral for Park.

What impressed me most about the meeting was the resolve of the attendees and their familiarity with the Korean security situation. Of course, Secretary Brown, General Jones, and I were fresh from our meetings in Seoul a few weeks earlier, but the other participants were equally cognizant of the situation.

While all of the principals naturally were shocked by the assassination and apprehensive about future developments, they were also emphatic that strong albeit defensive military measures had to be initiated promptly, both to stabilize the situation and to reassure the interim government in South Korea.

As a result of the meeting, the Department of State released the following statement:

> The United States Government wishes to make clear that it will react strongly in accordance with its treaty obligations to the Republic of Korea to any external attempt to exploit the situation in the Republic of Korea.

The meeting lasted only about an hour. I was instructed by Secretary Brown and General Jones to return to Seoul without delay. General Jones told me that he would go to the National Military Command Center and initiate the reinforcing actions that had been agreed upon in the meeting. Within an hour, I was flying toward Anchorage, Alaska, where the aircraft would be refueled for a non-stop flight to Osan Air Base, about 40 miles south of Seoul. In view of the unsettled situation, Ann and I decided that she should remain in Washington for the time being.

As I sat on the plane staring out the window at the beautiful Maryland countryside disappearing below me, I obviously had very limited knowledge of what was occurring back in Seoul. It was only after my return that was I able to piece together details of Park's death and its immediate aftermath. A great deal was happening in my absence.

Intelligence Director as Assassin

President Park had died slightly before 8 P.M. on October 26. At 9:30 P.M., the Korean National Police went on full alert throughout Korea. Shortly before that, the ROK army chief of staff had raised the alert status of all

Map 1. **Central Seoul**

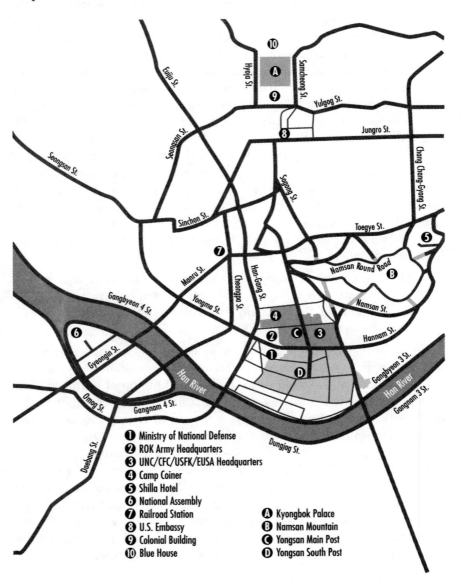

① Ministry of National Defense
② ROK Army Headquarters
③ UNC/CFC/USFK/EUSA Headquarters
④ Camp Coiner
⑤ Shilla Hotel
⑥ National Assembly
⑦ Railroad Station
⑧ U.S. Embassy
⑨ Colonial Building
⑩ Blue House

Ⓐ Kyongbok Palace
Ⓑ Namsan Mountain
Ⓒ Yongsan Main Post
Ⓓ Yongsan South Post

ROK forces to the counter-infiltration status known as *Chin Do Kae II*, a status approximately equivalent to Defense Condition Three, or near war footing for U.S. forces. Seoul remained calm that evening, mostly because of the long-standing security curfew that required all citizens to be off the streets by 11 P.M. (I was always amazed to see how strictly this curfew was enforced by the South Korean national police. It was a welcome relief for both Ann and me, since the curfew forced an early end to social engagements for the day.) Virtually no one knew of Park's death. The authorities in Seoul were keeping it quiet until they could decide what to do about the explosive situation.

To help with internal security, the ROK 9th Special Forces Brigade was summoned and arrived about 1 A.M. at the army headquarters, a military compound across the street from the Ministry of National Defense (MND) and within walking distance of my headquarters. Inside the imposing eight-story MND building, atop a small knoll in the Yongsan district of Seoul, a tense meeting began at approximately 9 P.M. It lasted almost until dawn. The attendees included the ROK Joint Chiefs of Staff, Prime Minister Choi Kyu-ha, Minister of Defense Rho Jae-hyun, and the director of the Korean Central Intelligence Agency (KCIA), Kim Jae-kyu. My Korean deputy, General Rhu Byong-hyun, in his capacity as the deputy commander of the U.S.–ROK CFC, also attended. From Rhu and others I learned what had happened in this crisis meeting.

I knew General Rhu quite well and had found him to be a remarkably able and level-headed officer. He was fluent in English and well read in Western media, with a sophisticated understanding of Americans. Before I arrived, he had worked closely with General Vessey in formulating the policy, design, and activation of the U.S.–ROK CFC, and I knew that General Vessey held him in very high esteem. In the difficult months to come, I would share that sentiment as I watched Rhu provide steady and brilliant counsel to both his countrymen and U.S. authorities. Eventually he would become JCS Chairman and ambassador to the United States. He would also become my best Korean friend.

The military leaders gathered for that meeting clearly faced a daunting challenge. President Park had been the source of his country's stability. Now, with unexpected suddenness, that source was gone. KCIA chief Kim Jae-kyu had been dining with the president at the time of his death. Kim was unwilling to disclose much about what had happened, so the rest of the men in the room knew little about the circumstances surrounding the assassination.

No immediate intelligence existed about North Korean reactions, although every effort was being taken to monitor its radio communications, including those signals emanating from agent networks. There was the alarming possibility that North Korean agents had infiltrated the grounds of the Blue House and killed the president. Aside from determining who was behind the assassination, the ROK military leaders also had to determine what actions should be taken to heighten military readiness without provoking the North. Almost half a million South Korean military forces and some 45,000 U.S. forces were under the operational control of the U.S.–ROK CFC, and the bulk of those forces would have to be placed on increased alert.

Early in the meeting the KCIA chief urged the ROK Joint Chiefs of Staff to name the army Chief of Staff, General Chung Sung-hwa, as acting president. Historically and institutionally, the ROK army chief was far and away the dominant member of the military chiefs. But Kim Jae-kyu's suggestion was not in accordance with the constitution, which designated the prime minister to assume full presidential authority in the event that the chief executive became incapacitated. Thus, Prime Minister Choi Kyu-ha became acting president upon Park's death; General Chung was designated martial law commander.

Chung was an unusual officer by traditional Korean standards. Bespectacled and intellectual, he had a reputation for modest behavior, thorough professionalism, and deep concern about the welfare, training, and equipping of the army. He was unassuming in his personal style and goals. Of even greater note, he also seemed to be honest, which was a very sharp contrast from some of his predecessors. Having met frequently with him on official business, I was impressed, as General Vessey had been before me, by his straightforward leadership, competence, and obvious sincerity. He was a devoted family man with four children and two grandchildren.

Despite his professional reputation, Chung's presence in the Blue House when Park was killed raised some doubts about his role, if any, in the assassination. Chung attempted to explain his presence as a mere coincidence; he was simply attending a friendly dinner arranged by KCIA chief Kim Jae-kyu prior to Kim's invitation to dine with the president. But doubts remained at the time.

Exactly why Chung was there, as with so many of the other details of that tragic night, has never been entirely clarified, although he was cleared of guilt in the assassination just a few years ago.

Late in the afternoon of October 26, a dinner for that evening was hastily arranged between the President and KCIA chief Kim. The arrangement was made by the Blue House security chief, Cha Chi-chul, who was a close confidant of the president's and a man who was thoroughly feared throughout the ROK Government. It remains unclear who requested the dinner—Park or the KCIA director—but in any event, Cha extended the formal invitation to Kim. There was speculation that within a few minutes after Cha called him with the formal invitation, the KCIA director picked up the phone and invited General Chung to dine with him. Strangely, the invitation was set for the same time and at a location very near the room where the KCIA director was scheduled to dine with the president. Kim's motives for arranging the evening that way never became clear, but his purpose may have been entrapment. He may have been trying to implicate Chung in the assassination so he could later capitalize on the army chief's martial law powers. During an interrogation following his confession, Kim maintained that he arranged the dinner with Chung long before Cha's invitation to him and that the two appointments just happened to coincide. In any event, Kim had two dinners on his hands, and he had to be clever about how he handled them.

When Park arrived for his dinner with Kim Jae-kyu, the KCIA director briefly excused himself and went to a nearby room where Chung was waiting. Kim explained to General Chung that the dinner with the president had been arranged suddenly and unexpectedly by Cha, and that if Chung would permit Kim's political officer to host him for the interim, he promised to return in two hours. Chung, of course, agreed, and Kim went back to the president's dinner.

Kim's security guards were waiting in a room adjacent to the one occupied by Blue House security guards, who routinely provided security for the president. During dinner there was a great deal of drinking, and a heated argument erupted between Kim and Cha. Kim hated Cha. He viewed Cha as a devious rival who undercut him at every opportunity, and the two of them had many differences over policy matters, several of which had reached an explosive point in October 1979.

In the weeks leading up to the dinner, severe labor riots had erupted in the cities of Masan and Pusan and then spread throughout Korea, becoming major demonstrations against Park's regime. The cause of the riots concerned two of "the three Kims," the most famous, enduring, and voluble political dissidents in the ROK.

One of the three Kims was Kim Jong-pil, a cashiered army officer who had masterminded the coup that brought Park to power in May 1961. Afterward, Kim Jong-pil had served in several powerful positions in Park's government, including prime minister, before the two men had a political falling out and Kim was thrown out of the president's inner circle. Kim had taken his political differences to the public.

The second was Kim Young-sam, a stately man who would go on to become president. Kim Young-sam was a moderate, democratic reformer who enjoyed wide popularity throughout the ROK; he was also an elected member of the ROK National Assembly.

The third was Kim Dae-jung, who is now president. Kim Dae-jung, also a legislator, was from South Cholla province, in the southwestern corner of South Korea, a province that considered itself distinct and disaffected from the rest of the ROK. The citizens of Cholla had legitimate grounds to be discontented, because Park and his inner circle, who came largely from provinces in the southeastern part of the country, had largely ignored the economic development in their region. There was a pragmatic explanation for this economic slight, because Cholla had no valuable ports, nor was it situated along the transportation corridors between South Korea's key ports and its most important cities. The province's stunted development stood in great contrast to the rest of the country, where the largesse of "guided" development was beginning to have a noticeable impact. The capital of South Cholla is Kwangju, a city destined to play a major role in the events covered in this book.

Kim Dae-jung, a democratic and social reformer, was the leading member of Cholla's political faction. Of the three Kims, he advocated the most dramatic and sweeping changes in the ROK political condition.

The labor demonstrations that began in Masan and Pusan, and quickly spread to other cities, erupted from public anger over President Park's ordered expulsion of Kim Young-sam from the National Assembly. Kim Young-sam had only recently become head of the opposition New Democratic Party, and Park had been angered by critical, public remarks Kim had made.

Blue House Security Chief Cha Chi-chul had argued for tough crackdowns against the dissidents and student protesters. KCIA Director Kim, however, had tried repeatedly to make the case for a more tolerant approach toward the demonstrators and those who incited them, specifically the "Three Kims." As a result, Cha had begun to blame the KCIA director for the spiraling situation, arguing that Kim was ultimately responsible for the demonstrations getting out of hand. In front of other cabinet officials, Cha had accused Kim of being too close to the Americans and their soft ideas on political liberalization and handling unrest. To his dismay, Kim had begun to sense that President Park agreed with Cha.

Cha had been with Park since the early revolutionary days after 1961, when Park first came to power. In fact, Cha was the only survivor of that era still in the government. He had become the president's closest associate, particularly after Park's wife was killed in 1974 by an assassin who missed his target. After that tragedy, Park, who was a retiring figure anyway, withdrew more and more from the public eye, relying on his most trusted advisers, such as Cha and Kim, to run the country. Park's eldest daughter, Park Kyun-hae, assumed the role of "first lady," but, despite her charm, she had little influence over matters of policy.

Kim had reached the conclusion that Cha's badmouthing was having a telling effect and that President Park would soon sack him. Adding to Kim's despondent mood were a series of personal failures that had accumulated as he filled successively higher positions, nearly all of which he had failed to earn on his own merit but instead were the fruits of his personal ties to President Park.

During his army career, Kim had advanced no further than colonel on his own merit. In fact, it was a startling surprise to everyone who knew him when President Park suddenly reached down into the ranks and promoted him to lieutenant general, giving him command of a prestigious front-line corps. The position far exceeded Kim's ability, and it wasn't long before he was relieved for incompetence. Nor was it long before President Park came to his aid again and appointed him as KCIA head.

Kim and Park were classmates from the second class of officer candidate school and had stayed very close during their army careers. Among Koreans, classmate connections from high school through college traditionally create lifelong bonds and loyalties, particularly inside the military. Indeed, Kim was by no means the only beneficiary of Park's loyalty. Park took care of many of his army cronies, a loyalty that was repaid by almost slavish personal support for the President and his policies.

Now there was growing evidence of Kim's inability to manage the KCIA and to retain the President's loyalty and ear. Rumors began to circulate that Kim would be thrown out of the cabinet, and those rumors worked their way to Kim's ears via several of his KCIA informers. Kim sensed he was on a slippery slope, and that made him desperate. There was some evidence that he had planned for several months to kill both the President and Cha and had only been waiting for a propitious moment.

During the bitter argument between Kim and Cha, which Park strangely tolerated, Kim abruptly left the room several times, claiming toilet needs. Finally, he returned with a pistol that had been hidden in a room upstairs. The moment he reentered the room, he confronted the President and reportedly asked him "how can we conduct politics with an insect like Cha?" Then he shot Cha and wounded Park in the shoulder before his pistol jammed. The noise from the shootings was the prearranged signal for Kim's security detail to attack Park's five guards, all of whom were killed in the ensuing fire fight. When Kim discovered that he had only wounded Cha in the arm, he grabbed another pistol from one of his guards, shot Cha in the chest, and then shot the President in the head, mortally wounding him.

Also in the room were several women entertainers, who had served dinner, and Blue House Chief Secretary Kim Kye-won, another army general, like so many cronies in the Park regime. For some reason, Kim Kye-won and the women were left unscathed in the shooting. In the ensuing confusion, the Blue House chief secretary took the president to a nearby military hospital, where doctors pronounced him dead on arrival.

Meanwhile, the KCIA director rushed coatless and shoeless, in a bloodstained shirt, back into the room where the army chief, General Chung, still waited. Having heard the shooting, Chung was alarmed and on his feet. Kim excitedly explained that a tragedy had befallen the president and that Chung must accompany him immediately to KCIA headquarters, where proper security and communications would be available to cope with the dangerous situation.

General Chung did not know specifically what had happened to Park. However, he suspected that the president may have been incapacitated, and he knew that his martial law responsibilities required him to go to the ROK army headquarters bunker, where military communications and security existed. He also feared that North Korea might capitalize on the situation, and that concern made it imperative for him to go to the bunker immediately, where he could direct the proper response. The two men argued for a while before Kim finally relented and agreed to accompany Chung to army headquarters. In the car, the former tried repeatedly to persuade the latter to assume not just his martial law responsibilities but also full presidential authority, so the two of them would be in a position to run the country.

Chung later said that he was appalled by Kim's blatant, self-serving opportunism. He also said that he began to sense that he had been set up by the KCIA director. In view of Kim's strange behavior, Chung began to entertain the suspicion that the KCIA director might have been responsible for the "tragedy" that had befallen Park. But despite his suspicions, he did not question Kim about the details of his role. He may have been worried about his own safety, because the car they were traveling in was being pursued at high speed by several black sedans with darkened windows. Kim eventually reassured Chung that the cars contained KCIA security guards.

Upon arriving at the ROK army headquarters bunker, Chung went to work on military matters. He had a reputation for coping with crises in a calm, no-nonsense way. He immediately ordered the national police and military forces to go on alert. Then he convened a meeting of the Minister of National Defense and Joint Chiefs of Staff. He also arranged for a special contingent of troops to provide protection for the ministry and the army headquarters. Calls went out to Prime Minister Choi Kyu-ha and to Blue House Chief Secretary Kim, who had disappeared after the assassination, he eventually was located with the prime minister at the Blue House.

During the meeting in the MND building, observers noted that Chung remained aloof and seemed to be trying to distance himself from the markedly nervous KCIA director, who for hours neither confessed to the slaying nor revealed any of the details of the event. Instead, Kim spent the time arguing strongly that it was a propitious opportunity for the military to take over the nation and to deal with the vexing problems of corruption and domestic unrest that troubled everyone. He said that the KCIA had done extensive research and that most of the population, at least in Seoul and the other major cities, had grown angry with the bureaucracy and would support a military takeover of the government.

When Prime Minister Choi and Blue House Chief Secretary Kim Kye-won arrived at the ROK army headquarters bunker, the atmosphere became more tense and confused. Choi decided to convene a cabinet meeting at the Ministry of National Defense, accessible by tunnel from the army bunker. Once in the ministry, the Blue House chief secretary acknowledged that he had been present at the scene of the assassination, but he refused to reveal any details or admit who did the shooting. The president's killer, still armed, was sitting at the table, and the Blue House chief secretary must have been confused and worried about his personal safety. He was apparently sizing up the situation to see who would emerge as the leader and how he might relate to him. Things were moving fast, and he was understandably frightened. Finally, just before midnight, Kim Kye-won pulled the defense minister and the army chief of staff aside and told them that Kim Jae-kyu was the assassin. Chung immediately ordered the military police to seize and disarm Kim and his bodyguards.

Amazingly, the military police had no ammunition for their weapons, perhaps because of simple incompetence. Some Koreans were later to cite that lack of preparation as proof that the military had no prior knowledge of the assassination or any involvement with it. Since the military police worked for General Chung, some argued that the cloak of innocence covered him as well.

Following Kim's arrest, the acting president, defense minister, and military chiefs decided to limit martial law to the mainland, deliberately exempting the large, populated island of Cheju, off the southern coast. As a result, Chung, rather than reporting directly to the president, as he would have under a full implementation of martial law, instead reported to the ROK cabinet and prime minister.

To their credit, Chung and his military colleagues supported the constitutional process and protected the mandate of civilian leadership. Each of them signed an oath of allegiance to Prime Minister Choi as the acting president.

Nevertheless, the fact that Chung had been near the scene of the assassination raised deep suspicions about his behavior and motives. In addition, after all that had happened inside the army bunker and at the defense ministry, concerns were growing about the extent of the conspiracy. Perhaps Kim Jae-kyu had accomplices. The fact that the Blue House Chief Secretary, Kim Kye-won, had been unscathed in the shooting and later appeared evasive at the defense ministry meeting raised questions about his role. As a result, the senior ROK leaders were worried about the dangers of a larger intrigue. Their personal security became a top concern. Once the meeting ended, they became difficult to contact, often changing locations, particularly at night.

After the meeting, the Minister of Defense and Joint Chiefs of Staff issued instructions that cautioned all military officers against taking any action for their personal gain during this troubled period. All officers were ordered to remain professionally oriented on the nation's defense and to place national security and the future of the republic above their personal interests.

One other portentous decision was made during those heated hours. The commander of the Defense Security Command (DSC), Major General Chun Doo-hwan, was designated by Acting President Choi to serve as the chief investigator of the president's murder. It was an invitation for the cat to enter the bird's cage.

Chun and the Road to Power

At the dingy headquarters of the DSC, in another part of Seoul, Chun began busily assigning trusted agents to round up information and potential suspects. It was a natural task for his agents, because the DSC functioned within the military as a powerful counterintelligence and internal security apparatus. Because of its unique mission, the DSC possessed separate communications and controlled a large number of specially selected operatives, who were positioned at every level of military organization down to battalion level. These operatives reported directly to DSC headquarters and took orders from no one inside the regular military chain of command.

When it was first formed, the DSC mission was to ferret out North Korean sympathizers and individuals in the military services who might harbor antigovernment attitudes. It was a mission that invited abuse. Without any kind of legal oversight, suspects could be apprehended, interrogated—sometimes brutally—and held for legal or even extra-legal action in the command's notorious prison. These unique powers and methods inevitably created temptations, and the command eventually evolved into something more than a watchdog, becoming a big brother-like tool for intimidating individuals who might be patriotic but were regarded as errant or unreliable by military and government authorities. Unsurprisingly, the members of the Korean armed forces regarded the DSC and its agents with wariness, if not outright fear.

Because of the sensitivity of the position, President Park had personally approved the assignment of Major General Chun to head the DSC. A shadowy figure to Americans, Chun had served in Park's government after the coup in 1961 and had remained close to the president.

The time in government had been formative for Chun. It had taught him a number of lessons about political power and how to manage the Korean bureaucracy and military, lessons he would put to good use in the months to come. It may also have nurtured in Chun a personal conviction that he was destined to "wear the purple."

Until this point, Chun had led a charmed career, one blessed with a series of rapid promotions. Regardless, he was disgruntled. He held himself in very high regard, and it was part of his nature to become frustrated, if not angered, over any impediments to his advancement. There was one impediment in particular that seemed to rankle him quite severely: older, more senior officers who enjoyed their perks, resisted retirement, and performed less competently than Chun thought they should. Chun was not alone in his thinking. Many of his contemporaries also believed that the nation deserved better leaders in the military and in government.

Included in this group of disgruntled contemporaries were six other army officers who had entered the army together and become known as the "Taegu Seven Stars." Several of them would play prominent roles in the events considered in this book and in subsequent development of Korea. Chun and Roh Tae-woo would both become presidents of the Republic. Chung Ho-young, who also aspired to be president, would become the army chief of staff, minister of defense, minister of Home Affairs, and an elected member of the National Assembly. A fourth, Kim Bok-tong, would become a lieutenant general and head of the Korean Military Academy, until he openly criticized Chun and was forced into early retirement.

These seven extraordinarily able officers were the first in their class to receive stars as brigadier generals. Patterned after the United States Military Academy at West Point, the Korean Military Academy had been dramatically revamped during the Korean War. The initial wartime classes had been severely compressed in order to meet the wartime need for officers. The "Taegu Seven Stars" graduated together in 1955 as part of the first, full, four-year class, designated as Class 11. All seven came from the historically dominant city of Taegu, from which many of Korea's political leaders had emerged.

Now, one of the group, Major General Chun, had just learned that his presidential patron was dead.

Assessing the Role of Commander in Chief

As the Air Force special mission aircraft headed for Korea, I jotted notes about the actions I needed to take. Time was going to be a factor, particularly if the North Koreans were in any way inclined to take advantage of the situation.

My first note dealt with the complicated command relationships that existed in Korea. That might sound like an odd concern, but it was

Chart 1. **Peacetime Command Relationships, 1974–1980**

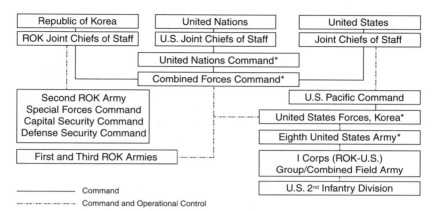

*The senior American general in the Republic of Korea is commander in chief of these four organizations.

crucially important. My reporting channels raised questions that could lead to confusion, even animosity, if handled incorrectly. As a military commander in Korea I wore four hats, each with differing responsibilities, authorities, and reporting channels. This arrangement was designed both to minimize the number of four-star generals in Korea and to ensure unity of command in the event of war. Unfortunately, it could prove awkward, even problematic, in a fast-moving crisis like the one we now faced.

One hat was as Commander in Chief (CINC) of the United Nations Command (UNC), with responsiblity for enforcing the armistice. In that hat, I reported directly to the Joint Chiefs of Staff in Washington and, if necessary, through the Joint Chiefs to the United Nations staff. The Department of State, of course, played a role in policy issues that concerned UNC. The important point was that the CINC UNC did not report to the ROK political or military authorities or to the Commander in Chief, U.S. Pacific Command. Also worth noting, UNC had virtually no forces, but was and remains responsible for all DMZ matters, such as shooting incidents and armistice violations. These matters were discussed at meetings of armistice representatives at the village of Panmunjom, inside the demilitarized zone.

Another hat I wore was that of Commander of the Eighth United States Army (EUSA), which controls all U.S. Army troops in Korea and serves as the Army component of the USFK.

In addition, I was the Commander of USFK, which is a subordinate, subunified command under PACOM. As commander, I reported directly to CINCPAC headquarters in Hawaii.

Finally, I was the Commander in Chief of the U.S.–ROK CFC. This position had unique, dual-reporting channels, because most of the ROK armed forces were under the command's operational control in both peace and war. The instructions for CFC required the U.S. commander to report directly to both the U.S. and ROK Joint Chiefs of Staff.

I was uneasy about these very complex command and control arrangements and how well they would work during this crisis. I recalled from my second tour in Vietnam the legendary problems that arose from the command relationships among the U.S. forces. The arrangements had not only provoked a great deal of unnecessary controversy, but according to the commanders, General Creighton Abrams, USA, and General Frederick Weyand, USA, they had also complicated the conduct of the war.

Yet, my predecessors in Korea had apparently been reasonably comfortable with the command and control arrangements. They had dealt with crises such as the "tree-ax incident," during the tenure of the General Stilwell, and not felt hampered. And, from my previous assignment as Director of the Joint Staff at the Pentagon, I could not recall any reported problems with the Korean command setup, so perhaps my misgivings would prove unfounded. I suspected, however, that I would have to be very careful. Besides, a new twist had been added to the equation.

CFC was a new and still untested arrangement. It had only been established in 1978. Previously, there had been no combined U.S.–ROK command, a fact that had become very sensitive to Koreans, who quite rightly felt that the old command arrangements failed to recognize or accommodate their status as an equal partner in their own defense. The solution had been establishing CFC, and the ROK had been very insistent that the command would report directly to both the ROK and U.S. Joint Chiefs of Staff. The significance of that was that the CFC commander did not fall under the authority of, nor report to, CINCPAC in Hawaii. It was understandable that South Korea would not permit its own forces to fall under the command of an American admiral located offshore. But this was something of a sore point since it meant that U.S. Pacific Command always could be effectively circumvented by CFC reporting and control arrangements, even though PACOM retained its responsibilities through USFK, which is a subunified command.

I had the leeway to pick and choose which command arrangement I wanted to employ. I could bypass Hawaii, reporting directly to the Joint Chiefs of Staff of both countries, and thereby minimize the complications that could arise from having too many chefs in the kitchen. Or I could be more inclusive. Considering the possibility of serious tensions, perhaps even hostilities, I decided that everything possible should be done to minimize any chance of controversy within the chain of command. I was convinced that success required emphasizing the combined nature of my command.

I decided that my reporting channel in the future must include CINCPAC. On personal messages to the Joint Chiefs and Secretary of Defense, I would add CINCPAC as an addressee. Also, I would seek CINCPAC's views on any key issues, not only because CINCPAC provided the U.S. forces and support in Korea, but also because I believed that the joint experience and judgment of the senior officers on the PACOM staff would prove invaluable to CFC. Besides, a long-time friend from my tours in the Pentagon, Admiral Robert Long, a former Vice Chief of Naval Operations, was about to assume duties as CINCPAC. I looked forward to the same wise counsel and support from him as I had learned to appreciate from Admiral Weisner.

Another note to myself dealt with my relationships with the U.S. ambassador, country team, and key officials in Washington. For an overseas commander, bureaucratic arrangements within the military are one consideration, but the arrangements with other departments are quite another. A misstep can prove disastrous.

I knew it was essential to strengthen those interdepartmental relationships through frequent messages, phone calls, and face-to-face meetings in Seoul and Washington. On my trips home, I planned to compare information with the Korea desk officers at State, CIA, OSD, and the Joint Staff. This would keep the channels of communication open and establish a common basis for analyzing developments. Not only would I learn a great deal from these visits, but they would solidify friendly contacts and cooperation at the working level. From my years in Washington, I knew that working-level contacts would help move my views and recommendations through the Washington bureaucracy.

I already had close relationships with a number of senior officials, including General Jones, Mike Armacost in the Office of the Secretary of Defense, Nick Platt on the National Security Council staff, and Assistant Secretary of State Dick Holbrooke. Keeping them informed of developments on a regular basis would ensure they had firsthand information as their basis for policy formulation. I would make each of them addressees on personal messages.

The ambassador and the CIA chief of station had their own channels of communications as well, and their responsibilities would, of course, require them to make frequent reports to Washington. I knew it would be vitally important that we keep each other well informed and present a unified front to Washington and the ROK.

Of course, this opened the question of why a military commander should become involved in extensive reporting on political matters. The reason is that the ROK military, particularly the army, ran Korea. President Park saw to it that nearly all of the elected and appointed members of the National Assembly, as well as most of his cabinet members, were retired military. The Minister of National Defense and all of his assistant ministers were retired military. Nearly all of the top positions in the large industrial firms went as perks to military retirees.

What was significant about that was that the Korean military believed it had a special friendship with the U.S. military, a relationship that dated back to the years before the Korean War. As a consequence, I found that my relationships with both active and retired Korean officers were very friendly and our dialogue was relatively open. Those relationships offered considerable opportunities to gain insights and understandings into key developments, insights that would be invaluable to those in Washington who handled Korea.

In Seoul, Ambassador Bill Gleysteen and I had already struck up a close personal relationship. Bill was a professional diplomat with a wealth of practical experience, particularly in the Orient; his parents had been missionaries in China. He had impressed me as a genuine intellectual with solid judgment, someone I could trust. Aside from other meetings, we breakfasted alone once a week and spoke on the secure phone virtually every day. It would be absolutely essential to minimize any surprises between us and to coordinate all our messages and recommendations. Not only would that help us to communicate unified positions back to Washington, it would also minimize any opportunities for the Koreans to find or exploit any daylight between us. Bill, of course, respected my broad responsibilities under the CFC charter and the fact that this position went beyond just U.S. interests.

The final note I recall writing down dealt with the immediate actions I needed to take after my arrival in Seoul. My staff, including the CFC deputy commander, General Rhu, would have to update me on the situation in Seoul and on any intelligence that had been gathered concerning the North Koreans.

I planned to increase our intelligence collection, primarily through the use of the additional airborne and electronic-intercept platforms that CINCPAC was already deploying to Korea. In addition to ensuring the proper deployment of the AWACS and P3 aircraft, I planned to order an increase in the flights of Army and Air Force intelligence collection aircraft already in-country, and to institute more intensive electronic monitoring of North Korean communications.

Also it would be important to see Ambassador Gleysteen and Minister of National Defense Rho Jae-hyun as soon as possible. I had condolence messages from Secretary Brown to deliver to the MND, which would afford me the opportunity to get Rho's sense of the situation.

I planned a series of immediate field visits to ROK and U.S. units, particularly those stationed along or near the DMZ. I planned to walk along portions of the southern fence, because the North Koreans regularly scanned the fence line with telescopes, and they would note a very senior commander inspecting the readiness of frontline troops. That would not only contribute to deterrence but also set a positive example for ROK commanders. I knew it would be vital to emphasize the absolute importance for these commanders to "face north," rather than look over their shoulders and worry about intrigues in Seoul. Given the way Park had manipulated military assignments, promotions, and perks, there was every reason for senior military leaders to be anxious about their personal loyalties, their connections, and the power plays occurring back in the capital.

From my first discussions with General Chung, the ROK army chief of staff, and General Rhu, my deputy, both officers had emphasized that a great deal of work needed to be done to improve the professional orientation of the ROK officer corps. We knew that it would take time and cautious leadership to change what had become deeply ingrained attitudes. Trying to change those attitudes by fiat or lecturing would only breed resentment. South Korea's military leaders had to be persuaded to elevate professional development and leadership as their top priorities.

After a few hours of fitful sleep, the steward awakened me with the news that we would land at Osan in an hour or so, which left just enough time for me to shave and change out of my jogging suit and into a uniform. There were no windows in the aircraft, so I could not see the dark countryside or the twinkling lights of the villages and houses scattered among the paddy fields and mountains along the heavily populated western coast of South Korea. On past flights, I had always marveled at the tranquillity of the countryside below. It was a touching scene, one that could not help but inspire a commitment to ensure that peace and stability were protected and maintained on the Korean peninsula.

This time, though, I was apprehensive. Dawn was about to break over the countryside, but I could see little daylight ahead. I would have been even more apprehensive had I known how much work would be cut out for me in the months ahead, or the challenges I would have to face.

Chapter Two

Aftermath of the Assassination

Return to Seoul

"Welcome back to Korea!" The familiar voice that boomed from the darkness at the foot of the aircraft steps belonged to Lieutenant General Evan Rosencrans, the chief of staff of the U.S.–ROK CFC and deputy commander of USFK. An Air Force pilot with a straightforward manner, Evan had become a trusted friend.

Accompanying him were Sergeant Jong Kim, USA, one of the two drivers assigned to the CINC staff, and Colonel David Lynch, USA, my executive assistant. I had recently selected Lynch for this job because of his reputation for extraordinary efficiency and professional talent. In the years to come, he would not disappoint me.

The cool night air of the Korean autumn was pungent with the smell of piles of rice husks smoldering in nearby paddies, a centuries-old practice used by farmers to help fertilize the soil. Koreans often refer to their glorious fall weather as *ch'on ko ma pi*, which can be roughly translates as "the sky is high and the horses are fat." The saying alludes to the benefits of full harvests and clear, blue skies over the countryside. It supposedly came from the Huns and their ancient practice of sending their fierce tribes on autumn raids into China. When successful, which they most often were, their superb cavalry rode "fat horses" of conquest.

Rosencrans and Lynch briefed me during the hour-long drive to the Hill Top House for breakfast. This residence was the U.S. commander's quarters in Seoul. As its name suggests, this relatively simple masonry house stood on the highest ground in the Yongsan U.S. military compound, just north of the Han River. The sprawling Yongsan compound, which is located adjacent to the ROK Ministry of National Defense and subordinate army headquarters, houses a number of American facilities, including several military headquarters, various family quarters,

27

and what used to be a fine golf course, before it was returned to the Koreans for conversion into a beautiful city park.

The Japanese originally constructed the Yongsan compound during their harsh occupation of Korea from 1910 to 1945. Some remnants of that period still remain, including an air raid bunker that is still in use as an operations facility. The post is in the midst of the city and stands in neat, orderly contrast to the jumble of narrow streets lined with shops and stalls, ripe smelling markets, and ancient housing crammed into every available space.

Living on a hill top has symbolic significance in Korean culture. For reasons of honor and prestige, the senior individual should either occupy the highest terrain or be as close to the top as possible. It is a matter of status and the notion of "face," which remains a very important element in social relationships. One must be careful not to give offense through demeaning behavior that injures an individual's "face," or *kibun*.

Kibun has no exact English translation, but can be described as self-esteem or the sense of status of a Korean. I was told by a language instructor that if I were to use Korean words in conversation with Koreans who were senior in rank or older than me, that I should include the suffix "nim" which means sir and connotes respect for an elder. Otherwise, I might offend. It was an interesting point and one that suggested I had a lot to learn about Korean culture and not much time to accomplish that task.

The drive north took us along a narrow two-lane rural road, much of it still gravel or packed earth. We rode through farmland, mostly dry rice paddies at that time of year, and sleepy villages that were just stirring with the early sunbeams of dawn. The countryside was dotted with low-lying, largely treeless hills, and my mind departed from the pastoral setting to dwell on the fact that the terrain would offer few obstacles to an armored attack by North Korean forces driving south toward Osan Air Base, our major airfield. To do this, the attacking forces would have to make an eastward bypass around Seoul, an attack option we believed the North Koreans might favor, because they would not want to become bogged down in urban fighting.

The villages we passed, like almost all towns in South Korea, consisted mostly of two-story homes, built from concrete, with blue- or red-tiled roofs. These modern homes were a vast improvement over the squat earthen huts covered by straw-thatched roofs that abounded in rural areas when President Park took power in 1961. To Park's lasting credit, he immediately adopted initiatives to improve the country's living standards and hygiene as he rebuilt from the war. All this progress stood to be destroyed in the event of another attack.

In our discussions during the ride, it was obvious that the situation was still quite murky. Most Koreans were in a state of shock and unable to provide much information to us. Even the U.S. Embassy had only limited knowledge about the assassination or the specific actions being taken by the ROK Government. General Rhu, the CFC deputy commander, was spending most of his time at the Ministry of National Defense, so he had been unable to provide much information to General Rosencrans. The ROK Government was preoccupied with Park's funeral arrangements, which had also interfered with our efforts to gather information. Dave Lynch, who had solid contacts with a number of ROK army colonels, said he was equally unable to gain much information. He noted, however, that an atmosphere of suspicion and uneasiness existed among the ROK officers assigned to the CFC staff. None of the Korean officers was willing to offer comments on internal events.

I asked Evan what Jim Hausman had been able to learn about the situation. Jim was a special assistant to the CINC and had been in Korea almost continuously since the end of World War II, when he had served as an army officer with responsibilities for helping the Koreans create an army. Many of the Korean army leaders regarded him as a good friend, or *cho-un chingu*, and his role now was to provide politico-military advice to the U.S. authorities and to ensure that our intelligence reporting was sound. It was a key responsibility.

Jim was on a first-name basis with virtually all of the senior ROK officers, who held him in very high esteem for both his sincerity and his intimate knowledge of the Korean scene. He could be counted on to report on Korean military thinking—at least what the Koreans wanted us to hear—but he could also be engaged when necessary to convey unvarnished views back to the Korean leaders. Jim's office included Steve Bradner and Bruce Grant, both of whom had lived in Korea for many years and spoke fluent Korean. Bruce, in addition to his mastery of Korean, was an accomplished Chinese language scholar. All three men had unique connections within ROK society, and Jim's advice, as well as his staff's, was invaluable to me, as it had been to previous CINCs.

This time, though, Jim was as surprised as everyone else. He was also immensely troubled by the potential for unrest as a result of Park's death. He noted as well that it was difficult to predict how North Korea would react; Kim Il-sung and his son had unchallenged authority over a closed, suspicious society, and it was impossible to know what decisions they would make.

Evan then reviewed the messages that had been released by the CFC and the ROK Joint Chiefs of Staff. *Chin Do Kae II* (second highest counter-infiltration alert) had been declared by the ROK authorities, and U.S. forces had raised their own alert status to Defense Condition Three (DEFCON 3). No incidents had been reported along the DMZ, although both sides were engaged in more frequent patrolling. The usual, coarse propaganda was blaring from North Korea's speaker system along the DMZ.

Evan told me that the ROK Ministry of Defense had notified CFC that it was withdrawing several army combat units from CFC control for deployment to Seoul. There was nothing unusual about that procedure. When CFC was established in 1978, the ROK Government gave operational control (OPCON) of almost half a million ROK military personnel from all services to CFC. This commitment was for defensive purposes only and did not extend to internal or domestic security matters, which remained the sovereign responsibility of the ROK Government. Thus, the terms of reference for CFC included the provision that in the event of internal needs, the ROK Government could withdraw any of its forces that were placed under the operational control of CFC, as long as it notified the command.

The Minister of National Defense told Rosencrans that he intended to hold these combat units in reserve, as a precaution against any disorder that might arise in the wake of the assassination and the upcoming funeral. The units would be returned to CFC as soon as possible. The ROK 20th Infantry Division, together with its artillery and three infantry regiments, fell back under ROK army control early on 27 October. The division was garrisoned only a few miles north of Seoul and had been trained extensively in riot control, as it was included in the ROK contingency plans for use during internal disturbances.

The North Korean Response

American signals-intelligence units began to report greatly increased activity in North Korean communications, particularly around the several major headquarters in North Korea's capital. I could not be sure what was happening, but I had a fairly good idea.

In Pyongyang, General Oh Jin-u, chief of the armed forces (eventually Marshall and Minister of Defense), probably was summoned sometime around dawn to an underground command bunker in the city's outskirts.

Deceptively youthful in appearance, General Oh had a well-earned reputation for toughness, harsh leadership, and professional competence. He was quick to take charge of events and he was intensely loyal to Kim Il-sung, a loyalty that was repaid with high trust and confidence from North Korea's leader.

When General Oh arrived at the bunker, the senior duty officer probably informed him that North Korean agent teams in South Korea were reporting a great deal of unusual activity by the national police and local security forces in all of the major cities. (One agent team in Seoul had actually furnished the information that a motorcade from the Blue House had driven late in the evening of October 26 to a nearby military hospital. This particular team had actually concluded, from the nature of the motorcade, that a senior official, perhaps President Park himself, must have been injured. The team even conjectured that a coup might be underway, although it had no evidence of it.)

The duty officer probably also informed General Oh that the radio communications among frontline ROK and U.S. units had suddenly increased. He may even have mentioned that intercepts from several ROK divisions had revealed that an increase in counter-infiltration alert had been ordered. Since the ROK armed forces lacked sophisticated communications encryption devices, their communications were easily penetrated, and General Oh had more than enough experience to realize that an increase in ROK and U.S. communications was consistent with an increase in readiness.

It became immediately apparent to me how General Oh responded to this news. That morning an order went out to all North Korean forces that placed them on a wartime footing. It included an alert of the forces along the DMZ and an order to disperse all aircraft. North Korea's intelligence collection also was increased, with particular emphasis on communications intercepts. Presumably, agent teams in South Korea were also directed to increase their reporting of military movements and activities in all major cities, particularly Seoul.

General Oh must then have left the bunker to brief Kim Il-sung, the 68–year-old president. The wily, enigmatic Kim remained in overall charge, although, because of his age, he had delegated the day-to-day operations of the nation to his erratic and peculiar son, Kim Jong-il. Kim must have approved Oh's recommendations.

Beyond that, it was hard to know what North Korea was thinking. The responses that were transparent to our intelligence signaled one of two alternatives. North Korea was either taking precautions in response to the signs of increased activity on our side of the DMZ, or it was preparing its forces to exploit any opportunities.

We did have one factor in our favor. It was fall, and that meant that large numbers of North Korean infantry and transportation units were still assisting the farmers with the rice harvest. That meant the North Korean army would require a few more weeks to restore its readiness to the levels required to undertake sustained combat operations. We had a breathing spell, but it was obvious that actions were underway to make sure it would not last long.

Chun Takes Charge of the Investigation

We now know that just before dawn, Chun presided over a tense meeting with his staff and the group of officers he had handpicked to gather evidence for the investigation into Park's murder. The mood was unusually somber. Chun had a distinctively brisk manner and spoke without emotion, although he chain-smoked continuously, an indication that he was under great personal strain. Ever since the coup of 1961, President Park had looked after Chun's career. They were so close that Chun often referred to Park as father. Now that he had suddenly lost his patron, he faced a future clouded with uncertainty.

Chun informed his staff that he had been at the fateful meeting in the MND when the KCIA Director Kim Jae-kyu had been accused of killing the president. After that, it had been decided that Chun and the DSC would have the sole authority to conduct the investigation into the assassination. He informed his staff that there had been other senior officers present at the Blue House when the assassination occurred, a fact that made the investigation both dangerous and sensitive. In his mind, it opened the possibility of a conspiracy within the ROK Government, the military, and the KCIA.

As the chief investigator, he was responsible only to the acting president and the minister of defense. He told his staff that he needed to know everything about the crime and who was involved, either directly or indirectly. Then he wondered aloud about army Chief of Staff Chung's whereabouts at the time of the crime and about his nervous behavior at the MND meeting. He said he had been amazed that Kim Jae-kyu and his guards had been allowed to remain armed throughout the opening hours of the meeting. No one else had weapons, except the military police, and it turned out they did not even have any ammunition.

Was Kim the lone mastermind of the plot to kill the president, or were there others, perhaps including Chung? Chun wondered why Kim had not been arrested immediately after the president's death and speculated that the delay was more than suspicious.

He noted that there were many unanswered questions about the objectives of the assassination, the extent of the conspiracy, and what actions might follow—musing out loud that some of these potential actions might affect the careers, if not the personal safety, of many senior officers and officials. All of which highlighted in his mind the need for urgency in concluding the investigation and identifying the culprits. The Korean people would expect nothing less, Chun emphasized, and he did not believe the North Koreans were implicated in any way, so the investigators should not spend much time on that possibility. Nevertheless, Chun warned them not to underestimate North Korea's capacity for malevolence and unpredictable behavior, or the very real possibility that the North Koreans could try to take advantage of the confusion. He mentioned that his friend, Bob Brewster, the CIA station chief, had told him that the United States would be increasing its presence in the region.

Chun then directed his investigators to be unflagging in their efforts to collect all of the details, to move quickly, and to brook no interference whatsoever. He instructed them to begin with KCIA Director Kim Jae-kyu and Blue House Chief Secretary Kim Kye-won. Chun wanted both men interrogated immediately to see if they could provide any further leads. If the investigators ran into any opposition at all, Chun was to be contacted right away so he could deal with it. DSC operatives throughout the military had already been ordered to report directly to Chun, via their separate channels of communication, on any unusual activities that might be related to coup plotting. He ended the meeting by ordering the investigating team to brief him at least daily and immediately after their interrogation of the assassin.

No one in the room was left with any doubts about Chun's take charge role in the investigation. Nor were there any doubts that he harbored deep suspicions that some senior leaders in the army and KCIA might have been involved in what he clearly thought was a full-blown conspiracy.

An oriental proverb warns that if you are going to ride a tiger, you had better stay on, because to fall off is to be eaten. Chun was now astride a tiger. The responsibility to investigate Park's death was not only an opportunity to acquire personal power, but also a threat to his very existence.

Coordinating the In-Country Response

After breakfast I drove downtown to the modern U.S. Embassy building to meet with Ambassador Gleysteen. The streets were almost deserted except for small knots of uniformed national policeman at almost every corner. As I approached the Embassy at the northern end of the main avenue, my eyes were drawn to a massive building in the Blue House compound a short distance away. The Japanese had constructed the building as their government headquarters during the occupation of Korea. The building blocked the view of the ancient and majestic royal Korean palace, *Kyongbuk-kong*, just behind it. Of course, that was exactly what the Japanese colonialists had intended.

The early morning sunlight illuminated the baroque-style architecture and the imposing dome, making the building seem oddly incongruous in this beautiful city. It had long since been converted into government offices and part of the national museum, but its very presence was still a displeasing reminder of a very ugly period in Korean history. (Under President Kim Young-sam it was razed.)

Walking down the narrow Embassy hallway to Bill Gleysteen's office, I was drawn to the pictures of the former American ambassadors, a few of whom I recognized, like Phil Habib and Sam Berger, whom I had known in Vietnam. More than a few of these former ambassadors had weathered crises as serious as the one we now faced, and there was some solace in that. There was even more solace in the fact that Bill Gleysteen was the current ambassador. He was a solid professional with considerable experience on the Korean scene. He also had the support of a strong and effective country team that worked well with the USFK and CFC staffs.

I summarized the results of the NSC meeting in Washington and outlined the military actions that were already in motion. Bill told me he had been in touch with Acting President Choi Kyu-ha, both to convey American condolences and to reassure Choi that he could expect strong support from the United States. Bill then advised me that it would be very important for me to use my contacts with the ROK military to commend the military leaders for their support of the constitution and to urge them to maintain that support until a new president could be elected. As I recall, he did not express any opinions about any of the potential candidates for president, except to note that the acting president would be a natural candidate.

Turning to the assassination, he said the CIA station chief, Bob Brewster, had gathered enough knowledge to conclude that the plot had been hatched by the KCIA director. However, it was still unclear just how far the plot extended or whether any military leaders were involved. Chun, who had been put in charge of the investigation, happened to be a longtime friend of Brewster's, so we should be in a position to gain reliable information as the investigation proceeded.

Finally, Bill approved an official letter that I planned to send to the acting president, through Minister of Defense Rho Jae-hyun, whom I would be seeing in a few hours. General Rhu had helped draft the following letter:

Dear Acting President Choi:

At this time of great national sorrow, the officers, men and women of the ROK/US Combined Forces Command reaffirm their total dedication to the Nation's security.

The Republic's loss is grievous. President Park Chung-hee was responsible for stimulating and directing the economic miracle that has moved the ROK to the forefront of developing industrial nations. The legacy he leaves in the nation he loved and served so well is long and distinguished. His achievements will remain an inspiration. The mark of his leadership is an indelible part of Korean history.

The nation united under your leadership insures that the fabric of Korean society will not be torn by this tragic event. The military leaders of the nation have closed ranks to assure the people that the shield of defense remains strong and impenetrable. I support the solidarity which will sustain Korea through this troubled period.

President Carter has reaffirmed the unwavering United States commitment to the security of the Republic of Korea. I affirm to you and the people of the ROK that should hostilities occur the Combined Forces Command will defend the Republic in accordance with directions from the national command and military authorities. I assure you that the Combined Forces Command will remain ready and totally dedicated to the security of the Republic.

My thoughts and prayers are with you as you carry out the important responsibilities of acting president during this difficult period.

Before I left, Bill asked for my assessment of North Korea's attack option and the readiness of our forces to handle such an eventuality. I told him that we had concluded that the North Koreans were not well prepared to launch a "standing start" attack, and that if they chose to do so, we believed the attack would be defeated along the first line of defense, the forward edge of the battle area (FEBA) ALPHA.

FEBA ALPHA was continually manned by full-strength infantry divisions and included substantial concrete obstacles to impede the movement of attacking mechanized forces. With even limited warning of an attack, our forces would have enough time to activate a series of more difficult obstacles, such as concrete drops over roadways and the emplacement of extensive minefields from our forward stocks. Moreover, our operational plans included extensive air strikes of North Korean military targets, and our South Korean and American air crews had been thoroughly briefed and updated on their assigned targets.

I also informed him that numerous North Korean army units had been scattered to farm areas to assist with the fall rice harvest, and it would take days, perhaps even weeks, to bring those units and their equipment back to full readiness. The CFC believed the North Koreans would require two to four weeks to attain a readiness level sufficient for an attack to be launched. We had also concluded that the North Koreans could not maintain a wartime footing for more than two to three weeks without disastrously degrading their force and materiel readiness—a problem we shared.

This assessment had also been transmitted to CINCPAC and to the U.S. Joint Chiefs of Staff, together with our recommendation that the U.S. military reinforcements—the AWACS, tactical air, and naval combatant ships—should remain in place, both for deterrence and intelligence collection.

The Investigators Report

Several days after the assassination, Chun received his initial briefing from the team of investigators. Chun and his associates probably found the conclusions deeply disturbing.

The investigators began by reviewing the results of their interrogations of KCIA Director Kim Jae-kyu, Blue House Chief Secretary Kim Kye-won, and Lieutenant General Lee Jae-jeon, Cha Chi-chul's assistant and the deputy head of the presidential security force. (Cha, the head of the security force, had been murdered along with President Park.) The investigators also outlined all of the information that had been gathered in the early days of their work.

They reported that the KCIA director had simply ranted about his patriotic motives and reiterated that he was a national savior for killing the president and Cha Chi-chul. Kim Jae-kyu claimed that the vexatious security chief was detested by nearly everyone in the government—which was true—and that he himself had rid the country of Cha's influence. Kim insisted again and again that everyone believed that Park had been in office far too long, that he had greatly abused his power, and that his continued rule was endangering the nation. The investigators concluded that Kim was not very cooperative, hewing completely to these wild recitations.

The KCIA director steadfastly refused to implicate any others in the plot. More importantly, he specifically avoided any adverse comments about General Chung, claiming that Chung only happened to be near the site of the assassination, because Kim had invited him to an informal dinner weeks before. The dinner with President Park, according to Kim, had been hastily arranged only a few hours before, and therefore the army chief's presence was merely a coincidence.

As for the interrogation of the Blue House Chief Secretary, Kim Kye-won, little had been revealed beyond the facts the investigators had already known. The Blue House chief secretary appeared to have been a terrified bystander at the murder scene, although the investigators were still dubious about how he managed to escape without any injuries. Kim said he tried to save the president by taking him to a nearby military hospital, but Park died before he could get him medical help. Kim was at least able to corroborate many of the details about the dinner and the murderous actions by Kim Jae-kyu and his security guards.

Notwithstanding the KCIA director's testimony, the investigators informed Chun that they were still suspicious about General Chung's role. They might have been playing to Chun's own doubts about the army chief of staff, but the investigators were also bothered by their inability to determine the full extent of Chung's actions on the night of the assassination, or why he happened to be near the site of the murder.

So far, the investigators had not been able to arrange for the interrogation of Chung. They undoubtedly were aware of how awkward that would be, because of Chun's rank and Chung's authority as the martial law commander.

At the end of the briefing, Chun's chief investigator asked to speak with him in private. When they were alone, the investigator whispered to

Chun that, in the course of gathering information, he had heard rumors about the imminent moves of a number of senior military officers. Given all of the uncertainty in the aftermath of Park's death, the rumors might be nothing more than sheer speculation, but the investigator considered his sources fairly reliable.

According to what he had heard, Chung apparently suspected some officers of being unreliable or too politically ambitious, and he was worried that these officers might cause trouble during the tenuous transition period before a new president could be elected. Chung had said that in order to ensure a constitutional succession, it would be necessary to retire several senior officers and to shift some others into less influential and powerful positions. As the martial law commander, he was in an unchallenged position to control army assignments and promotions, and because of the role he had played in making Prime Minister Choi the acting president, Chung could expect tacit approval for whatever decisions he made.

Chun asked the investigator if the rumors happened to include any names. The investigator said that yes, in fact they did, and that one of the names was Chun himself. The rumors indicated that Chun probably would not be retired, but that Chung was thinking about reassigning him to the East Coast Security Command. Remote from Seoul and the vital historical invasion corridors north of the capital, the East Coast command was viewed as a backwater, retirement assignment. Chun had heard the same rumor from other sources, but he was stunned nonetheless. He thanked the investigator for the report and then told him to get on with his important work.

Although armed only with rumors, Chun seems to have concluded that he had to initiate actions to safeguard his own future. His principal mentor and "father" figure, President Park, was dead, so there would be no help from that quarter. But, Chun had been appointed the chief investigator of the assassination, and that left him reporting only to the acting president and the minister of defense. He had been dealt an interesting hand of cards and had to play it right.

He was not without resources. For one thing, he controlled the extensive network of the DSC, an organization with extraordinary power. He was also buoyed by his Korean Military Academy Class 11 connections, particularly among the ambitious "Taegu Seven Stars." They, like Chun, were fed up with the slow pace of promotions and disgruntled by what they saw as a military hamstrung by incompetent senior officers and a nation misled by self-serving politicians.

This frustration would bubble over as a result of several developments during the troublesome transition period. One development in particular—one that was strongly encouraged by American officials—was the attempt to foster more liberalized treatment and attitudes toward the ROK opposition parties and dissident leaders. That was a hot-button topic for the conservative ROK military leaders, most of whom deeply distrusted two of the three Kims. The third Kim, Kim Jong-pil, had at least been a career military officer, which gave him a certain reputation within the military, although he was considered corrupt and overly ambitious. But Kim Young-sam and Kim Dae-jung were held in special contempt, as they were both considered by many ROK officers to have been draft evaders during the Korean war who held soft views on how to deal with North Korea. At one point during the transition, the three Kims sought to arrange a series of visits to some frontline military units, an effort that was viewed with great disgust by many in the ROK officer corps as a self-serving and politically manipulative attempt by the Kims to improve their poor images.

For the moment, Chun found himself in a position that combined both great risk and remarkable opportunity. His formative experience as a protege of President Park had taught him how to maneuver successfully in accumulating power and, of equal importance, how to deal with Americans. Moreover, by virtue of his DSC responsibilities, Chun had developed a close working relationship with the CIA station chief, Bob Brewster. That friendship would enable Chun to keep Americans informed, if not influenced, to his advantage.

A Meeting with the Minister

After visiting Ambassador Gleysteen, I drove straight to the MND building for a scheduled meeting with the Minister of Defense Rho Jae-hyun, a former army general. Rho exercised considerable power in the government and would play an important role during the transition. He was tall by Korean standards, graying, somewhat reserved, and humorless. When he spoke, it was with conviction and firm self-assurance, an attitude no doubt fortified by his physical stature and the respect he enjoyed among senior ROK military officers. He had fought in both the Korean and Vietnam wars and had been hand picked to head the ministry by President Park himself. Thus, his credentials were impeccable, and Secretary Brown, General Jones, and I had all been impressed by his detailed knowledge of the issues and his professional conduct at the recent Security Consultative Meeting held in Seoul.

At the ministry, I was met by the always smiling Mr. Han, the minister's personal interpreter and assistant. Han was and still is a revered fixture at the ministry, having served a number of ministers and participated in many Security Consultative Meetings. He was a flawless translator, a skill helped considerably by his complete mastery of nearly every security issue that affected our two nations. Like most expert interpreters, Han would carefully study the speech habits, inflections, and usages of the men he was translating, and then quickly adapt his translations to mirror their habits. His experience and skill assured reliable translations of often complex and nearly always sensitive issues. As for Minister Rho, like many ROK officers he understood far more English than he would acknowledge, but he always used an interpreter, both to ensure clarity and to buy time for himself to compose more thoughtful answers.

Mr. Han escorted me past the armed security guards and through the foyer with its marble walls and floor. We rode the elevator to the second floor of the eight-story headquarters and entered the conference room. It was decorated with the usual array of colorful Korean paintings, scrolls, and celadon vases, as it was the room where the minister normally met with his visitors and held official ceremonies. After a few moments, Minister Rho walked in from his adjoining office. He was accompanied by the chairman of the ROK Joint Chiefs of Staff, General Kim Chung-hwan, who deferred to his senior and said very little during the meeting.

During those years, the ROK chairman did not exercise the same power or influence as his counterpart in the United States. For protocol purposes he ranked above all of the other ROK chiefs of service, but in reality the army chief of staff was far more powerful than any other officer in the country.

The traditional cups of ginseng tea with pine nuts were served while I conveyed the personal condolences of Secretary Brown and Chairman Jones. Minister Rho reflected silently for a few moments before he thanked me. He then explained that an investigation by the DSC was underway to determine whether a plot existed and, if so, who was involved, admitting to me that the motives and many of the details were still unknown. He recounted what had happened that evening, although I noticed that he was careful not to elaborate or speculate on the motives of those behind the president's death or on the extent of the suspected conspiracy. It would have been unseemly to press him for more details.

Turning to the current situation, Rho said that the South Korean people naturally looked to the military for both the defense of the country and the maintenance of domestic stability. Everyone was aware that North Korea's forces and terrorists might attempt to take advantage of the confusion. He accentuated the need for heightened security measures, even as he mentioned that it was for that very reason that he had decided to temporarily withdraw the 20th Infantry Division from CFC operational control.

Based on my earlier discussion with Bill Gleysteen, I told Rho that the ROK military were to be commended for their support of the cabinet and the constitutional process. I told him that it would be essential for the military to continue this firm support.

As soon as this meeting ended, I drove across the street to the ROK army headquarters for a brief discussion with the army Chief of Staff, General Chung. Appearing very fatigued, Chung's manner indicated great grief and bewilderment with the situation. He had known President Park all of his life and had been personally selected by him to serve in the powerful position of the army chief of staff. I was sure that his grief was sincere and could only imagine what must have been running through his mind.

Throughout our discussion, Chung did not comment or even hint at his personal circumstances or the details of the assassination. Nor did he elaborate on the details of the meeting in the Ministry of Defense that occurred the night of the assassination. Rather, he turned abruptly to military matters and explained, as the defense minister had done, why the ROK army had withdrawn the 20th Division from CFC. He mentioned as well that there might be a need for more forces to be withdrawn in the future, and that he would inform me whenever the occasion arose. For the time being, he saw no need to actually use military force to handle domestic disturbances inside the country, but he wanted to be prepared.

He made a careful point to express his total dedication to the constitution and the maintenance of law and order. He repeated this several times to be certain I understood. To make his point, he told me that he had deliberately vetoed the effort to install him as the acting president, prevailing on his peers to exclude the island of Cheju from the realm of martial law, specifically to limit his own powers and authority. As we spoke, Chung's executive officer, a highly decorated infantry colonel, served as our interpreter.

Chung mentioned that we should continue to meet regularly to share information and discuss security issues. I agreed, even as I had no idea what was in store for him, although I remember thinking how difficult it probably was to be in his shoes.

A few nights later, General Rhu, the deputy commander in chief of CFC, came to dinner at the Hill Top House. Rhu spoke fluent English, so there was no need for an interpreter. He told me that he had been at the Ministry of National Defense on the night of the assassination, and then went on to recount everything that he had been able to learn. There was nothing new in what he said, but it was a helpful corroboration. Then he reviewed the details of the decision to exclude Cheju from martial law authority and the joint decision to sign a pledge of support for the acting president. He assured me that there was total support among the military leaders for the cabinet and the constitutional process. He said he knew of no dissent or unrest.

Nevertheless, he was deeply concerned. He predicted a great deal of maneuvering among the nation's politicians and said he was concerned about the possibility of domestic unrest. He felt that any sign of unrest would present a picture of weakness to North Korea and perhaps invite attack. He added that it was imperative for the acting president to announce a strong plan of action for the next several months. Rhu and a number of other senior officers were already cautioning the Korean officer corps against taking any actions for their personal gain. Of course, there was still the possibility that the president's death was the result of a conspiracy. Rhu said that he intended to avoid sleeping in the same place each night.

With General Rhu, Deputy Commander in Chief of Combined Forces Command, during command briefing.

Visiting the Troops

Before dawn the next day, I headed out of Seoul by helicopter for several days of visits to combat units, including several infantry regiments, some ROK naval patrol aircraft squadrons, the NIKE and HAWK air defense batteries, and a few ROK Air Force fighter squadrons. My initial visits were to some frontline troops along the DMZ and the headquarters of our major operational units. These included the I Corps (ROK-U.S.) Group, commanded by a U.S. three-star general, which controlled the defenses of the infamous Chorwon invasion corridor; the Third ROK Army (TROKA), which was responsible for the defense of Seoul and the invasion corridors to the north and west; and finally, the First ROK Army (FROKA), which defended the mountainous and relatively unpopulated terrain far to the east of Seoul.

Four-star generals commanded both of the forward ROK armies. The Second ROK Army (SROKA) controlled all the terrain and defenses south of Seoul. SROKA did not come under CFC OPCON because its mission largely involved rear-area security and the training of reserve and support units.

I was relieved to find that everyone appeared to be "looking north" and did not seem overly preoccupied with political developments back in Seoul, although the ROK soldiers I met with clearly were troubled by President Park's death. That was more than understandable. Park had led their country for nearly two decades, and many of the younger soldiers had never known any other national leader. His passing heralded a new and uncertain era.

Still, I was impressed by the toughness, serious demeanor, and professional competence of South Korean soldiers, as well as their intense motivation to protect their homeland against attack or infiltration from the North. Their toughness was the product of rigorous training and Spartan living conditions. When not on duty, soldiers stationed along the DMZ lived in small communal buildings without running water or much heat and slept side-by-side on hard, wooden floors. Winter temperatures frequently dipped below zero, and biting winds blew from the northeast, bringing both a frosty chill and balloons filled with North Korean leaflets. The ever present din of propaganda broadcasts created an eerie atmosphere.

The readiness of the ROK army combat units also was the result of quality leadership. While cultural differences and low pay left the ROK army with few professional noncommissioned officers, virtually all of the combat battalion and company commanders were college graduates or products of the Korean Military Academy. The officers also received first-class professional instruction at the military's infantry, artillery, and other schools, all of which were patterned on the U.S. military system.

One visit in particular made a deep impression. I went to a ROK infantry division that was stationed on the demilitarized zone, in the mountains northwest of Seoul, very near the Chorwon valley. Major General Oh Ja-baek, a graduate of officer candidate school, commanded the division. Oh was a uniquely talented officer who would eventually be promoted to three stars and given command of the ROK National Security Agency, which has a mission similar to its American namesake. He would also become a very close friend.

Late in the day, Oh met my helicopter. We drove together in his jeep to an observation post at a high point along the DMZ fence line. We were met at the windy observation post by the ROK corps commander and several staff officers. General Sennewald, the CFC operations officer, also was there. One of the purposes of this visit was to review the plans for replacing warning signs along the center of the demilitarized zone.

With Ann on the demilitarized zone.

The signs were made of metal, painted a faded-yellow, and set on concrete posts that were spaced several hundreds yards apart along the 150–mile DMZ. Black lettered warnings written in Chinese, Korean, and English had been installed after the armistice in July 1953. Their purpose was to mark the center of the demilitarized zone. Weather had obliterated the warnings on many of the signs. Others had been overgrown by foliage or had simply collapsed from years of erosion.

The plan, which had actually required the approval of the Carter administration, authorized the repair of the signs, but under the auspices of UNC, which was responsible for the terrain along the southern portion of the zone. Most of the signs could be reached only with some difficulty. Although it sounded like a simple, mundane mission, it actually entailed considerable dangers. An earlier effort to refurbish the signs had been aborted as a result of casualties from North Korean ambushes and fire fights.

Bob Sennewald and I were privately skeptical of the plan, which had been prepared and approved months before our arrival in Korea. The risk of casualties would be great, and we were not convinced that it was worth the cost. The North Koreans would probably see the refurbishment as a further manifestation of the permanent separation of the two Koreas, a symbolic issue that was sure to draw their violent opposition.

The plan would require multiple patrols, each consisting of about 11 soldiers, to replace all of the signs that could be reached safely. The patrols would occur over several months. Each patrol would have mine-clearance capabilities and enough security to cope with potential ambushes. We intended to begin the repairs in General Oh's sector, because his outposts either had visual observation of the signs or were on ground high enough to dominate the areas where the signs would be repaired. In the event of a mine explosion or an ambush by North Korean forces, Oh's forces would be capable of providing covering fire to extract the patrols with minimum casualties.

Peering down at the nearest sign, several kilometers away, we reviewed the details of the plan and how General Oh would control the initial patrol. I was struck by the peacefulness of the scene in the valley below. Dense, lush foliage covered the ground, and the absence of normal human activity had turned the zone into a nature preserve, home to many rare and endangered species. There was no sign of human activity along the southern DMZ fence, and I could see nothing on the North Korean side.

Without revealing my skepticism, I asked Oh what he thought about the operation. He reflected for a few minutes and then pointed to the nearest sign. Using field glasses, he observed that the warning words were recognizable to him, although faded. He asked Sennewald and me to verify that with our binoculars.

Then he explained that in his opinion, this particular sign continued to serve its original purpose and that, for a variety of reasons, he believed that the North Koreans would not be at all keen about the overall endeavor to replace the signs. In any event, because of the plan's instructions to limit the effort to only those signs that could be safely approached, clearly the UNC would be able to repair only a fraction of the signs, so what was the purpose of fixing just a few of them? He assured me that he was fully prepared to execute the order, but if I wanted a frank opinion he considered the mission "unnecessary and overly dangerous. The signs, such as they are, continue to fulfill their purpose, and ROK forces have more important things to attend to."

The story is worth recounting because Oh's candor broke a cultural norm that had long been a worrisome aspect of his army's military professionalism. Respect for age and seniority often prevented Korean officers from disagreeing with their seniors, even when they were given orders that flew in the face of common sense. On a fluid, fast-moving battlefield, that kind of cultural obedience could prove very costly and troublesome. Making Oh's frankness all the more astonishing, he voiced his view in the presence of his superior corps commander and several other senior ROK officers.

It revealed a great deal. It displayed the open relationship that had matured over the years between ROK and U.S. officers, and it revealed that despite the corruption of the officer corps that President Park's cronyism had strongly encouraged, there were still many officers with personal integrity, professional talent, and sound leadership abilities. We immediately canceled the plan for replacing the DMZ signs.

Calm Before the Storm

After President Park's state funeral, I continued my visits to ROK military units and attended more meetings with senior ROK officials. I was careful to include meetings with certain retired senior officers, such as Generals Chung Il-kwon, Min Ki-shik, Paek Sun-yup, and Lee Hyong-kon, all former army chiefs of staff or chairmen of the JCS. General Chung Il-kwon had held other high political positions, including that of prime minister. These men had played key roles in the history of the Republic and had valuable and timely insights into what was happening in the capital and considerable leverage and prestige within the ROK military. I knew they could help persuade the current generation of senior officers, many of whom had served under them, to act responsibly and professionally during this time of change.

While Secretary of State Vance was in Seoul for the funeral, he had met with a number of the leaders of the ROK Government and key opposition parties. He had reaffirmed to all of them that the U.S. military augmentation would remain to help deter hostilities and had cautioned them all on the need to maintain domestic stability. At the same time, he had urged government leaders to move more rapidly toward political liberalization, to relax media censorship, to release some of the numerous political prisoners, and to lift Emergency Measure Nine, which sharply restricted dissent.

Ambassador Gleysteen was making the same points with his contacts in the ROK Government and with opposition leaders Kim Young-sam and Kim Dae-jung. In early December, Gleysteen encouraged Kim Young-sam to strengthen his ties with the military and to demonstrate his party's concern for the country's security in an effort to help the military overcome its strong distrust of the political opposition.

Kim Young-sam faced a steep uphill challenge with the military. In the words of Minister Rho, he was regarded as "a Korean war draft-evader who over past years has made many indiscrete and irresponsible remarks and was adept at manipulating, to include the United States through the embassy." South Korea's military leaders also disparaged Kim Dae-jung, who had just been released from house arrest. They considered him "untrustworthy and willing to do almost anything for political expediency." The ROK military did not have a very laudatory view of professional politicians, and especially not of the Kims.

Bill Gleysteen was very effective during this difficult and dangerous transition period. We compared notes almost daily. Bob Brewster, the CIA station chief, also met with me at least once a week. He offered a great deal of helpful advice on how to deal with various senior Korean leaders. Even though he was suffering from a serious disease that eventually would claim his life, his service was superb and enormously helpful.

But back in Washington, there was a peculiar confidence about the progress in Korea that those of us in-country did not share. For some reason, Washington believed that South Korea's political progress was still on track and that the North Koreans were being effectively deterred by American warnings and military reinforcements.

The U.S. election process also had begun to deflect attention from Korea. The presidential election was held in 1980, and the candidates were already on the stump, focusing their rhetoric on the dismal state of the U.S. economy, with its high inflation, sluggish growth, and double-digit interest rates. Ronald Reagan was energetically belittling the Carter administration for inept foreign policies and for endangering national security through military budget cuts.

Meanwhile, Minister Rho told me that the North Korean threat was the overriding rationale for limiting the freedoms of the opposition political parties. Almost weekly shooting incidents or infiltration attempts along the DMZ constituted strong grounds for this claim. Despite this concern, a number of senior Korean military leaders were also assuring me that political change was absolutely necessary, and that they were willing to tolerate a degree of dissension in order to achieve progress. At the same time, they emphatically rejected any notion of allowing an opposition party to lead the country. To my ears, that sounded illogical, but they were completely blind to the contradiction. That was the result of a kind of in-bred paternalism that is repugnant to Americans. More than once, I heard from ROK patriots that professional military officers regarded themselves as the faithful guardians of the nation, a fail-safe mechanism to keep the people from making mistakes.

I met frequently with Minister Rho and my deputy General Rhu, primarily on military matters, but nearly always the conversations edged over into political updates. No doubt, both men were also using me as a sounding board for their views, and, of course, they wanted me to carry back the message that ROK military leaders fully supported the constitutional process and acting President Choi.

All the military leaders I spoke with, including a number of senior and well-connected retirees, assured me of their desire to "get back to business as usual." They were very concerned that the state of political drift was harmful to the economy and that it could trigger domestic turmoil. Consequently, the military was privately pressuring the caretaker government to quickly enunciate a coherent program to get the economy back on track and to deal forthrightly with the nation's political matters. Sensing that this impatience might imply some threat of a coup, the military leaders were quick to point out to me that Korea in 1979 was quite unlike the Korea of 1961, when General Park Chung-hee had seized control. "The structure of the nation and its management are much more complicated and require broader leadership and technical talent than the military could provide," I was told.

Rhu emphasized again and again that the military fully supported the constitutional process. Reminding me, as Jim Hausman frequently did, that Korea does not have a history of peaceful transfers of political power, Rhu asked me to be sure to tell him if I heard of any rumors or detected any hints of political activity by active duty officers, because he and other senior military leaders would act quickly to put an end to it. He believed that setting a good example would be the most important legacy he and the other four star officers could leave to the Korean people and the younger officers who would follow in their footsteps.

Given the potential for trouble during the transition period, Rhu and Minister Rho urged me to keep the CFC force readiness above normal levels and to persuade the United States to keep its force augmentation in country, at least until after the presidential election. Both men were convinced that the North Koreans would increase their infiltration of agent teams to collect intelligence and target military facilities.

In the meantime, martial law commander and army Chief of Staff General Chung delivered stern warnings to both Kim Dae-jung and Kim Young-sam against taking any actions that might threaten internal law and order. Both men were warned formally that punitive action would be taken against them if they were unrestrained in their public comments. The Kims responded positively and agreed to abide by Chung's cautions. Newspaper editors, aware that censorship would continue, were warned not to contribute to speculation by "reporting irresponsible stories or stories of behind the scenes maneuvering. They should confine reporting to factual material."

As the days and weeks went by after the assassination, Minister Rho seemed to become more and more confident. He was self-assured by nature, but his confidence seemed to swell as a result of his role in Acting President Choi's "inner cabinet" and his deft handling of events. Rho confided to me that he would be kept on as the minister of defense after the election of Acting President Choi, an electoral win that he felt was all but assured. (Acting President Choi was, in fact, elected interim president on December 6 by the National Conference for Unification, to fill the rest of President Park Chung-hee's term of office, but did not officially become president until December 21.)

Despite Rho's optimism, I began to receive troubling reports in late November and early December about unrest among some of the younger generals. One of my sources was retired General Lee Hyong-kon, a former army chief of staff and chairman of the Joint Chiefs of Staff. General Lee approached me out of patriotic concern to inform me that a number of younger generals appeared to be intensely unhappy with the transition process and the fact that political opposition leaders were being allowed to foment unrest and dissent. The younger generals believed that America's policies were encouraging the liberalization of the media and the outspokenness of the opposition leaders. The officers were also openly bitter about the corruption in the government and business community, and they were restless over the prospect that the current military power structure would remain in place and inhibit their own promotion prospects.

This clique of younger generals, he said, came from Korean Military Academy classes 11 (1955), 12 (1956), and possibly 13 (1957). He was worried that they might try to seize power before the election of the president. He gave me no names, but at the time those three classes contained only a few generals, so it wasn't difficult to determine who might be involved.

He told me there were three broad factions within the ROK military. The first included the military's most senior leaders, the chiefs of the services and major unit commanders. This group, he said, "owes its loy-

Acting President Choi greeting me as Admiral Long, Commander in Chief, U.S. Pacific Command, looks on.

alty to the current political leadership and therefore is committed to minimum change and wants to maintain the status quo." The second faction began with Korea Military Academy class 11, some of whom were now major generals and brigadiers in key positions. The second faction views "with great skepticism politicians whom they regard as corrupt and not serious about national security. They desire some change to establish a broader basis of popular support, but they have deep mistrust of the politicians and they remain uneasy about the willingness of senior military and political leaders to tolerate change." The last faction, composed of lower ranking officers and enlisted men, "is closer to the people and the students. They essentially are impatient for change, but they do not want to be placed in a confrontational role against the people."

On December 4, I told Minister of Defense Rho about my unusual meeting with Lee. Rho replied, "Your informants, including General Lee, really have no feel for the pulse of the military. Of course there would be much speculation over the months to come, particularly by those who have little knowledge or responsibility for events. But be assured that the military will continue to support the political authority and the people." He repeated it twice to be sure I understood.

When I told the story to General Rhu, he was equally dubious. He said I was right to bring the information to his and the minister's attention—since that was exactly what they had asked me to do—but he also reminded me that as Koreans, he and the minister would always have more information about the domestic scene than would ever be available to an outsider. He told me I'd probably be the last one to know of any real political maneuvering or coup plotting.

Still bothered, I recounted this conversation to my political adviser, Jim Hausman, and he reminded me that General Carter Magruder, the American CINC at the time of General Park Chung-hee's coup in May of 1961, had absolutely no advance knowledge of what was about to occur. In that case, ROK troops under Magruder's command were even employed, without his authority, by the coup leaders.

Rhu and Minister Rho both were exceedingly confident that my information was without substance. They were wrong. Early in the evening of December 12, Korean history took a dangerous turn.

Map 2. **Yongsan Main and South Posts**

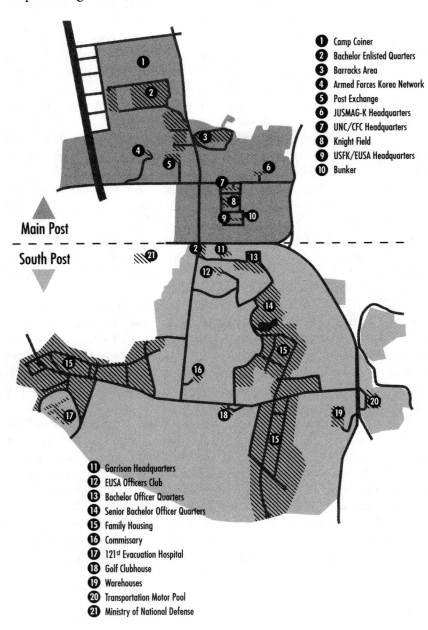

1. Camp Coiner
2. Bachelor Enlisted Quarters
3. Barracks Area
4. Armed Forces Korea Network
5. Post Exchange
6. JUSMAG-K Headquarters
7. UNC/CFC Headquarters
8. Knight Field
9. USFK/EUSA Headquarters
10. Bunker

Main Post

South Post

11. Garrison Headquarters
12. EUSA Officers Club
13. Bachelor Officer Quarters
14. Senior Bachelor Officer Quarters
15. Family Housing
16. Commissary
17. 121st Evacuation Hospital
18. Golf Clubhouse
19. Warehouses
20. Transportation Motor Pool
21. Ministry of National Defense

Chapter Three

The "12/12 Incident"

A s dusk fell over Seoul on December 12, the command center phone rang in the Hill Top House. Ann and I were alone, and soldiers from the United Nations Honor Guard company had just been posted at their nighttime guard posts around the exterior of the house. The clock showed about 7 P.M. It was pitch dark and almost freezing outside.

In a hushed tone over the secure phone General Rhu told me I had to come immediately to the underground bunker located next to the U.S. Forces, Korea/Eighth U.S. Army headquarters building. He had just arrived at the bunker and had taken the precaution of calling for the full CFC crisis staff. A series of unusual developments was transpiring around Seoul and apparently in other major cities as well. There were reports of ROK army units moving around the capital, securing key communications facilities and the bridges over the Han River. There were also reports of scattered small arms fire.

What units were involved and who was doing the firing was a mystery. Nearly all of the units of the ROK 20th Infantry Division had been returned to CFC operational control, and there had been no subsequent notifications from the ROK authorities that they were withdrawing any more combat units. That left a limited number of military forces under ROK military control, including the Special Forces brigades and a few battalions from the Seoul-based Capital Security Command.

Adding to Rhu's alarm, he and the staff in the bunker had been unable to contact any key Korean officials, including Defense Minister Rho; ROK Joint Chiefs of Staff Chairman, General Kim; and army Chief of Staff, General Chung. Even the duty officers at the ROK army headquarters were unable to reach them and had no idea where they were or what was happening.

I asked about our communications within the Combined Forces Command and Rhu told me that the operations staff was beginning to check telephone and radio connections with our subordinate headquarters and that, so far, solid communications existed with all of our major commands. He said that intelligence had detected no unusual North Korean communications or movements along the DMZ. I told him to put out an intelligence alert and that I would join him in the bunker.

Before leaving the house, I called Ambassador Gleysteen on the secure phone. I quickly explained the situation and asked him to join me at the bunker. Bill said that he and the embassy staff had no idea what was happening and he wondered if the activity might be related to North Korean infiltrators or, perhaps, to some sort of "muscle flexing" among elements in the ROK military. His comments hinted that he suspected a coup, but he did not make the full leap to that conclusion. He told me he would meet me at the command bunker within the hour.

Chun's Secret Meeting

In another part of Seoul, a group of conspiring ROK army generals had been cloistered at a secret meeting place since mid-afternoon. Several lieutenant generals were in attendance, but the "heavy" in the group was Major General Chun, the commander of the Defense Security Command. Chun had carefully selected the officers who were invited to the meeting. He knew each of them personally and, in fact, had approached them weeks before, in mid-November, about their willingness to be part of this group. Included were Lieutenant General Yoo Hak-sung, the assistant minister of defense for logistics; Lieutenant General Cha Kyu-hun, the Capital Corps commander; Lieutenant General Hwang Yung-si, the ROK First Corps commander; Major General Roh Tae-woo, the commander of the 9th Infantry Division; Major General Park Jun-byong, the commander of the 20th Infantry Division; Major General Paek Un-taek, the commander of the 71st Infantry Division; and Brigadier General Park Hee-do, the commander of the First Airborne Brigade.

Chun reportedly opened the meeting by sharing his deep concern about the growing political unrest within the country and his view that things were going to get quickly out of hand unless strong actions were taken. The revered "father" figure President Park was gone, a political vacuum existed, and the nation needed strong, new leadership. The current crop of aspiring presidential candidates was not up to the task. The three Kims—Kim Young-sam, Kim Dae-jung, and Kim Jong-pil—were all weak, self-serving, or corrupt. Acting President Choi, notwithstanding the

respect he earned for his ethics and professional talents, was an ineffec-
tual bureaucrat who lacked the qualities of a decisive leader.

Chun shared another concern as well. General Chung seemed to
be implicated in the assassination and was refusing to be interrogated, a
fact that aroused even further suspicions about his conduct.

Then Chun told the other generals that Chung was planning to
retire or reassign a number of officers, an indication that he was laying
the groundwork to seize power himself. Chun told them that his own
name was on the list for reassignment and that several others in the room
were slated for retirement. He knew the effect this revelation would have,
that it would cement their support for him to seize power. He had
reached the conclusion that his own survival depended on removing
Chung from the position of army chief. Unsurprisingly, the group of generals quickly agreed that Chung had to go, and they decided they had to
act immediately. They knew that waiting would run the risk of leaks.

They urged Chun to immediately dispatch a team of interrogators
to General Chung's residence. He replied that he was prepared to do just
that. In fact, Chun already had directed the DSC staff to plan the army
chief's arrest. In early December, the staff had suggested that, for the plan to
succeed, the commanders of certain key units who were expected to be loyal
to Chung had to be diverted. In fact, a dinner had been arranged for that
night, and all of the suspect commanders had been invited.

If Chung refused to meet with the DSC team that was sent to in-
terrogate him, he would be arrested and brought immediately to DSC
headquarters. The generals recognized that these actions might be regarded as highly irregular, but they concluded that Defense Minister Rho
and Acting President, now President-Elect, Choi probably could be persuaded to approve the arrest—after the fact, if necessary. Chun now had
the green light to arrest Chung.

Some of the generals in the room were already aware of a plan
Chun had prepared to establish complete military control within Seoul.
The plan would make use of units from the Special Forces brigades and
the 9th Infantry Division, commanded by Chun's military academy classmate, General Roh. Chun had already been in contact with the combat
leaders selected to perform the mission and was sure they were ready and
willing to support his plan.

Then came some spirited discussion about how to deal with the
Americans. Everyone in the room knew the United States was going to
take a very dim view of this kind of military action, and that could prove

troublesome. Chun confided that he had a solid working relationship with the CIA station chief, Bob Brewster, and said he would exploit that friendship to persuade the Americans, particularly the U.S. ambassador, that what they were doing posed no threat to American and ROK national security interests, to internal stability, or to the process of political liberalization. The Americans would be told that the group's objectives were quite limited and did not extend to the seizure of the nation's political leadership. Besides, Chun assured the others, he and several others in the room had the benefit of having worked for President Park early in his regime, where they had observed firsthand how Park dealt with the Americans. Although the situations were not entirely analogous, there were many lessons that could be applied to this case.

Chun assured them that he would also enlist the help of his friend, Major General Kim Yoon-ho, the commander of the Infantry School. Although Kim was not yet aware of Chun's plans, he could be helpful in persuading the Americans that Chun and his associates were only pursuing limited objectives to "clean house" in the military. The other generals knew Kim as a highly competent professional, fluent in English, and an independent and innovative thinker who was apolitical and trustworthy. They knew that Kim also had a warm friendship with Bob Brewster, that their families were equally close, and that Brewster had actually given Kim the nickname, "Bo Bo." The generals all agreed that Kim could be very helpful, and they were right.

Then Chun and his companions turned to the possibility of opposition from the U.S. military, particularly me. They all remembered that President Park had encountered serious difficulties with General Carter Magruder, the United Nations commander during and after the coup in 1961. Furious that the coup leaders had used forces under his command without his authority, Magruder had launched vigorous protests to the ROK and U.S. Governments. He ended up so thoroughly antagonizing his ROK counterparts, including Park Chung-hee, that he departed Korea and retired from the U.S. Army only a few months afterward. His retirement may have been voluntary, but it was certainly helped along by Park's protests to Washington.

Chun said he believed that I was close to the U.S. ambassador and that, like the ambassador, I would be critical of the actions about to be taken, especially because Chun's plan relied upon using ROK troops that were under CFC operational control. One of the generals suggested that it might be possible to mute or thwart my anticipated opposition by cleverly garnering support from other American generals. That struck a number of the generals as a sound idea, and they decided to move in that direction. Some of their efforts would be focused on Lieutenant General Eugene Forrester, commander of the I Corps (ROK-U.S.) Group north of Seoul.

Galvanized by their support, Chun put his plan into action with a phone call to dispatch the team of interrogators to apprehend General Chung. The interrogators would arrive at Chung's official residence shortly after 6 P.M. The diversionary dinner for the commanders loyal to Chung was already underway in Yonghi-dong, western Seoul, so there would be no one Chung could turn to for immediate help. Among the officers at that dinner were the commander of the Special Forces Command, the commander of the Capital Security Command, and the ROK army Provost Marshal.

Chun made hasty telephone calls to the units he had already colluded with, putting into motion the seizure of selected critical installations in Seoul. The troops would be moving under cover of darkness. He also put out instructions that DSC operatives at every level were to watch for any orders or actions that might interfere with Chun's plan.

Everything was now in place. The generals sipped their coffee and awaited further developments.

Events in the Bunker and at the Ministry of Defense

As I left the Hill Top House to go to the command bunker, a platoon of about 30 armed soldiers from the UN Honor Guard company began surrounding the hillside. Our three Dalmatian dogs barked at the commotion. The arrival of the platoon struck me as an ominous sign, even though I knew it was a routine protective action during any kind of crisis. My driver, Master Sergeant Ron Larmer, drove me the short distance down a steep hill to the bunker. Ron would play an important role that night.

On the way to the bunker, I had a sense of *déjà vu*. Minister Rho's and General Rhu's protestations aside, it looked like the information I had recently received about rumblings among the young generals from KMA classes 11, 12, and 13 was turning out to be valid.

It also occurred to me that while the North Koreans had probably been caught off guard by Park's assassination, they were not likely to be so unprepared this time around. We had reliable intelligence that North Korea's forces were now in a high state of readiness.

Around 7:30 P.M., I arrived at the bunker and saw that it was secured by armed military police. Inside, it was a bustle of activity. Its dimly lit interior was not much larger than an average house. The main room was the command center, cluttered with wall maps, extensive communications gear, and desks for duty officers; several smaller rooms were available for planning and meetings. A quick review with the duty officers from the U.S. and CFC communications centers revealed no major problems. Our intelligence indicators showed no unusual change in North Korea's posture, and our intercepts of North Korean communications revealed no surge in activity, but maybe it was still too early to draw any reassuring conclusions.

The crisis staff was beginning to arrive. We still had no contact with any of the key ROK officials, although we were persistently trying to locate them. I put in secure phone calls to the PACOM operations center in Hawaii and the National Military Command Center in Washington, DC, informing the senior duty officers of the situation. Shortly afterward, I talked with CINCPAC, Admiral Long in Hawaii, and JCS Chairman, General Jones, and apprised them of what was happening. After that, we maintained open secure lines with them and their staffs.

Bill Gleysteen rushed in shortly after 8 P.M. and immediately tried to contact President-Elect Choi but was unable to reach him or any of his close aides. Bill remained with us for most of the night and participated in virtually all of the discussions. His vast experience and coolness under pressure were invaluable.

Although we tried constantly over the next several hours, we could not reach any of the ROK military leaders. Then, around 11 P.M., to everyone's surprise, Defense Minister Rho and ROK JCS Chairman General Kim, accompanied by several of our security guards, came bursting into the bunker. Rho and Kim were in civilian clothes, ashen-faced, disheveled, and quite obviously unnerved. They knew little about what was going on but reported hearing gunfire close to their homes. The firing appeared to come from General Chung's quarters. Upon hearing gunfire so nearby, Rho and Kim both jumped out windows in the backs of their homes and fled into the darkness on foot. That explained their scratches, rumpled clothing, and late arrival at the command bunker.

We provided Rho and Kim several rooms in the bunker, plus communications and staff assistance to help them make contact with ROK military units. I urged Rho to give clear instructions that no ROK military units were to be moved until dawn, because in the darkness and confusion clashes inevitably would occur. Rho replied that he already had made contact with the Capital Mechanized Division and the 26th Infantry Division, both reserve divisions of the ROK First Corps, and had ordered them to prepare for deployment into the city. He said he intended to use them to secure vital installations and to thwart insurrectionist movements.

The room became very tense. Bringing these units into the city was likely to lead to widespread fighting, perhaps even a civil war. That was obviously problematic from an internal standpoint, but it would open an unmistakable opportunity for the North Koreans. A civil war in Seoul was nearly an invitation for intervention by the North.

I repeated to Rho that I thought it would be prudent to wait until daylight when we could clarify just what was happening. Rho reflected on that for a few minutes before he reluctantly agreed. It probably crossed his mind that if this was a coup, and it turned against him, he would be much better off if there were no bloodshed.

He quickly rescinded his instructions to the two divisions, then he and General Kim began establishing contact with all the major ROK military headquarters. Rho received a large number of assurances of loyalty, but a few of the headquarters reported that some of their subordinate units had already headed into Seoul. The movement orders had been based on instructions received from DSC chief Chun and several other general officers. That was our first inkling of who was behind the firing in the streets. With that knowledge, Rho's frustration and resignation began to grow.

At that point, Bill Gleysteen tried to contact Chun to warn him of the obvious danger from North Korea, should fighting erupt between ROK military units, and to caution him about the threat to political stability posed by the night's actions. His calls were rebuffed. Chun and his group refused to have any contact with U.S. officials until the outcome of their action became clear.

In the meantime, several infantry battalions from Roh's 9th Infantry Division were moving into the city. The 9th Division, a forward-deployed combat unit, was supposed to be under the operational control of the CFC. It had important wartime roles under the general defense plan. Thus, in the absence of any notification from the ROK authorities that elements of the division were being withdrawn from their wartime responsibilities, the movement of the division constituted both a clear violation of the CFC Terms of Reference and a risk to the nation's defense.

Now I was just as angry as Minister Rho, although my anger was over the breach of the chain of command and the unauthorized diversion of troops away from their defense mission north of Seoul. Of course, we were completely powerless to do anything about it. We might have attempted to order those units back to their operational positions, but by the time we could discern exactly which units were on the move, it probably would have been too late anyway. After all, the units had only a few miles to drive before they were inside Seoul. Besides, the orders would probably have been ignored. We were forced to accept the situation.

We soon learned that some Special Forces units and some battalions from the Capital Security Command were also maneuvering around Seoul. Contrary to the belief held even today by many Koreans, neither the Special Forces brigades nor the Capital Security Command had ever been under CFC operational control. Both units were considered to have overriding national missions to protect the central government and vital installations in Seoul and, therefore, had never been committed by the ROK Government to CFC peacetime control.

As the night wore on, I sensed rising apprehension and fear among my ROK counterparts, including General Rhu. The younger ROK officers in the bunker were particularly tense because it was clear that internal trouble was brewing, and they were worried about their own futures and the safety of their families. An air of resignation began to settle over the room as everyone began to realize that Minister Rho and General Kim were on the losing end of events. There were many hushed discussions in the corners of the room, as the ROK officers tried to reason through what all of this meant for them.

Rho and Kim eventually were able to contact President-elect Choi who confirmed that something ominous was taking place but then mysteriously distanced himself from the situation by saying that the military must sort things out. Despite pressure from Minister Rho, the president-elect feebly refused to accept any responsibility and, in fact, told Rho to talk with Chun. Choi told him that Chun had very properly ordered an interrogation of the army chief of staff, but when the interrogators reached Chung's official quarters, they ended up trading gunfire with Chung's aides. According to Choi, the trouble was entirely Chung's fault, because he refused to accompany the interrogators and ordered his aides to begin shooting. A few minutes later, Ambassador Gleysteen also talked with Choi. He was left with the impression that the president-elect was too afraid to do anything.

After some delay, Rho and Kim finally were able to speak by phone with Chun and his cohorts. That was when we first realized the extent of the conspiracy.

The phone discussion was heated enough that I could overhear nearly every word. Rho, Kim, and Rhu already knew they were playing a weak hand. They had concluded that a *coup d´etat* or something equivalent to it was in progress, if not already concluded. The president-elect's reluctance to become involved left them shocked and disappointed, because they needed his authority to initiate legitimate counteractions, and that authority obviously was not going to materialize.

The coup officers told Minister Rho that General Chung was completely at fault for the night's troubles. They said that Chung's actions on the night of Park's assassination had left a number of lingering and still unexplained suspicions about his role. The officers were all having dinner together and they agreed that Chung should be interrogated, so they had sent an armed escort to confront him at his quarters. The escorts and Chung's aides became involved in a shooting incident, just as Chung was descending the stairs in his home, and Chung was subsequently apprehended without injury to himself. However, several others were seriously hurt and one man was killed. General Chung was now in the prison in the basement of the DSC headquarters.

The conversation became more heated until one of the coup officers told Rho to "shut up" and listen carefully to their litany of complaints. Rho became visibly angry, but he held the phone and listened. First, the generals were "upset with liberal trends in the nation, which the government seemed to be tolerating if not encouraging," and they "deeply distrusted the opposition parties as well as the media for their self-serving actions which fomented unrest in the countryside." The generals feared that this unrest could get out of hand and provoke a North Korean attack. It had to be stopped without delay or compromise.

Second, they also demanded that Rho "approve in writing our action in arresting army Chief Chung." Then they demanded that Rho officially remove Chung from his duties as both army chief of staff and martial law commander, and that Rho appoint a new army chief, whom they were prepared to name. Apparently, Chun had offered the position to General Lee Hee-sung, who was the acting head of the Korean Central Intelligence Agency.

The fact that the coup officers required the minister's approval of their actions after the fact, and not before, seemed to be a tacit admission that their actions were illegal and in complete defiance of proper constitutional processes. We were later to learn that during the night a number of senior army commanders who were loyal to Chun and his cohorts rushed into Choi's office and demanded his approval of all actions taken by the coup group. Of course, the actions had already been taken, and President-elect Choi, faced with a *fait accompli* and bereft of any real power base within the military, sadly decided to distance himself from the night's events. Obviously, that was why Choi had told Rho to meet with the group of officers and accede to their demands.

In another ultimatum, the coup officers told Rho to remove the commanders of the Special Forces Command and the Third ROK Army, both of whom had resisted Chun's actions. Finally, the group insisted that Rho meet with them immediately at the president's residence, the Blue House. In choice, earthy terms, they said that Rho's continued presence at the U.S. military bunker in Yongsan would be viewed as a disgrace by all patriotic Koreans.

After the call ended, I urged Rho and Kim to remain in the bunker where their safety could be guaranteed and they would be able to maintain communications with the ROK military and national police. Traveling downtown at night to meet the coup group at the Blue House was risky, and Rho had no loyal Korean escorts to accompany him. It would have been unseemly for him to travel with American guards. Furthermore, the outcome of the coup was still uncertain and probably would not be clear until daylight.

Rho and Kim agreed to stay, but about 1 A.M., the Vice Minister of National Defense telephoned Rho from his office on the ministry's second floor. He assured Rho that the building was completely secured by loyal troops and that Rho should come there right away, because his presence was needed to manage the situation. The conversation lasted several minutes as the vice minister repeatedly sought to convince Rho that "all would be OK, including your personal safety." Rho finally, although somewhat reluctantly, agreed to go to the ministry, even though I urged him to stay until dawn. Since he had no vehicle, I instructed Ron Larmer, my driver, to take him, Kim, and Rhu to the MND building in my official sedan. The ministry was only a few hundred yards away, close enough that from outside the bunker I could see the lights on every floor of the building.

After the party arrived at the ministry, they strode by the ROK security guards and went upstairs to Rho's second floor office, where the vice minister awaited them. Then, gunfire erupted outside as Special Forces troops loyal to the coup leaders assaulted the building from hidden positions. Bullets shattered the front entry and the marble foyer as the Special Forces soldiers stormed the building and rushed upstairs to apprehend Rho and Kim. Rhu was caught in the struggle, but he was unharmed. He told me later that he faced down several of the youthful ROK soldiers by telling them who he was, that he was a true patriot, and that he had a son about their age who was also serving in the ROK army.

Ron Larmer was waiting in the parked sedan and he feared for his life as the gunfire erupted all around his vehicle. I could hear the shooting from the Eighth U.S. Army headquarters office.

Ann was at the Hill Top House and she could also hear the shooting, although she was reassured by the presence of the UN honor guard security around our quarters. My executive officer, Colonel Lynch had been telephoning Ann throughout the night to keep her aware of what was happening.

Shortly after midnight, I sat in my Eighth Army office on the second floor of the old Japanese building across the parade field from the CFC headquarters and drafted a message back to Washington and Hawaii. It struck me that General Magruder probably had sat at the same desk during the coup in 1961. As I wrote the report, my mind kept turning over the same issues that had probably troubled Magruder.

The message I wrote outlined my first impressions of the dangerous events unfolding in Seoul.

> A coup is in progress by a group of middle level officers, plus several senior officers who seek to restore tougher domestic controls. The "heavy" in this group has not emerged but seems to be Chun Doo-hwan. MND Rho still appears to be in charge of some elements within the military, but he is anxious to negotiate and avoid bloodshed. However, the coup officers are committed, and the evidence of their action suggests that a struggle of potentially serious dimensions will continue in the ROK army. While the Ambassador has conveyed the United States' distress at the developments and warned the coup group about the negative U.S. reaction, the ROK military will have to solve this crisis on their own terms and in their own way. Our role must continue to be that of urging moderation, full recognition of the risks inherent in the coup, and preparedness against the enemy threat. The ROK military has

gone to *Chin Do Kae,* which is the highest state of counter-infiltration alert. It compares roughly with DEFCON two but in a counter-infiltration mode. On the U.S. forces side we have taken measures to increase intelligence watch, organization of crisis action teams, and restriction of off-post activities. If other actions appear appropriate they will be taken.

I knew that some parties in Washington were going to be very disenchanted with my conclusions, as they were also obviously intended to serve as recommendations. The Carter administration had spent years pressuring the ROK to liberalize and to reduce the influence of the military in running the nation. A military coup was a complete reversal of everything President Carter had tried to accomplish, and my message argued for a hands-off response.

Officials in Hawaii and the Pentagon would no doubt recognize that the Koreans would have to solve this problem themselves. It was not our place to interfere, to dictate solutions, or to pick South Korea's leaders. Besides, the United States had limited influence with this sovereign partner. Of course, we had obligations under the mutual security agreement, and it was, therefore, quite proper for us to object to actions that jeopardized our mutual security, which was exactly what we were doing.

But the overall situation in Korea in 1979 was quite different from the period after Park seized power in May 1961. Said bluntly, we had far less influence. The Korean War had ended barely eight years before Park seized power. As a result, Park tended to listen to Americans—at the beginning of his presidency, anyway. His country needed all the help it could get to launch the Korean economic miracle that was his most cherished goal, and that made him somewhat open and amenable to American advice. Moreover, in Park's time the U.S. military deployment in South Korea was larger and more powerful, including two infantry divisions and a large air division that was spread across multiple bases in South Korea. The sheer size of that presence was a powerful chip, but so was South Korean belief in the continuity of the American commitment. When the United States became preoccupied with the war in Vietnam, substantial South Korean force commitment to that conflict also helped further cement the relationship between our two nations.

By 1979, though, ROK leaders were far less willing to take American advice. The economic miracle had already begun to blossom, and the results of that progress had instilled greater self-confidence. The South Koreans demanded equality in our partnership and were becoming more sensitive and more easily slighted by any treatment they considered high-handed or condescending. Twenty-six years of relative peace and stability had also dimmed the memories of the Korean War, particularly among those born after 1950, and the result was lessened dependence, if not in reality, then at least in the minds of many ROK citizens.

The era of America's paternal influence over the ROK had passed. Moreover, since the United States had significantly reduced its military deployment to one infantry division and a smaller air division and had recently threatened to withdraw even those forces, ROK leaders doubted the reliability and continuity of America's commitment. Coming on the heels of the disastrous withdrawal of U.S. forces from Vietnam, South Koreans began to worry that American prestige and influence were waning throughout Asia. Added to that, President Carter's lukewarm support of Park's government, in hand with the administration's avid encouragement of liberal activities and human rights, not only raised hackles among conservative Korean leaders but also stirred doubts about the enduring nature of the U.S. security pledge. Anyone who believed that we were in any position to order a halt to this coup was badly out of date.

Events at the MND had taken a turn for the worse. From his sedan outside the MND building, Ron Larmer saw ROK army officers brusquely escort Rho through the bullet-pocked Ministry entrance and force him into a military sedan. Rho was taken to the Blue House, where the coup group confronted him and obtained his written and obviously tardy approval for the arrest of General Chung. Rho also acceded to their other demands, which for the most part were the same ones they had discussed with him on the phone. Once Rho had given his written approval, President-Elect Choi formally acquiesced as well.

By dawn, for all intents and purposes the coup was over. Chun and his cohorts had achieved their initial goals with a minimum of bloodshed. There were still scores to settle within the ROK army with those who had not supported the coup group, and in the days ahead various military leaders and members of the cabinet were quietly replaced. But otherwise, for the time being anyway, it was over.

After sending a wrap-up situation report to CINCPAC's command center and the National Military Command Center in Washington, I left the command bunker for my quarters. I asked General Rhu to join me for breakfast so we could have a private discussion. We were exhausted, so our discussion did not last long. Rhu appeared weary and tense, some of which I attributed to his encounter with the armed soldiers

Chart 2. **Major South Korean Military Commands, 1979–1980**

Commands under ROK JCS command and operational control	Commands under CFC operational control
Second ROK Army	First ROK Army
Defense Security Command	Third ROK Army
Special Forces Command	ROK units assigned to I Corps [ROK-US] Group (redesignated Combined Field Army in March 1980)
Capital Security Command	

Units that supported the "12/12 Incident" violating operational control of ROK JCS or CFC	Units temporarily recalled by ROK from CFC operational control during Kwangju tragedy
9th Infantry Division	20th Infantry Division
Special Forces Command	30th Infantry Division
Capital Security Command	

in the MND. Still, and despite the night's activities, he expressed the hope that the officers involved in the coup would continue to support the president-elect and the constitution. He was deeply worried about the North Koreans and also about the potential for retribution within the military. Rhu considered himself at risk and said he was going to avoid sleeping in the same place at night. I offered him use of one of the guest quarters in the Yongsan compound.

Power Consolidation and American Appeasement

Flushed with their initial success, Chun's group decided that President-Elect Choi should be retained as a figurehead, at least for the time being, to give the impression that the constitution was being upheld. They knew they needed to pacify the Americans and, at the same time, keep the leaders of the political opposition at bay. Of course, they planned to control the nation from behind the scenes and eventually maneuver one of their group to become the "elected" president, but they were following the template of General Park's experience in 1961 and early 1962. They were creating the structure for control before moving on the presidency itself. In fact, striking parallels between their actions and Park's would emerge in the months ahead.

However, the immediate tasks for the group were to assuage the Americans, to garner American support or acquiescence, to solidify their military power base, and to impose their stamp on the government and its policies. Those were daunting tasks for military officers who had had only a few weeks of preparation after the assassination.

General Kim Yoon-ho, the highly respected Infantry School commander Chun had earlier promised his cohorts he would try to enlist, assisted Chun and his group in defining their goals. And, just as Chun had predicted, Kim's earnest explanations of the night's events and the motives behind them were entirely persuasive to his many American acquaintances, and particularly to his long-time friend Bob Brewster. For his efforts, not to mention his vast professional talents, Kim eventually would be promoted to full general, given command of the prestigious FROKA, and, later, appointed as the Chairman of the ROK Joint Chiefs of Staff. Based on extensive experience over the next several years, I found him to be one of the most able, imaginative, and apolitical officers in the ROK armed forces. The coup group had made a great choice.

To justify their motives, the coup leaders described their actions on December 12 as the "12/12 Incident," completely denying that it was a coup d'etat. A great deal of thought probably went into the choice of those sterile words for describing their actions, and that was the way the events of that night would be referred to in the future. In fact, Ambassador Gleysteen, while fully recognizing the immense power now held by the generals who seized control of the army and nation that night, noted that from a technical viewpoint the word "coup" really was not an accurate depiction of what had occurred. After all, Choi was allowed to remain as the president, even if only in a figurehead status, and the ROK constitution had not been suspended.

In a late December message that I forwarded for internal guidance to the senior U.S. military leaders in Korea, Bill formally retracted his initial assertion that a coup had occurred. I am sure he felt it was necessary to build bridges of communication with Chun and his supporters and wanted to avoid the acrimony that would result from accusing them of having conducted a coup. Bill certainly was not naive. He knew the December 12 "incident" was a planned action by a group of officers who now intended to play a powerful background role behind the curtain of a weak civilian government, even if they did not intend to take full control just yet.

Still, I did not agree with the conclusion in Bill's message. I was convinced that Chun and his partners fully intended to seize absolute power but had simply lacked a comprehensive plan for how to go about it. Perhaps they just had not yet had enough time to flesh out the details. But, once they decided to arrest General Chung and to occupy Seoul with loyal military units, there was no turning back. At some point, they had to seize total power. There were still men in powerful positions who were not sympathetic to their goals. At some point, those men would inevitably act to reverse their actions and perhaps punish them and their families for what they had done.

Chun surely understood that from the beginning, and the rest of his group would appreciate it soon enough. However, I had no specific evidence at the time to challenge Bill's conclusion so I simply passed his views to my subordinate commanders for their knowledge and guidance.

On December 13, as I walked through the entry, I saw that the doors to the MND building and the marble foyer were pocked with bullet holes. The firefight the night before had been intense.

Minister Rho looked ashen and beaten down, and the usual spark in his manner seemed to have disappeared. He began the discussion in a very subdued, grave manner, and he smoked continuously. I was surprised to note a tape recorder, barely out of sight, that was being used to record our conversation. That had never been done before, at least that I had ever noticed, and I guessed that Chun and his clique wanted to hear firsthand what the American commander had to say.

From the outset, it was clear that Rho had been told to provide a carefully crafted message for me to convey to my superiors back in Washington. As we talked, he repeated several key points to be sure the translation was clear and that I understood them fully.

He said he was sincerely sorry about the hectic events of the night before and emphasized the importance of sustaining the state of martial law. Then, almost as though he and I had not observed most of the night's activities together, he launched into an excuse of the events and the motives behind the general's actions that was almost identical to the one used by the president-elect the night before. It was a rendition that completely vindicated Chun and his partners.

Aware that my comments were going to be studied carefully by Chun and his group, I asked Rho if he wanted me to be very candid. I did not want to lecture, harangue, or be disrespectful, but I believed it was important for Rho—and therefore Chun—to understand how the American authorities felt about the situation. Rho said he welcomed a frank discussion as he always did during our regular meetings. Bill Gleysteen and I already had discussed the points I was about to make.

I told Rho that his explanation was duly noted, but entirely implausible and unconvincing. The actions initiated by the group of generals not only jeopardized the political progress of recent weeks, they also threatened the internal stability of the republic and opened very real risks of a North Korean attack. Thereby, they raised deep concerns about the future relationship between the United States and the Republic of Korea. Those concerns could lead to a full review of all American policies toward Korea, including policies concerning troop withdrawal, technology transfer, missile development cooperation, foreign military sales of U.S. equipment to the ROK, economic assistance, and several current proposals to increase the authority and responsibility of the Combined Forces Command.

Rho was clearly shocked. He came forward in his chair, looked straight at me, and expressed his hope that the situation would not degenerate further. He beseeched me, as a friend of the Korean people who was responsible for defending them, to do my best to protect this relationship so vital to the future of Korea. I replied that the nature of my mission was military, and that the burden of restoring our relationship could not rest with me, but with the group of generals who seized power yesterday. I urged Rho to convey this message to this group of generals. Although I did not suggest any specific actions that Chun and the generals should take, I did say that their subsequent actions must demonstrate complete support for the constitution and an orderly and moderate political process.

Rho suddenly became quite agitated. Waving his arms, he reiterated that the current situation was simply the result of a misunderstanding over the apprehension of General Chung. He was completely sure that no harm would occur to the political process or the ROK constitution. The generals were well aware of the crucial importance of the close relationship between the United States and the ROK, and they were "very patriotic and will do their best for the Korean people. The generals have absolutely no intention of intervening in the political process."

We spoke for a few more minutes, each of us reiterating the points we wanted conveyed to other parties—in my case to the generals who now controlled the ROK, in his, to my superiors in Washington. It was not until I was departing the conference room that Rho told me in confidence that the ROK chairman of the Joint Chiefs of Staff probably would retire from the military and be given a cabinet post, and that General Rhu, my deputy at CFC, would become the new chairman. Rho did not hint at his own fate, but I sensed from his demeanor that he would be leaving.

After reflecting on this important meeting, I wrote the following conclusion to my superiors in Hawaii and Washington:

> It is clear that the coup group has extensive support and planned this operation ahead of time. It is, of course, a shock that absolutely no inkling was leaked to us in advance, although apprehension existed about political factions in the military. The coup group is moving to solidify control of the military by changing commanders and positioning selected officers. Much of the current political and military apparatus will be shucked although the group, for legitimacy, will retain the powerless president and prime minister for his economic value. The MND will be replaced by someone who is pliant and sympathetic. It is clear that we are in a hard ball game with professionals who feel they can run the country better than their peers and are flush with the first round of victory. In my judgment the course of political events has been fundamentally and unalterably changed. We now must work closely with the emerging leadership to see how much of the recent political progress can be restored, and to assure that internal political as well as military stability is maintained thereby denying North Korea any incentive to intervene.

Even as I was meeting with Minister Rho, Ambassador Gleysteen was in another part of Seoul, meeting with President-Elect Choi. Recalling his exasperation with Choi's reluctance the night before, Bill stressed to Choi that the U.S. Government regarded the activities of the night before as a serious setback and wanted to reiterate the absolute essentiality of civilian control over the military and the continuation of political liberalization throughout the nation.

Unfortunately, Bill came away from the meeting even more convinced that Choi and his administration were too weak to reassert control over the military. Choi was a gentle, soft-spoken civil servant with long experience in the government, but he seemed powerless in this situation, largely because he had no solid relationships with the military. Thus the shift in power was a "done deal."

In Washington, Assistant Secretary of State Holbrooke met with the South Korean Ambassador to the United States and emphasized the same points that Bill Gleysteen had conveyed to President-Elect Choi. The South Korean Ambassador, even more removed from the situation and less influential than Choi, simply noted Holbrooke's concerns and said he would pass them on to Seoul. I'm sure he was concerned about his own future.

On December 13, an official statement was released from Washington. The statement had actually been drafted by Bill Gleysteen. But it had to be issued from Washington because the U.S. Embassy had no access to the South Korean media. Moreover, a Washington dateline would have more impact on ROK leaders:

> During the past few weeks we have been encouraged by the orderly procedures adopted in the ROK to develop a broadly based government following the assassination of President Park. As a result of events (yesterday) in Korea, we have instructed our Ambassador and the Commander of U.S. Forces in Korea to point out to all concerned that any forces within the ROK which disrupt this progress should bear in mind the seriously adverse impact their actions would have on the ROK's relations with the United States. At the same time, any forces outside the ROK (read North Korea) which might seek to exploit the current situation in Seoul should bear in mind our warning of October 27 (after President Park's assassination).

The U.S. Government obviously was out of sorts over the "12/12 Incident". It was a setback to the democratization process in the ROK and a poor harbinger for the human rights goals that were central to President Carter's foreign policy. It also opened new complexities in our relations. The legal ROK Government had been turned into a figurehead overnight by a group of army generals who were barely known to most American officers in Korea, much less to officials in Washington. The ROK was a vital American ally, but the American news media had long been critical of its governing habits. The actions taken by Chun and his clique weren't going to sit well and would become even more problematic if they led to further domestic turmoil.

But my responsibilities as the CFC CINC were clear. The North Koreans could intervene at any moment, and the bulk of my efforts naturally had to be devoted to military matters. Chun's actions the night before had simply added to that challenge. As difficult as it had already been to keep the ROK officers "facing north," Chun had just made it all the more so. There were now very tangible reasons for the ROK military to worry about political-military maneuvering back in Seoul.

I also had to be seen as evenhanded in my dealings with all the various factions in the ROK Government and military. Those who seized power, of course, were anxious for me to be supportive of them, but many Koreans were suspicious of them. As a result I had to keep my distance from Chun and his cohorts. At the same time, Chun now controlled the military power and the future of Korea.

The Birthday Card

In Washington, General Chung's son, who was a college student in the United States, contacted Army Vice Chief of Staff General Jack Vessey to inquire about the status of his father. Because General Chung had been in prison, with no outside contact since his apprehension the night of December 12, Jack asked me to check into the matter and pass word to Chung's son.

Bill Gleysteen and I had made a number of discreet inquiries about General Chung. Our views were that the public explanation for his apprehension seemed insufficient to warrant severe punishment and that excessive harm might beget retribution from Chung's followers in the army, who were numerous. I told Jack Vessey that we had no information about the nature of punishment or administrative action that might be meted out, although I had been assured by the new Minister of Defense, Chu Yong-bok, and the Blue House chief secretary that Chung would not be executed. However, the group of generals who had seized power probably would have to arrange for an important conviction and punishment in order to justify their insubordinate actions to the public.

A fortuitous birthday note from me may have had some effect on General Chung's circumstances. My practice was to write birthday notes to senior ROK officers with the list of names drawn up by my Korean military aide. My note to Chung reached him in prison. According to eyewitnesses, Chung and his wife wept after reading the note. For them the note meant that a "lifeline" existed to an important military friend and government.

I was told later by Korean officers and by Jim Hausman, who obtained reports from his wide military contacts, that the note carried significance beyond birthday greetings. To Chun and his group, the note meant that the Americans retained a strong friendship with General Chung and official concern over what happened to him. Thus Chun could not deal harshly with Chung.

In fact, Chun became so incensed with the note's import that he went to see Ambassador Gleysteen and complained bitterly about my "upstart action." Chun said that I was interfering with the Korean legal process and that I had absolutely no right to communicate with someone Koreans regarded as a "non-person in prison." Bill brushed off Chun's complaint with the explanation that my note was merely a personal birthday greeting and that, as a matter of fact, if it were Chun who was in prison instead of General Chung, that perhaps he would have received a similar note. Chun was not at all amused. (Eventually Chung was punished with reduction in rank to private, the forfeiture of all pay and allowances, and imprisonment for a period of time. In 1997 the Seoul District Court reversed Chung's conviction in relation to the Park Chung-hee assassination, returned his back pay, and recovered his qualifications to retirement as a general officer.)

In my message back to General Vessey, I summarized the internal situation in the ROK armed forces "as very uneven. The ROK air force and navy chiefs privately assured me that they have been and will continue to be totally supportive of civilian authority, and we should have no worry about them. The ROK army, on the other hand, faces a period of settling down from the swift seizure of power by younger KMA graduates. Many changes in command and staff positions are taking place despite my pleas to General Lee Hee-sung, the new army Chief of Staff, and to the new Minister of Defense, Chu Yong-bok." I believed that widespread changes would adversely affect readiness.

Gleysteen Meets with Chun

On December 14, Ambassador Gleysteen decided it was time to meet with Major General Chun himself. Bob Brewster arranged the meeting, trying to reassure both Bill and me beforehand about Chun's professional military orientation and limited objectives.

During the meeting, Chun was understandably nervous, but he listened intently to Bill. To his credit, Chun recognized the importance of establishing effective relations with the ambassador. But from the moment Bill was done expressing his concerns, Chun sought to convince him that the goals of the "12/12 Incident" group were indeed limited, entirely patriotic, and not at all self-serving. "Trust me to demonstrate this."

With as much chagrin as he could summon, Chun gave Bill the same rendition of events about the "12/12 Incident" that we had already heard from President-Elect Choi and Minister Rho. He put the blame squarely on General Chung, who, after all, had been in the Blue House when the president was killed and subsequently refused to be interrogated, even ordering his aides to shoot Chun's interrogators when they were sent to get him.

Chun then assured Bill that he had no ambition beyond a successful career as a professional soldier. Ever since he was a boy he had only wanted to be a soldier, and a good one. That was what his training at the Korean Military Academy prepared him and his classmates for. Politics was "not a hobby" for Chun. Until the death of the president, he had always considered himself a happy warrior. However, events in life sometimes thrust an individual into unhappy circumstances. He insisted that he and the others would "go back to the barracks" after this episode was over. He repeated that point for emphasis, then insisted that he supported President-Elect Choi and his efforts to further the political liberalization process. In nearly the same breath, he said he had in mind some specific changes within the senior military leadership, changes that would strengthen the professionalism and unity of the ROK armed forces. He and many others were convinced that there were too many old, corrupt, and self-serving military leaders who not only blocked the promotions of more capable younger officers, but also did not serve the nation well. The same could be said for a number of political and business leaders, he said.

After his meeting with Ambassador Gleysteen, Chun sought to meet with me, probably to offer a similar explanation for the "12/12 Incident." Again, he used Bob Brewster as his messenger; however, Bill Gleysteen urged me not to see Chun at this time. Bill considered it important to highlight how seriously the U.S. Government viewed the breach of the chain of command and the dangers that could result from internal instability. Furthermore, he wanted to make sure that we did not dignify Chun's actions or his position in any official way.

An Insightful Discussion

At my request, General Lee Hyong-kon, former ROK CJCS and army chief of staff, visited to give me his insights. He was the man who had come to me in late November with warnings of unrest among a group of officers from classes 11, 12, and 13 of the Korean Military Academy.

General Lee told me that immediately after our previous discussion he had seen Chun and had counseled him about the importance of keeping his hands out of the nation's political affairs. In response, Chun had intimated nothing about his plans for the night of December 12. However, he had complained that he and a number of other KMA graduates were quite concerned about political developments in Korea, as well as certain army matters, such as the plans for the early retirement of some senior officers and the "banishment" of certain others to remote outposts.

Lee said that Chun and his colleagues had been very close to President Park and were sympathetic to his policies. That meant that their political views would be "hard line" and probably not appreciably different from those Defense Minister Rho and former army Chief of Staff Chung had supported before their downfalls. As to the effect on the rest of the military, Lee said there was a great deal of uneasiness, particularly at the lieutenant colonel and colonel levels, where careers were on the line. Right now the word was out not to talk to the Americans because it would arouse suspicion.

According to Lee, the Korean people were very suspicious about the events of December 12–13. Lee believed that there was general support among the people for liberalization in the political arena, and that the people sensed that Chun's actions were harmful to political progress. He anticipated that the spring months would become particularly dangerous, because there was likely to be widespread student unrest that would lead inevitably to situations in which the army would be pitted against the people and the students.

Lee confirmed that Chun and his close-knit group—a handful of generals and colonels, mostly from the DSC—were the new power in the country. General Lee Hee-sung, the new army chief of staff, had been chosen by Chun because the two of them were personally close, and because Lee Hee-sung was completely supportive of Chun's goals. Lee also said that the new Defense Minister, Chu Yong-bok, a retired air force chief of staff, would be little more than a figurehead and would have very little influence over the army. Given the army's preeminent position in the nation, the choice of a former air force officer to be minister of defense was simply a clever move to buy off the other military services.

I asked Lee what advice he might give under the present circumstances. Without hesitation, he said the Korean people knew very little about the situation and were completely ignorant about U.S. policy. Censorship had eliminated virtually any explanation or mention of American policy in the media, and any contacts with Americans were being heavily discouraged. Any Korean who attempted to violate that embargo ran the risk of being detected and reported to Chun's Defense Security Command. Lee was convinced that the U.S. authorities must find a way to explain their policies to the South Korean people.

Finally, he said that my principal task must be to assure the preparedness of our combined forces. At the same time, he urged me to become "actively involved in the domestic scene in order to assure that the internal situation does not turn sour and invite intervention by the North." He said the two tasks were intertwined. "This is why many senior Koreans continue to look up to the CINC as protector of the nation and its people, just as Koreans did during General MacArthur's era. Whether you like it or not, the CINC must help stabilize the domestic situation, and this will take some care as you attend to your overriding military responsibilities."

Lee's parting comment was not at all encouraging. "Koreans have never informed the Americans of insurgent activity. We did not tell them before the coup in 1961, we did not in December 1979, and we will not in the future."

I wondered whether General Lee was telegraphing another event, just as he had a few weeks earlier.

Chapter Four

The Struggle for Dominance

A Countercoup Declined

It was early morning when the visitor was ushered into my office in the CFC headquarters. His visit was unexpected, which was unusual, because Koreans rarely show up unannounced. Although I had known him for several months, our official contacts were infrequent and seldom on a personal basis.

He was a lieutenant general stationed in Seoul, impressive-looking and, from what I knew about him, well-connected in the army. His English was fluent enough that he did not need an interpreter, and he specifically asked that none be asked to attend our meeting. We talked alone with the door closed for more than half an hour.

It was obvious that he wanted to speak in confidentiality, and it soon became evident that he trusted me to keep our conversation in confidence. After a short period of candid talk about the existing situation and the North Korean threat, he asked if he could speak frankly about the incident on December 12. When I told him he could, he bluntly asked if the "Americans would be prepared to support a countercoup. The purpose of this counter-coup would be to eject Chun and his group of supporters and restore power to legitimate civil and military authorities." He said he "spoke for an important faction within the military that was very upset with events and what they might portend for the future." Leaning closer, he said he "was deadly serious with the proposal and did you understand it?"

I was astonished. Only a few days earlier, General Lee Hyong-kon had told me that Americans would be the last people to get any reliable information about the possibilities of insurgent action. This was more than information—it was advance warning.

Before responding, I took a moment to think through the ramifications. As a minimum, his group obviously wanted a tacit go-ahead for their endeavor, and it probably wanted an assurance that the United States would withhold the kind of withering criticism that was being heaped on Chun. But perhaps he and his faction wanted more than political support. Perhaps, just in case things went awry, his faction wanted assurance that U.S. military forces would intervene on their behalf.

Obviously, I could not speak for the U.S. Government or Ambassador Gleysteen. But we had already come close to civil war on the night of December 12. The general's offer reopened that possibility with all of its inherent dangers, both for America to become caught between several contending factions, and for North Korea to exploit the situation. I was tempted to ask him about his military faction, the scope and nature of their plan, and their specific goals, but those kinds of questions might easily have been misinterpreted as more than passing interest on my part.

I told him that "the United States is not in the business of supporting coups and absolutely would not support any counteraction by the military faction he represented or any other faction." He paused for a moment, apparently to be sure that he fully understood, and then awkwardly thanked me for the opportunity to discuss such important matters. His face and manner revealed his disappointment, but he expressed his appreciation for my unequivocal answer. When I escorted him out of the building, we parted amicably.

I probably should have consulted with Bill Gleysteen and my military superiors before I answered him, but I thought that any delay might have been misconstrued as interest. As soon as he was gone, though, I immediately briefed Bill on the secure phone. He agreed with what I had done, but we wondered whether my response was enough to stop the general's faction dead in its tracks, and even if it was, whether other factions would appear in the months to come. Bob Brewster and his operatives had surfaced any number of reports of unrest within the military over Chun's actions.

In hindsight, I suppose a critical argument could be made that by spurning the proposed countercoup, we were thrust into the position of tacitly supporting Chun and his group. It was U.S. policy not to do so at the time, but rather to keep Chun at arm's length and to deal only with the legitimate authorities, although the faction the general represented undoubtedly perceived my response as a vote of support for Chun.

There were a great many what ifs. Perhaps the general and his faction were sincere in their promise to restore civilian leadership and the constitutional process, in which case my response was antithetical to the Carter's administration's avid desire to advance the democratization of South Korea.

But the reality was that we knew nothing about this particular faction. Another reality was that it would have been wrong to meddle in our ally's political fate. We could protest and cajole, but a direct intervention, or an alliance with an internal conspiracy, was out of bounds.

Bob Brewster visited me a few days later for one of our regular weekly meetings. Bill Gleysteen had already told him about my meeting with the general who represented the countercoup faction, and Bob said he was in complete agreement with my response. Aside from the other considerations, if Chun were to discover U.S. support for an effort to overthrow him, we would face real trouble.

Bob then went on to point out that Chun was the "only horse in town and we have to work with him, even if it has to be at arm's length." He said, "We have to do our best to assure that Chun's movement toward total control over the political structure, if that's what Chun intends, is accomplished in legitimate ways and without jeopardizing domestic stability or provoking a North Korean intervention."

He said he recognized that U.S. policy was to avoid any actions that implied an endorsement of Chun or what he had done, but it was still "absolutely essential to maintain an open dialogue with Chun and his cohorts." Chun could not be ignored, since he had already moved with surprising swiftness to grasp control over the military and to install his own people in a number of key positions, including the minister of defense and the army chief of staff.

I told Bob that my intelligence advisers, Jim Hausman, Steve Bradner, and Bruce Grant, shared his practical views, although they were less congenial toward Chun. Of course, they did not know Chun and were therefore suspicious. Bob answered that he had developed a close relationship with Chun—not close enough to have been apprised in advance of Chun's move on December 12, but close enough that the two of them frequently consulted on important matters. He offered me that channel if I ever needed it.

Chun Restricts Contacts with U.S. Officials

Chun must have realized that there were pockets of resistance forming inside the military. Instructions were issued from DSC headquarters to all of its agents to report immediately on any unusual meetings, secret gatherings, or comments by senior officers that hinted at resistance to Chun.

Map 3. **The Defenses of South Korea**

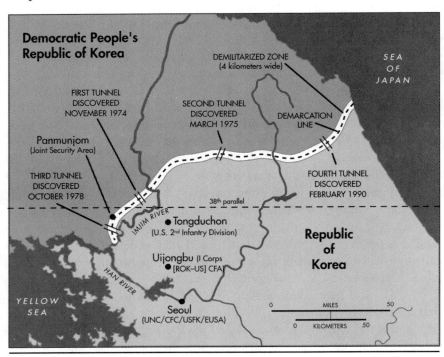

Officers known to have been loyal to General Chung were to be watched closely, and those holding command positions were to be replaced as soon as possible with officers who were loyal to Chun. That was one of the first instructions given to the new army Chief of Staff, General Lee Hee-sung.

Chun also seemed to recognize that the Americans might be approached by potential countercoup groups, so he issued blanket instructions that all high-level contacts with American officials were to be cleared with the DSC. Hidden tape recorders were to be used at all high-level meetings, and the transcriptions were to be reviewed by key officers in the DSC. Any suspicious items were to be reported directly to Chun. Also, Chun instructed that all official sedans would have their windows blackened so that observers on the streets and any potential assassins could not see who was inside. Chun was taking no chances.

My office was notified that it was time for a routine reassignment for my ROK army aide. A new aide, a ROK army lieutenant colonel, began work right away. After a few weeks, he was observed rifling through some in-boxes in the outer office, obviously searching for information. We had him checked, and it turned out he was a DSC officer and had been making secret reports on his observations. Afterward, we made certain that all office correspondence and sensitive conversations were shielded from him, and that no important discussions were held in the official sedan or the command helicopter whenever he was present.

Tactical Seminars on Korean Defense

I held several lengthy discussions with the key American military leaders in Korea to obtain their sensing of the situation and how we should redirect the military's attention toward security matters. Included in these discussions were my level-headed deputy, General Rosencrans; Major General Robert Kingston, USA, commander of the 2nd Infantry Division; Major General Kenneth Dohleman, USA, my chief of staff; General Sennewald, the CFC operations chief; and General Forrester, the commander of the I Corps (ROK-U.S.) Group (soon to be redesignated as the Combined Field Army). I Corps Group was responsible for defending perhaps the most dangerous invasion corridor into the ROK. Forrester had arrived in Korea only a few months earlier.

Nearly all of us agreed that the ROK military needed to be less absorbed with intrigue in Seoul and more absorbed with professional matters. I was struck, however, by the fact that Forrester was less troubled than the others by what he observed in the ROK military. He insisted that he had not sensed any undue concerns about the intrigues in Seoul and said that the senior ROK officers he had daily contact with were not overly alarmed by Chun's actions. In fact, he believed that many of them strongly supported Chun. He implied that the United States should be more understanding of Chun's situation.

Gene's views surprised me. I knew that two of his corps commanders, Lieutenant Generals Yu Hak-san and Kim Yoon-ho, were participants in the "12/12 Incident." Yu had been much more directly involved than Kim, but both of them were part of Chun's clique. Gene undoubtedly was being barraged with daily justifications about why Chun and his group had acted as they did and why they could be trusted. Still, I was bothered and shortly afterward I shared Gene's views with Bill Gleysteen. He was equally surprised.

The result of these meetings with my U.S. leaders was an idea for CFC to hold a series of "tactical seminars," to be conducted over several months at each army corps and tactical air wing, and at the naval base at Chinhae. Forrester wholeheartedly agreed with the idea and suggested that the seminars should begin in his command in early 1980. The stated purpose of the seminars was to review our war plans and identify areas that needed improvement. An equally important purpose was to get the ROK military to "face north," to become focused on their war plans and our preparations for war.

We decided to start with the corps commanded by Kim Yoon-ho, which occupied a key defensive position in the CFA area of operations. Kim was the Infantry School commander who had been recruited by Chun after the night of the 12th and had just been promoted to three stars. He had a reputation for professional competence, and his experience heading up the Infantry School meant that he should be conversant on the newest military doctrine. We wanted to use Kim first in the hopes that he could set an impressive example for the other corps commanders. He did, although there was some criticism among the Korean officers because he conducted a fast-paced seminar, completely in English, and acted like an overbearing tactical instructor.

The seminars unfolded even better than we had hoped. The first day of each seminar began with a terrain walk to study the ground of the battle. The second day focused on discussions about how to fight. The seminars improved as we moved among the corps, tactical air wings, and the naval base. The audiences grew in size as junior officers began to see the seminars as opportunities to acquire greater professional knowledge. The discussions were frank and informal.

One of the last corps seminars was conducted by Lieutenant General Chung Ho-young, who was one of Chun's core group. After a few minutes of broader discussion, Chung suggested that the current war plan was seriously flawed because it withheld any offensive actions until adequate ammunition and reinforcements could be introduced into the Korean peninsula. Thus, the plan was too defensive. It could take up to two months to bring in enough ammunition and troop reinforcements to mount a continuous counteroffensive. Chung felt that was too long. In a very forceful presentation around tactical maps in the CFA conference room, he proposed that CFC should go on the offensive within several weeks of a North Korean attack and not wait for reinforcements. Capitalizing on the existing ammunition reserves in Korea, the CFC counteroffensive would be designed to break the momentum of the North's attack by seizing a pocket of high, defensive ground just north of the DMZ.

It was a good point and the CFC plan eventually was altered to accommodate a variant of the option suggested by Chung.

Meeting the New Army Chief

In the latter part of December, General Lee Hee-sung, the new army Chief of Staff, came to visit me at CFC headquarters. The proper form would have been for me to call on him first, but as a courtesy he insisted on coming to CFC. Lee was taciturn, reserved, and very self-confident. That attitude was physically reflected in the way he strode up the stairs and down the hallway to my office. I had been told by others that he was a very logical thinker but not aggressive in his manner, nor personally ambitious. While he had not been an original member of the insurgent group, he was sympathetic to their goals and had played a key role on the night of December 12 as a liaison between the group, the president-elect, and Minister Rho.

Lee started by telling me his four goals as army chief. First, he wanted to ensure a frank flow of information between the United States and South Korea. He wanted to understand our views and wanted us to help him do his job better. Second, he believed it necessary to restore cohesion in the military, because that was essential to handle the North Korean threat. Third, he would continue and, in fact, improve on all programs related to combat readiness. Fourth, for as long as the state of martial law persisted, he would execute the law, "consistent with political developments and in a democratic way." He repeated that phrase twice.

I agreed with his objectives and welcomed the opportunity to work closely with him. Since he had invited frankness, I then gave him a very frank assessment of how the United States viewed the recent developments in Seoul and military involvement in the nation's political affairs. I reviewed the same concerns Bill Gleysteen and I had discussed with so many other officials and warned him that these concerns might lead to a complete reassessment of the American defense programs in country.

Lee strongly disagreed with my statement about the military involving itself in political affairs. He told me he had been with the president-elect, the prime minister, and the Blue House chief secretary to the president during the night of December 12–13. He was a direct witness to what occurred and insisted that the president-elect had been in firm control of the military's activities and that it was Choi issuing the orders, not the military. In other words, the constitutional authorities were in charge.

Although it was the first time I had heard that justification, I bit my tongue and nodded. Then I told him that, while my principal responsibility was military preparedness and the defense of South Korea, instability and insurrection within the military had a direct bearing on that responsibility. Recent events had left all of us greatly concerned. What we needed to do now was restore our relationships and determine how best to proceed. ROK interests would be best served by recovering the political progress made before December 12 and by the military's demonstrating solid support for the constitutional process. Lee's eyes narrowed, and he replied sharply that politics was for the president, that his "mission and that of the military is simply defense of the ROK and to insure that the government can execute its activities."

Despite the frank exchange we parted on friendly terms. He was obviously anxious to work closely with the United States, although it did not escape my notice that he saw absolutely nothing wrong with the actions initiated by Chun. No doubt, General Lee's version of events represented the new line the insurgent generals wanted to sell to the American authorities and the Korean people, because they knew that they needed legitimacy and maneuver room to accomplish their ultimate goals. Lee probably was chosen as army chief because of his seniority, and because Chun could rest comfortably that Lee would do no more than passively preside over the ROK army. I did not find him to be as strong or intellectually capable a leader as his predecessor, Chung Sung-hwa.

Discussions at the Ministry

Shortly thereafter, I met with the new Minister of Defense, Chu Yong-bok, at the MND. The entrance still showed the evidence of gunfire, although workmen were busily replacing tiles and the glass doors. In an unusual courtesy Chu met me at the entrance. He was short, very affable, and energetic, and he spoke some English, although like many, he understood it better than he spoke it. Chu had been the ROK air force chief of staff for five years, an unusually long time and an indication that President Park held him in high favor.

It was a lengthy discussion, and Chu smoked continuously, lighting each cigarette with the discarded one. I took that as a sign that he was anxious and noted a tape recorder in operation, even though the interpreter, Mr. Han, was making copious notes.

I began by congratulating him on his appointment. I noted that he enjoyed a fine reputation among U.S. officials for his superb leadership of the ROK air force. He laughed and recounted some humorous "war stories" of his long service in uniform, a career that began when Japan still occupied Korea. I told him that Minister Rho and I had developed a very close relationship, that we had always been frank with one another, and that frankness was essential if we were to achieve a better understanding of each other's positions on complex issues. As I was telling him that I looked forward to establishing a similar relationship with him, he quickly interrupted to say that we should meet every week, perhaps even at breakfast or lunch.

Because he had retired from active duty before CFC was created, I explained my roles as CFC commander and senior U.S. military officer, then reiterated much of what I had told General Lee about our concerns over the December 12 incident and its potential for souring our relationship.

Chu listened carefully and smiled often, which struck me as odd but appeared to be a natural part of his manner. He replied, "I am devoted wholeheartedly to reestablishing a firm chain of command system in the military. Throughout my 30 years of service I was dedicated to the principle that military officers should be neutral in political affairs. I will make every effort to assure that this principle is observed in the future." Laughing, he said he knew how to deal with generals. "Rest assured that the generals will behave themselves under my command as minister of National Defense!" He said he would hold a meeting of commanders on December 26, "to emphasize, among other things, that the command authority and chain of command must be strictly observed."

Elaborating on his goals, Chu said he fully recognized the threat from North Korea and promised to devote his efforts toward improving the readiness and training of the military. As a last thought, he assured me that he had no political ambitions and no objective other than defending the nation.

I passed him a memorandum that reviewed the missions of CFC and listed the ROK units placed under the operational control (OPCON) of CFC by Strategic Directive One. My memo noted that several units under the OPCON of CFC had been moved without authority during December 12–13, raising serious concerns about the nature of CFC control over the ROK units and the effectiveness of the chain of command. My memo respectfully requested an official explanation. After a quick glance at it, Chu said that this type of incident would not happen again, and he regretted that units were moved without my knowledge.

I noted that any U.S. officer who moved a unit without authority from the legitimate chain of command would be court-martialed. I was surprised to see that the officers who had been involved in the incident of December 12 had either been promoted or moved to positions of increased authority. At that point, Chu became highly agitated and began waving his arms in the air. His earlier joviality was dropped and he began to read from a clutch of notes placed in front of him. He said he wanted to be sure that I had the facts with regard to the December 12 incident. Since assuming the position of minister, he said, he had researched the incident, to include calling in the generals individually to query them. All of them had said that there was no plot, that the incident was "blown out of all proportion by Chung Sung-hwa's action to begin shooting at his quarters, and the incident was purely accidental." Chu then proceeded to read to me the same version of the December 12 incident that I had heard several times before, emphasizing the spontaneous nature of the generals' actions. He apologized for going through this formality but insisted that he had to do so. Then Chu leaned back and asked for my comments.

I told him I had great respect for his judgment and personal views and that I took note of the explanation he had just read. However, I suggested that he must give me some credit for my knowledge of what happened that night and that I could not believe the explanation he had just read. I told him I had evidence that the insurgent group had begun plotting as early as November 30, almost two weeks before the incident. Also, as a professional soldier I knew that the nighttime seizure of a number of key installations in and around Seoul by major elements of several divisions could not have been carried out as swiftly and efficiently as it had without advance preparation. It simply was not credible that the events of that night were the result of a spontaneous order sent out after 8 P.M. Chu merely took notes as I spoke.

That first meeting with Chu lasted more than an hour and a half, with many cups of ginseng tea. It was for the most part a friendly discussion, until Chu felt obliged to convey almost in rote form the story that the insurgent group wanted portrayed. He left me with the impression that he would have difficulty becoming the strong minister his predecessor had been. His word-for-word recitation of the insurgents' explanation suggested that he was unlikely to be his own man, at least in the beginning, and that while his stated objective was to restore cohesion in the army, he had little idea of how to go about it, except by issuing orders. When I pointed out that the sweeping assignment and promotion changes being made in the army could lead to speculation and unrest, he merely nodded and gave his curious smile as he explained that it was necessary to remove Chung's supporters. He said he had always been suspicious of Chung's involvement in the assassination. Now that he was the minister and knew all of the facts, he was convinced that not only Chung but also the former TROKA commander, General Lee Kun-young, and the former Special Forces commander, Major General Chung Byong-joo, were all implicated in the plot to kill Park.

Not long afterward, a chance meeting between us took place at the CFC headquarters following the honor ceremonies for the new CFC Deputy CINC, General Baek Sok-chu, who replaced General Rhu. Chu approached me and asked if we could have a private word in my office. He began by asking—in fact he used the word begging—the United States to accept the fact that the generals had "made a gross error with the December 12 incident and we must forget it. We must work on the future. We Koreans are keenly aware of what the United States wants from us." Surprised by his emotional plea, I answered that American security interests were served by maintaining peace and stability on the peninsula and by improving our mutual capability to deter external aggression. I continued, "At the same time, our long-term interests in the military, economic, and political arenas must be taken fully into account." Chu agreed, then assured me, "Chun Doo-hwan is a devoted soldier, concerned with combat readiness and I am confident that no wrongdoing by him will happen again. You should pay no more attention to this matter or be nervous about reoccurrence of this wrongdoing!"

In short, Chu was telling me that the insurgent generals admitted they had made a mistake, promised that it would not be repeated, and asked Americans to put it behind us. Chu said he preferred not to give a formal, written response to the memo I had given him concerning the unauthorized movement of units under CFC OPCON, but rather to let his oral, frank explanation suffice. I accepted. I knew a written one probably would be less frank and that insisting upon it would have been counterproductive, if not insulting. Chu said he appreciated that. Then he told me that he had uncovered some unrest within the military. He and the new army chief of staff, General Lee, had agreed to eliminate 15 major generals who were "talking too much and were not sufficiently concerned with their military duties." In addition, to placate some senior elements in the army, three major generals would be promoted, but only for a limited two-year term, and then retired.

Unrest, of course, had nothing to do with the decisions. Most, if not all, of the eliminated generals had probably been loyal to General Chung and were being purged. I checked, and the lieutenant general who had visited me with the countercoup proposal was not among the group to be retired, so the plot remained secret.

Thursday Morning Golf Club

Another inside source of information turned out to be an unusual one. Every Tuesday at daybreak, a small band of hardy golfers would play nine holes of golf, rain, shine, snow, or even dense fog notwithstanding. The absence of visibility seemed never to deter the game, and, remarkably, the caddies always seemed to be able to find the balls. The group was known as the "Thursday Morning Golf Club," even though it met every Tuesday. This was a mystery to all concerned, although to the best of the oldest member's knowledge it had always played on that day.

After the round of golf we would breakfast together at the Eighth Army Golf Club, sharing camaraderie and talking openly and amiably about any topic that struck a member's interest. Much to everyone's amusement, whoever won the round of golf had his handicap summarily reduced by a former ROK chief justice, who was a leading member of the group.

Others in the group included the CINC, deputy CINC, senior generals from USFK, the American and Japanese ambassadors, and a number of retired officials, including a former prime minister (the army chief of staff during the Korean war and then head of the nation's largest political party), two former service chiefs, several former government ministers, and, eventually, the chairman of one of the *chaebol,* the largest commercial firms in Korea.

While the retired officials were not always current on developments, no one could accuse them of being bashful with their counsel or insights. In fact, as the Chun movement began to gather momentum, word came to me from his inner circle that I should no longer associate with this group or listen to the views of my golfing partners, because they were "out of touch with the real world, and very unhelpful."

In their more candid moments, these golfers offered some interesting and wise advice. They deplored Chun's actions and harbored no doubt that what he had accomplished was a coup. In their view, he had clearly usurped political authority and had his eyes set on the Blue House.

However, they also considered it a *fait accompli* that probably could not be reversed. "Americans need to accept this reality and move on," several of them made a point of telling me. Furthermore, they contended that some of Chun's goals were not all that bad for Korea. Reducing corruption and assuring domestic stability during the transition to a newly elected political administration were seen by them as reasonable and prudent goals. In any event, trying to restore the status quo might lead to an internal disaster that, in turn, could lead to intervention by the North Koreans.

Indeed, many of the members thought that the United States should encourage the opposition political parties and the media to behave moderately. They urged that the United States continue its support for the current government of President-elect Choi, but at the same time nurture a careful, low-key dialogue with Chun and his group. American pressure would be helpful to convince Chun that, if he contemplated a move toward the presidency, his moves must be designed and carried out so as to assure domestic stability, support from the Korean people, and the maintenance of a strong military posture.

One point the golfers made again and again was that the United States had to avoid using the threat of troop withdrawals as leverage with Chun and his group. They believed fervently that further withdrawals of U.S. forces by the Carter administration would be a calamity. Past troop withdrawals already had unsettled the Korean people, raising doubts about the durability of the U.S.–ROK alliance. All in all, I thought it was very canny and useful advice from a group of golfers.

North Korean Infiltrators

It was a dark, bitterly cold, early January night when the report came in. A light snow was falling, just enough to obscure visibility. A few kilometers north of the DMZ and slightly east of the truce village at Panmunjom, a team of North Korean paramilitary agents waited until darkness. The two infiltrators had rehearsed for several weeks for this special mission. Their task was to infiltrate into South Korea, to make contact with other North Korean agents already in the South, and then to gather firsthand information on the unusual political and military developments in Seoul. The agents had been briefed on the most recent intercepts of ROK military communications, which suggested that there was growing political unrest in Seoul, enough unrest that a number of army units had been placed at a high state of alert and been ordered to prepare to cope with domestic instability.

The agents were to cross the DMZ, infiltrate through combat elements of the U.S. 2nd Infantry Division and the ROK 1st Infantry Division, cross the swift, icy Imjin River, and make their way to Seoul, where they were to contact agents already in the city. Their routes had been carefully chosen to avoid the known locations of ROK army ambush patrols and ROK field police listening posts. These locations had been detected and pinpointed by previous infiltrators and agents already in the South.

As the night became darker, the agents, clad in black and without any identification, crept into the DMZ. They had been warned that U.S. troops relied on radar and night vision devices to detect unusual activity, so they stuck to the trails used by the abundant wildlife and wound their way through the dense foliage inside the zone. The frozen ground and wildlife trails also helped the infiltrators avoid the numerous antipersonnel mines that were still scattered throughout the DMZ from the Korean War.

An alert ambush patrol of U.S. combat troops detected the sounds of movement near them. They were authorized to shoot at any suspected targets and immediately opened up with small arms and machine guns in the direction of the noise. At the same time, the patrol reported the possible contact to Outpost Oulette, located on a hilltop several hundred meters south of the Military Demarcation Line that marked the center of the zone. The other U.S. outpost, Collier, was further south and also on a hilltop, and it was similarly notified. However, the combination of darkness and light snow prevented any radar or infrared detection from either outpost.

The agents eluded the defenders and within two hours reached the northern bank of the Imjin River near Liberty Bridge, a rusting, single lane military link over the river. Donning wet suits and small inflatable vests, they entered the frigid, swiftly flowing water. As they made their way along the southern bank they repeatedly had to climb over wires that spanned the river to interfere with infiltrators and to catch debris. A ROK ambush patrol along the bank detected activity in the water and opened fire. In the ensuing confusion both agents escaped again. They continued their journey into Seoul, although it became more difficult because one of the agents had been wounded.

Shortly after dawn I visited the site of the encounter because I wanted to see firsthand just what was going on with infiltration attempts. CFC had been receiving numerous reports of infiltration activity all along the demilitarized zone.

The ROK commander showed me the blood trails and the abandoned swim gear near the river's edge, an indication that at least one of the agents had been wounded. He was obviously pleased that his soldiers had been alert enough to detect the infiltration, but he was also disappointed that the weather conditions and visibility had hampered their ability to kill or track the agents. He told me that the reports of agent activity in his sector had increased, with several "hot" trails a month. No agents had been captured or killed, although some may have drowned in the river. The highly trained agents were very difficult to detect, and they would either fight to the death or kill themselves to avoid capture.

This incident and the many others reported along the DMZ were a matter of growing concern. They indicated that the North Koreans either were trying to improve their intelligence about the political unrest and military dispositions in the South or were augmenting their already extensive agent network in preparation for a possible attack. In addition, our ongoing tunnel detection work had noted an increase in unusual sounds in a number of locations, possibly because of digging. Extensive drilling and acoustic analysis by experts did not discover any new tunnels,

Speaking with opposition leader Kim Dae-jung.

but the underground noises continued to alarm us. We already had discovered and destroyed two tunnels that had been carved through solid granite underneath the DMZ. With a diameter about the size of a standard auto, each tunnel was large enough to permit the transit of a regiment of several thousand combat troops within an hour or two.

As the reports continued, we kept CFC forces at a high state of alert and increased our intelligence collection efforts.

Chapter Five

American Reprise, Korean Influence

Assessing the Coup

Bill Gleysteen and I had many discussions about the "12/12 Incident" that inevitably brought us back to one question. Both of us recognized that Chun and his group had at the very least seized control of the ROK military but, curiously, had not displaced the existing government. That left the United States faced with a conundrum: how to deal effectively with Chun, yet neither dignify his position nor so alienate him and his supporters that we would lose whatever influence we still retained.

On a regular basis Bill would convey his assessment of the evolving situation back to Washington, together with recommendations for how American policy should respond. He generally took the line that, while Chun's ultimate intentions remained obscure, his actions did not bode well for the complex political challenges facing South Korea, nor for relations between our two countries. Bill and I agreed that power and authority had become so diffused within military and political structures that it would require substantial consolidation by Chun if he intended to achieve a civilian takeover. Bill, however, did not believe we could yet conclude that Chun intended to replace Choi. He reported that Chun's group had publicly denied any intention to overthrow the civilian government or to obstruct the process of political evolution. In fact, Chun's group had widely circulated a "white paper" that attempted to explain that their actions were motivated simply by patriotism, without any intention to seize political power. After reading their "white paper" I termed it a "whitewash" to my superiors.

While Bill did not disagree with my assessment, he did believe that, for the time being, Chun and his cohort might simply content themselves with a powerful background role. President Choi seemed to be living under the optimistic pretense that he could survive without becoming

Chun's puppet or losing the respect of the Korean people—in fact, he had said as much to Bill. My own view was more tempered. Choi was not blessed with a reputation for strong leadership or for holding strong convictions, and his connections with the military, though based on genuine respect, were weak. He had never served in uniform or in a security-related position in the government, and prior military service was a litmus test among the ROK officer corps.

We were faced with a murky situation, and Bill believed we should use our influence to nurture positive changes in the ROK. President Park had exploited his vast power to manage the nation in a highly centralized fashion. His death led many Koreans to look toward the United States for guidance on how to manage their domestic functions. Bill's position, therefore, was that we should maintain strong support for Choi's government, so long as it demonstrated an ability to advance the country's political progress and to remain reasonably independent of Chun's group. We should carry on normal business, but we should refrain from pressuring Choi to liberalize the constitution and laws, although we should be willing, if necessary, to express concern over any instances of police brutality, press censorship, human rights problems, or overly harsh administration of the nation's martial law. Bill also urged that we deal with the ROK army through normal military channels, rather than through Chun and his group. At the same time, we should convey to the ROK military authorities our distress over recent events, particularly use of military forces in violation of the CFC chain of command. We should encourage unity of command in the ROK armed forces, the maintenance of civilian government and support of the constitutional process, moderation in the conduct of martial law, and patience among the political and dissident elements in Korean society, particularly when the students returned to their campuses in March 1980.

In many ways my frequent reports up the military chain in Hawaii and Washington paralleled Bill's reports, although my principal focus was on military aspects of the situation. In one key report two weeks after the "12/12 Incident", I provided the following summary of the situation:

Although the facade of civilian government has been retained, we in the military are faced with the *fait accompli* of illegal power seizure by an insurgent group of generals. By swift insertion of its members in key leadership positions the insurgent group has assured oversight if not control of policy and events. Further, by retaining control of the Defense Security

Command counter-espionage apparatus, which includes a separate reporting channel and teams in every battalion, regiment, and division throughout the ROK armed forces, the insurgent group can monitor suspicious actions and troop movements but not necessarily prevent a countermove.

This lawless seizure of power has interrupted the political progress of recent weeks and displays utter disregard for certain objectives we have been pursuing, to include development of a professional military which would abide by law, remain apolitical, and support the constitutional process. Even if political progress is allowed to be resumed, the insurgent leadership will retain oversight.

I and other senior U.S. officers, in past weeks after the death of President Park, have talked with hundreds of middle- and senior-level officers in all of the armed services about their performance since the assassination. We commended them for their support of the constitutional authorities and emphasized the importance of continued support for civilian leadership in the future. There is evidence that these views were widely circulated and welcomed in ROK military circles. But in our view the events subsequent to 12 and 13 December mock these views. Unless the United States now takes a strong position concerning actions by the insurgent group, young officers who know what the U.S. position and advice was after Park's assassination will conclude that in future circumstances U.S. views are to be regarded as hollow or hypocritical.

The insurgent group for its own purposes will attempt to sell a benign explanation of events and motives. They will seek to reestablish a business as usual relationship and profess no political interests. The group may also of necessity tolerate for the time being a degree of political movement to allay concern in the ROK and the United States.

The insurgent group consists of generals who can be described as "politicians in uniform." They made decisions on 12/13 December which have serious political implications. Hence it is likely that their decisions will continue to be political in nature. They cannot stop where they are now—they have stepped across the political line and there is no turning back. The 1961 scenario of power takeover may be one way to achieve power in the months to come. But we must try to discourage the insurgents from an outright takeover of the [government], encourage them to leave politics to the civilians, and allow the process of liberalization to continue.

Further, the intelligence gap associated with this event indicates that in the future we may be susceptible to being led by planted information, suggesting that the insurgent group in fact is benign and can be trusted. Also we probably will have no advance knowledge of further crisis events. The latter we cannot do much about, but we should be wary of the former.

The bottom line for me is that the insurgent group and those who follow them have betrayed U.S. trust and jeopardized U.S. as well as ROK security interests. Their willingness to engage in insurgent actions, to use forces illegally, and to make a mockery of CFC by moving forces without the authority of CFC all raise serious questions about whether we now can deal with this group on the basis of mutual trust and reliability. In view of this, as a minimum, we should reconsider programs which are premised on trust such as sharing of technology, intelligence, missile cooperation and expansion of CFC through additional OPCON of U.S. forces and other operational improvements.

Consequently we face several realities: First, the insurgent group will adhere to their benign explanations. Second, a civilian government technically remains in place. Third, the United States has limited leverage with regard to domestic developments. . . . And fourth, U.S. security interests continue to be served by strengthening the ROK, by maintaining a close alliance with Korea, and by ensuring peace and stability in the area. As a consequence we cannot and should not punish [South Korea] by spiteful actions which ultimately could hurt U.S. security interests in the region. For this reason we should not reopen the troop withdrawal issue until 1981.

Accordingly, we should pursue a course of action which accepts what has occurred. However, we would make certain that ROK leaders recognize the depth of U.S. outrage, that we will not tolerate any repeat of events, and that we will not accept influence of the insurgent group on the civilian government. In addition we would review programs of cooperation where reliability is a factor such as technology cooperation, missile development, intelligence sharing and increased OPCON of U.S. forces to CFC which the ROK military have been anxious to achieve. Essentially this course of action is a hard-nosed one designed to contain if not diminish the influence of the insurgent group and to make unequivocally clear the risks of further insurgent activity. We could refrain from dealing directly with leaders of the insurgent group, unless absolutely necessary, and we would take no action to dignify or legitimize their control of events. We would, however, work with the legitimate leadership structure of the [government] and military.

My judgment and that of the senior U.S. military officers here is that we should pursue the foregoing course of action. We are convinced that the United States cannot tolerate actions taken by insurgent groups which threaten U.S. security interests, and we cannot condone lawless, insubordinate actions which jeopardize unity of the chain of command and establish unethical precedents for junior officers to follow. Moreover, we cannot permit such behavior to invite North Korean attack.

Accordingly, unless otherwise directed, the U.S. military team in country will pursue this course of action. We will be prepared to moderate this action as concrete developments demonstrate that the military is restoring cohesiveness, is staying aloof from politics, and is permitting continuation of the political progress we wish to see. The ambassador generally agrees with these views.

My superiors in Hawaii and Washington generally accepted my analysis of the situation and my recommendations.

A Stray Helicopter

Early one morning, an OH–58 scout helicopter with a pilot and enlisted observer took off from Camp Page northeast of Seoul. The weather was miserable. A light snow was falling and an ice fog blanketed the ground, obscuring the terrain features from the air. Helicopter flights near the DMZ obviously were carefully controlled, because the mountainous terrain and the lack of a clear southern boundary made navigation very difficult. The fog and snow made navigation even more treacherous. All pilots who were assigned to MEDEVAC or reconnaissance missions had to complete a preparatory terrain course and be certified for flight near the demilitarized zone. Nevertheless, aerial incidents had occurred over the years, a number of which had led to shooting incidents.

On this particular winter morning the OH–58 flew directly into North Korea, almost as though that were part of its flight plan. ROK outposts along the southern edge of the DMZ were caught by surprise but spotted the aircraft. They fired warning shots and when the aircraft continued its flight, the outposts actually attempted to shoot it down because they believed it was defecting. Once the aircraft entered North Korea, it flew north for several kilometers with the North Korean soldiers withholding their fire probably because they also thought a defection was in progress. Then the dumbfounded pilot realized his error and abruptly turned south, causing the North Koreans to unleash a barrage of intense antiaircraft fire. It was only by good fortune that the pilot and his enlisted observer made it back to Camp Page unscathed.

An immediate investigation followed. The pilot was grounded and disciplined, in part because he had not been properly cleared to undertake flights along the DMZ. The pilot's defense during his disciplinary review was that he was a recent arrival in Korea and that his navigation mistake was the result of the weather conditions. Neither defense excused his error.

The incident could have been much worse. It might have resulted in the death or capture of two American soldiers with all of the potentially serious political ramifications about negotiating their release. At the very least, it could have triggered a major fire fight.

Given the very tense situation, General Sennewald and I thought a great deal about how to avoid such incidents in the future. We had to continue flying near the demilitarized zone for reconnaissance, intelligence, and MEDEVAC purposes, so suspending flights or flying farther south of the DMZ were not reasonable solutions. Yet, even with extensive preparatory and refresher training for our pilots, the mountainous southern boundary of the DMZ remained so obscure that the possibility of an inadvertent flight into North Korea could never be ruled out.

The solution we came up with was to install large, brightly-colored, permanent markers every 300 meters along the 150–mile southern boundary wherever pilots would be unable to detect natural terrain features, such as roads or rivers. These markers would be constructed of angle iron, about a meter square, embedded in concrete, and be painted international orange so that they would stand out during daylight, fog, or snow.

Surprisingly, the notion of installing the markers caused considerable controversy. Many of my colleagues, U.S. and Korean, considered the concept unnecessary, an indication that I was too safety conscious. Probably they were right. Having commanded the 101st Airborne Division and its 400 helicopters, including during the REFORGER exercise in Germany, I had come to the conclusion that when it came to safety, particularly when it came to helicopters, too much was infinitely better than too little. During that exercise in 1976, the division had tested very tight flight safety procedures and found that it both saved lives and aircraft and actually improved operational capability. We had suffered only two aircraft incidents during bad weather, and neither had been serious.

Despite the doubts, the markers were quickly installed by the ROK military. Their worth was demonstrated by the fact that no further aerial incidents occurred during the next two-and-one-half years of my tour in Korea.

The Mun Talks

Over the next several weeks I had a series of lengthy but invaluable discussions with retired General Mun Hyong-tae, chairman of the National Assembly Defense Committee. A former JCS Chairman, Mun was a distinguished soldier with an engaging manner. He spoke English well, which allowed us to converse frankly in my office without fear of being overheard. I liked Mun from the moment I met him. He held a powerful position in the legislature, and from all reports was highly regarded by the ROK military establishment, particularly the more than 400 retired generals.

It was unclear why Mun first came to see me. Perhaps, like other senior ROK officials, he realized that the "12/12 Incident" had jeopardized relations with the United States and that the situation might be getting out of hand. Mun had a reputation as a great patriot and a strong friend of Americans who had worked hard to establish close relationships with Congress. His motive may have been to capitalize on his wide experience and to help restore good relations. More likely, Mun, who knew Chun from his army days, had come to the conclusion that the agitated American leaders needed some calming.

He began by revealing what he had discussed with the Japanese prime minister, who had just returned from a visit to Beijing. The prime minister said that China's leaders had assured him they would not support an attack by the North, but at the same time had warned that the North Koreans, perhaps the world's most xenophobic people, feared a possible attack from the South as a result of domestic unrest. The prime minister informed Mun that he had told the Chinese not to worry about democratic progress in South Korea or that an attack would be launched against the North. Further, although the subject of U.S. troops never arose officially, in "unofficial" asides the Chinese military told the chairman of the Japanese Self-Defense Force that U.S. forces must remain in South Korea for "purposes of stability." The Japanese of course agreed.

Then Mun abruptly changed the subject and asked me about some rumors he had heard that the United States wanted to restore the previous military structure, including the former army chief of staff, General Chung. The leader of the Defense Reform Party, and mastermind of the coup that brought Park to power in 1961, Kim Jong-pil, had been the source of the rumors. Kim, incidentally, saw himself as a candidate for the ROK presidency and probably wouldn't have been displeased to see Chun isolated or his plans sidetracked. I told Mun, "the rumors are totally false—the United States cannot turn the clock back." I reassured him on the steadfastness of the U.S. commitment to deter hostilities and to improve the capabilities of the CFC. He could see what we were doing with our forces.

Mun welcomed all of these views, particularly the points about strengthening deterrence and not turning the clock back. He said, "We must put behind us what has happened . . . it was a mistake that cannot happen again. People are very disappointed in their army, which they believe must be above politics, but at the same time the people recognize that the army is the basic power in the land, and that the current civilian government is hollow." He reflected for a moment, as if for emphasis, and then offered some advice: "Our army and nation still are very young, and we desperately need advice and help from our true ally. The young leadership that has taken over the army is immature, and you must work with them to develop an international sense as well as a more responsible attitude toward politics and their profession. You must understand that these young generals are motivated in part by fear that the political progress after President Park's death would be too rapid, hence their objective of influencing events in a more orderly, evolutionary way." I thanked Mun for his advice and told him that the United States basically was trying to move in the direction he suggested, and that I would welcome further discussions with him.

Our next meeting came a few weeks later and focused on the attitudes of ROK senior military and political officials. Apparently, after our last discussion General Mun had arranged to meet with a number of army generals, all the way down to division level. In addition, General Chun had met with the members of the National Assembly Defense Committee, of which Mun was the chairman, to explain his motives in the "12/12 Incident." Mun told me that he had used these meetings to carefully explain the U.S. concerns as they had been expressed by Bill Gleysteen and me. To be sure the generals would understand the broader implications of their actions, he said he had pointed out the potentially dire economic circumstances facing Seoul in the months to come, when a severe credit squeeze might force the closure of significant portions of the nation's industrial capacity, including defense-oriented firms. Mun told them that the credit problem stemmed directly from declining international confidence in the internal stability of South Korea. As a final point, he emphasized the critical importance of maintaining a strong and open relationship with the Americans. Without the United States, South Korea would be in deep trouble economically and militarily.

Chun and his group of generals bristled as Mun lectured them, but they told the members of the Defense Committee that there was absolutely no plot behind the "12/12 Incident", no *coup d´etat* in mind, and no intention to meddle in politics. Chun then insisted that it was his intention to "allow constitutional reform and elections to take place under civilian guidance." Then Chun repeated his benign explanation for the arrest of the army chief of staff, an explanation that mirrored the group's white paper.

Mun apologized to me for taking so long and said he had one final comment to make: he personally had no ax to grind or power to accumulate. His career had been full and successful, but in his capacity as chairman of the Defense Committee he wanted "to assure solid support for security and serve as an intermediary during these difficult times." He said he was trying the best he could to understand the motives and objectives of the new leaders in the military. In the meantime, he would continue to urge moderation in his regular meetings with Chun.

After this lengthy exposition Mun smiled and watched for my reaction. I told him that Chun's explanation of events was very familiar, that the ambassador and I had heard it countless times and from numerous sources, and that it seemed to both of us that there was some room for doubt, particularly since General Chung had never been given the opportunity to state publicly and freely his side of the story. Would Chung ever be given such an opportunity, I asked him. Mun said he did not know. As to Chun's assurances that he would stay out of politics, I told Mun that I would have to wait to see whether his actions lived up to his assurances. I told him that my skepticism had been reinforced by recent information I had received that Chun was considering the use of his martial law authority to arrest a number of corrupt politicians and other individuals who might be troublesome to his plans; that was just the kind of action that struck me as a military incursion into political affairs.

Mun said nothing, merely nodding his head as though he agreed, so I went on to reiterate the principal concerns of U.S. leaders about recent events. First, the internal instability caused by the "12/12 Incident" could be a perfect opportunity for North Korean intervention, and our intelligence suggested that North Korea's forces were on high alert and far stronger than we had previously believed. Such an incident must not be repeated. Second, the "12/12 Incident" involved insubordination and defiance of the legitimate chain of command and civilian authority. As a lifelong professional soldier, I knew that Mun would understand the gravity of that point. The CFC CINC could not be undermined by the unauthorized diversion of forces under his command and still be expected to perform his mission. There had to be trust up and down the chain of command. Mun readily agreed. He understood my responsibilities. Third, in the likely absence of strong political leadership, with Choi Kyu-ha at the helm, there were obviously strong temptations and rich opportunities for the army to intervene directly or indirectly in political affairs. Were this to occur, it would have a tragic impact on U.S.–ROK relations and on international financial confidence in South Korea.

Mun said he fully recognized these points, then went on to assure me that "things were settling down in the army after the recent shifts of general officers. No political meddling will occur." He acknowledged, however, that these assurances were merely talk and that only time could tell whether actions backed up the talk. He also noted that an atmosphere of uneasiness pervaded the army senior ranks, because officers were unsure about their futures and, therefore, the welfare of their families. Mun sensed that the atmosphere was similar to what he had experienced after Park's coup in 1961. He said that only "time could heal." Unfortunately, much damage might be done during the wait.

The third time we met was toward the end of January, after I had returned from congressional testimony in the United States. That time,

Mun called and requested an urgent meeting. After some opening pleasantries he told me with some emotion that there were widespread rumors circulating in Seoul's political and military circles that I was being held responsible by the U.S. Government for the "12/12 Incident" and its aftermath. According to the rumors, I was going to be removed soon because the U.S. authorities were unhappy with my performance, especially that I was unable to control the ROK military and did not have close, harmonious relations with Chun and his group.

I was stunned. I had no inkling of any dissatisfaction with my performance, not from Secretary of Defense Brown, General Jones, Admiral Long, Assistant Secretary of State Holbrooke, Ambassador Gleysteen, or any of the other key officials whom I knew in Washington. I had tried my best to keep everyone informed of developments in Seoul, to work harmoniously with my Korean counterparts, the ambassador, and my immediate superior in Hawaii. Most of all, I had worked hard to keep the lid on military problems so that hostilities would not break out.

Where could such a rumor have originated? And why at this time? Perhaps it came from the Korean cultural outlook that suggested that when things went wrong the top official had to be held responsible. Korean ministers were commonly treated as sacrificial lambs to atone for failures, even those that were entirely beyond their control. Koreans knew that the United States was deeply distressed over Chun's actions, especially his rollback of the progress toward political liberalization in Korea. And there was a U.S. presidential election coming up in 1980. The worrisome setbacks in Korea, on top of the agonizing and humiliating Iranian hostage crisis, would not be regarded as helpful by the Carter administration, which was involved in a hard-fought reelection effort. Consequently, Koreans might have surmised that my recent trip to Washington was to defend my actions and performance in Korea.

On the other hand, it was just as possible that Chun and his generals had fabricated and circulated the rumors through their various contacts in Korea and the United States, hoping that I would be replaced by someone more in tune with their objectives. At the very least they may have hoped to frighten me into becoming more sympathetic toward them and their goals. Of course, I might have been making too much of the issue, but clearly some intrigue was underway that I did not understand and that might affect my future.

I looked back at General Mun and I could see that he was anxiously awaiting my reaction to the rumors. Without revealing my personal

uneasiness, I told Mun that so far as I knew there was absolutely no substance to them, just as there was no content to the rumors that the Americans were seeking the removal of Chun and his group of generals. I added
that if he had heard any rumors that there was American support for a
countercoup, it, too, would be false. Mun smiled broadly.

I had already discovered that Chun had written letters to a number
of American generals who had served previously in Korea, explaining his
benign motives and soliciting their personal support for him and his goals.
In addition, he had sent a personal emissary to the United States to brief
various senior generals and to give General Vessey a copy of Chun's white
letter. Chun's emissary had also tried to solicit General Vessey to offer Chun
an invitation to travel to the United States to explain his motives or, barring
that, for General Vessey to come to Korea for the same purpose.

When I mentioned Chun's letter campaign to Minister Chu and
JCS Chairman General Rhu, they exhibited quite different reactions,
which I thought was understandable, given their loyalties. Chu told me
that he had not authorized the initiative, but did feel it was completely
understandable as an "act of good will based on previous friendships." He
admitted that he recognized the irregularities this presented with regard
to respect for the chain of command problems and promised that he
would look into the matter. Needless to say, I did not expect much to
come from his investigation. Rhu, on the other hand, was extremely irritated by this development. He said it clearly represented a bypassing of
the chain of command and was "not a good sign at all."

I was confident that most of the generals Chun wrote to were entirely unreceptive and unsympathetic to Chun's initiative, regardless of
their abiding friendship for Korea and possible acquaintance with Chun.
However, some U.S. generals might have concluded that I had fouled up a
few things because I was the "new guy on the block" and a new four star
at age 51. I had no way of knowing whether any American generals had
answered Chun's letters, but I did learn that Chun had mentioned to his
associates that he did not expect answers.

One retired Army lieutenant general did accept Chun's invitation
and traveled to Korea in May while I was in the United States on official
business. He met with General Forrester and a number of senior Koreans, including Chun. The Deputy Chief of Mission, John Monjo, accompanied him on the Korean office calls and heard absolutely no criticism
of any U.S. officials from the Koreans, even as the retired American general verbally excoriated the current U.S. leadership in Korea, as well as

several recent military commanders. The general left a trail of venom. Although I was unable to positively identify the source of his criticism, I was left with a few suspicions.

When I asked General Rhu about the American general's diatribe, he exploded with uncharacteristic bluntness: "What he says is pure bull. . . . In the past 20 years I have served in a number of key positions and have had the opportunity to observe closely and work with U.S. ambassadors and CINCs; in my opinion the current ambassador and CINC are the best that I have seen because of their understanding of the Korean situation during this difficult period, their close personal relationship, their effective working relationships with ROK counterparts, and their interface with Washington bureaucracy." I was, of course, quite appreciative of Rhu's support, although I recognized that our close personal friendship made him a natural ally.

I sent a message to General Vessey summarizing what I had learned so he would not be surprised. Still, I felt blindsided by the retired American general's unhelpful visit and strongly suspected that he had a source within my command structure—that a high-ranking American officer was disloyally feeding the visiting general information. The meddling by a retired U.S. Army general with absolutely no official responsibility in Korea greatly troubled me. Intrigue and backbiting were distractions in the best of times, but they were even more dangerous and complicating, given the issues we faced at the moment.

In my meeting with General Mun, I mentioned Chun's letters to various generals in the United States, including General Vessey. Mun just shook his head in disgust and commented that the initiative was a bad move, because it violated established channels of authority and reflected gross ignorance by Chun about the role played by the U.S. Ambassador and CINC in Korea. Mun described Chun and his group of generals as unsophisticated and lacking in experience in dealing with the matters suddenly thrust on them, echoing the same point he had made in our earlier meeting. Thus, in his view, Chun was not being malevolent, just clumsy. Chun and his group basically were very patriotic and they were well aware that the Korean people did not want another military dictatorship. Chun had repeatedly assured him that he had absolutely no political ambitions. Nonetheless, Mun asked me what advice I would give Chun about his letter-writing campaign. I told him that Chun needed to reduce his visibility and avoid any implications of political action, and that he should most certainly display evidence of his support for the established chain of command and political authorities. Let actions speak louder than words, I told him. Mun said he would pass on these comments.

Looking ahead, Mun described the worst-case scenario for internal developments. He said that some 370,000 students would return to the campuses in March, and intelligence indicated that a series of massive demonstrations was being planned. The demonstrations probably would challenge the activities of Chun and his group after the "12/12 Incident", particularly the strong enforcement of martial law. In addition, the country's economic position was looking very bleak as a result of serious cash flow problems that were affecting large and small companies alike. Mun estimated that there could be as much as $5 billion in bad credit, which might lead to widespread factory closures and large-scale layoffs. The combination of unemployment and income problems, together with the student violence, could lead to serious confrontations, particularly if the ROK military had to be called in to back up the police. Mun's predictions of trouble paralleled those I had heard from a number of other retired ROK officers and officials.

Mun said he felt that North Korea would try to exploit the domestic unrest by increasing the infiltration of agents and commandos and possibly by instigating a major incident to foster worldwide concern about ROK internal instability so that foreign investment would dry up. Mun believed that such a worst case scenario would seriously strain the ability of the politically weak, caretaker government to control the situation. That, in turn, might provoke a desperate move by Chun and his group.

I wondered about Mun's motives. Here he was preaching moderation and responsible action to his extensive military and official contacts, yet he seemed to have a very pessimistic assessment of the future. He had told me several times that he was increasingly troubled by what he described as the sight of "many senior officials trooping to Chun and showing abject deference to him. And Chun appears to enjoy this heady influence." Nevertheless, I could not help but notice that Mun himself was in frequent contact with Chun, and thus was himself one of the "many senior officials" who were passing through Chun's doorway.

I concluded that, like Bill Gleysteen and me, Mun was caught up in the web of a complicated political situation and was clearly trying hard to maintain channels of communication between senior American officials in Seoul and influential elements in the ROK military. He was trying his best to perform a difficult balancing act, and his warnings about the troublesome spring that lay ahead probably were intended to prepare us for the difficult challenges we were going to face. He foresaw domestic turmoil and knew that could involve serious armed confrontations between the populace and the military, something that was rare in Korean history.

In his own way, he was not being disingenuous about Chun. He knew Chun's power was rapidly increasing, even as he continued to assure me and the ambassador that he was continuously warning Chun to stay out of politics. Like everyone in Seoul in those days, he was trying his best to walk a straight line on a curvy road. He knew Chun could not be stopped and was worried that America might try to punish the ROK by lessening its support for his country's defense.

Chapter Six

Maneuvering Toward the Presidency

Korean Army Morale

The harsh, freezing temperatures, snow, fog, and ice of winter were still with us. There was something about Korea's cold that caused it to penetrate deeply. Notwithstanding, I had decided the time was right to begin a series of terrain walks along portions of the demilitarized zone.

The patrol lanes along the southern edge of the demilitarized zone were for the most part in very rugged and remote terrain, particularly in the eastern and mountainous portion of the peninsula. The lanes were observed by outposts and roving patrols of ROK army soldiers who spent their days walking or, more often, climbing the steep, arduous trails near the 8–foot-high barbed wire fence that traced the southern edge of the zone. Dirt roads or rain-gutted trails for jeeps were often the only way to reach most of the patrol bases.

The more I went out to the DMZ, the more I realized that improved road networks, particularly lateral roads, were absolutely essential to execute our operational plans, which depended entirely on the rapid lateral movement of reserves, supplies, and reinforcements. Plenty of commanders before me had probably insisted on improvements in the road network, but from what I could see, the condition of the roads and trails indicated they had met with little success. In fact, early in my tour I had met with Defense Minister Rho and army Chief of Staff Chung, both of whom agreed that the roads were a serious problem, but they were removed by Chun before they could initiate the programs needed to remedy the situation. Therefore, I carried the same message to the new team of Defense Minister Chu and army Chief of Staff Lee, and both assured me they would make it a top issue with the minister of transportation and their army engineers. I was not optimistic. The progress over the next several years continued to be excruciatingly slow, largely because frontline road improvements fell well below ROK national priorities for improving telecommunications, constructing railroads, and laying oil pipelines.

A number of South Korean soldiers along the fence line had mixed-breed dogs, both for companionship and for detecting suspicious activities inside the DMZ. To the best I could tell, there did not seem to be any command policy about the dogs, so whether a soldier had a dog or not seemed to have been left entirely to individual choice. The keen hearing and acute sense of smell of the species actually made them extremely effective in detecting infiltrators, and I would have liked to see more dogs involved with security, but for cultural reasons dogs did not exist in large numbers in Korea. Food was still scarce, and the fate of dogs often was dictated by the belief that eating them strengthened masculinity.

From the DMZ outposts you could catch glimpses of the sniper towers built about every 25 meters by the North Koreans. Sharpshooters were placed on each tower and their job was to kill potential defectors. You could also hear the loudspeakers blaring propaganda 24 hours a day in an effort to unnerve the defenders. From what I could tell, none of our soldiers were unnerved, but more than a few were irritated when the constant noise interrupted or interfered with their sleep. Soldiers are soldiers, and sleep ranks high on the hierarchy of needs.

I hoped that my constant walks would set an example for ROK commanders, many of whom were acutely and constantly concerned with the growing domestic unrest and the political maneuvering in Seoul. I could not blame them, but I still hoped to make them pay more attention to the readiness issues in their commands.

One visit in particular left an impression. I visited a division commander whose unit was in the process of improving the mine fields in his sector. All divisions had to accomplish some routine minefield maintenance. The task was inherently dangerous. While it would have been unnecessary and costly to mine the entire southern portion of the DMZ, in those sectors where limited visibility, weapon coverage, or access to prime attack corridors were a factor, minefields were usually essential. After the mines were laid, they were carefully recorded and then had to be periodically checked for reliability. Sometimes they were moved as defensive plans changed. It was not easy work. The records that were supposed to show where mines were laid often were unreliable because of dense foliage and the heavy rains that sometimes caused soil runoff—and scattered mines. There also were many old mines left over from the Korean war and no records to show where they were located. We were constantly mindful that the ancient mines were still there and still active, as wildlife and unsuspecting patrols occasionally tripped one off.

This particular division commander's sector lay in the mountainous east. He told me he used only volunteers to search for old mines or to check existing fields. Volunteers were always better motivated, he told me, and fortunately there were always enough men who were willing to step forward. After extensive training the soldiers would spend several months searching for and checking the mines, then returned to their original assignments. For that, the reward was usually a three-day pass to visit their families, although I sensed from his praise that they probably would receive some special incentives as well. He told me that during his command a few soldiers had lost feet or perhaps a hand but these were the most serious injuries. Deaths were almost unheard of.

He wanted me to handle the very large, heavy, protective shoes crudely constructed from half-inch thick sheet metal and sections of rubber tires. I had difficulty imagining how anyone could walk with these cumbersome shoes, particularly in dense underbrush and mountainous terrain. But the shoes were absolutely necessary. Small plastic antipersonnel mines were undetectable to the electronic sensors on the mine detectors, so protective gear was needed for the soldier's feet and lower extremities. He said that ROK army engineers had fabricated the heavy shoes by copying, and then improving upon, a design originally observed with the U.S. forces in Vietnam.

I wasn't sure that I would have been willing to volunteer for this duty. I remember looking at the proud faces of the volunteers the commander had assembled and being struck by the courage and the sacrifices that Korea's sons continued to endure in defense of their country.

Meeting with Chun

General Mun came to see me several more times to report on his discussions with Chun Doo-hwan. He also told me there was growing dissent among the retired military community and urged me to meet with Chun. I agreed to do so in February, which Bill Gleysteen agreed would be an appropriate time.

As he began the discussion, Mun warned me that I had to recognize that his own interests were Korean, but that his political background and his position in the National Assembly gave him an understanding of American interests, as well as the interests of a broad section of the Korean people, including the students and opposition elements, and how to work things out in Korea's complex society. Thus he felt he could be most helpful as an intermediary.

Mun agreed that U.S. authorities must not deal directly with Chun because he was not in the direct chain of command and we might inflate his position by excessive direct contact. However, occasional meetings with Chun would be useful. I asked Mun whether he thought it would be helpful if I were to invite Chun and several other commanders who were not subordinate to CFC to our next commanders conference. He said he thought it was a good idea. Additionally, I asked Mun what he thought of the notion of inviting several prominent civilian scholars on politico-military affairs from the major universities to attend some CFC conferences. The purpose would be to initiate a productive dialogue between the military and the academic groups in an effort to bridge the animosities and differences between the two groups. Mun heartily approved.

Since I had already agreed to meet with Chun, Mun then recounted the details of a long discussion he had with Chun. The discussion concerned the country's growing political problems and domestic unrest. Mun said he opened the talk by telling Chun of his close relationship with President Park. Mun had been a close confidant of the President's, and the two of them often had talked about the extraordinary problems of running Korea. Mun said that Park had told him that a military takeover was never an easy task, and that the big problems really begin after the coup. In Park's opinion the military were ill equipped to deal with the country's internal pressures, external political negotiations, and particularly the complex economic issues. Knowing how much Chun admired Park, Mun felt that Chun needed to hear Park's unvarnished views. He also told Chun that Park had believed that American support was absolutely essential to the security of the ROK and to any regime that sought to assume political power. Further, Mun emphasized that "all Korean authorities must work with the U.S. team in country because the team provides virtually all the persuasiveness in the formulation of U.S. policies which emanate from Washington." Mun told me that his comments were designed to serve as subtle criticisms of Chun's letter-writing campaign and his invitation to General Vessey. Chun had merely listened to Mun's discourse, neither agreeing nor disagreeing.

Mun then relayed to Chun the results of his extensive talks with many retired and active duty flag officers. He said that a large number of generals had concluded that "Chun and his associates had carried out a coup in all but name and eventually would move to seize total power."

Chun dismissed their views as sheer nonsense, noting that if he and his associates had wanted to achieve a coup, they could have done so because they controlled the key military installations in Seoul and most military units were not in any position to counter their efforts. Chun said that in his judgment the Korean people did not want another military government now that Park was gone. Given the popular dissatisfaction with the later years of the late president's regime, there was little or no support for the military to take over the government.

Then Chun strangely offered an opinion about the current political process: if elections were held in the next few months it would be an absolute disaster because neither Kim Young-sam or Kim Dae-jung had any experience in government affairs and they were unreliable. Further, the military deeply distrusted both of them. As for Kim Jong-pil, Chun said he was neutral toward him, although Chun also remarked that he had a reputation for corruption and a notable lack of allegiance toward the military. However, Chun expressed some support for Prime Minister Shin Hyon-hwack because he had "played a very helpful role during the night of December 12." Chun flatly told Mun that whoever ran for president, military support would be "crucial for acceptability." I commented wryly to Mun that Chun did not sound like a man who professes no interest in politics. Mun just smiled.

I mentioned that Chun's DSC appeared to be moving well beyond their military sphere. The command had organized a separate organization to handle domestic political and economic affairs. Mun acknowledged this development and said he had discussed it with Chun. He said that Chun's response was to minimize the issue by pointing out that the new office was merely the reinstitution of a domestic intelligence function that had existed within the command until 1978, when Park had discontinued it. Moreover, Chun said that President Choi had recently approved his request for the DSC to become more involved in domestic intelligence activities, to include political as well as economic affairs. I suggested that creating the office seemed odd at this particular time. Given their professed disinterest in governing, why would Chun and his associates want to establish a military organization to give them political and economic advice? Why would they want to duplicate a KCIA function? Wasn't that the reason Park disbanded the old office, to end a duplication of effort? Mun just shrugged.

Mun's candor during our discussions was a welcome relief and nearly always a sharp contrast to my talks with other Korean officials.

Defense Minister Chu, for example, always assured me that I "should not worry because all is well in the military, and I continue my forceful instructions to general officers about their responsibilities toward the chain of command and avoidance of involvement in politics." I often sensed that most of Chu's comments were designed to tell me what he thought I wanted to hear. One day he suggested that in any future public statements U.S. officials might make about the current domestic and military scene, we should be careful how we describe the situation. He said, "the public already is alarmed about actions taken on the night of December 12 and the role of the military." If Americans "continue to say that the military needs to be watched then the public will continue to be alarmed, and worse the North Koreans may sense opportunities to exploit unrest." Rather, U.S. officials should say, "The situation is calming down and moderating actions are being taken." Not only was Chu telling me what he thought I wanted to hear, he was asking me to tell him what he wanted to hear.

The Magruder/Kim Memo

Major General Chun came to CFC headquarters in late February. We had met briefly before but this was my first opportunity to develop a relationship with him. We met in my office, seated around the coffee table without any distinction of protocol as usually existed in Korean offices. He was about my height and balding and sometimes wore glasses, and he looked physically vigorous, though he seemed to be a chain smoker. His facial features and actions suggested a very strong, direct personality—a tough man who was sure of himself. Overall, he was an impressive-looking soldier, and his competence had been attested to by his very rapid promotions through the ranks.

Our meeting turned out to be cordial, but correct, and lasted more than two hours. I intended to do more listening than talking at this first meeting and not resort to lecturing him about American views. I was sure he knew our views quite well. I wanted to use this opportunity to size him up as a leader and to understand better where he was coming from. I'm sure he wanted to do the same with me.

Chun brought along his military interpreter, and I included Bruce Grant, from the Special Assistant's office, because it was helpful to have an American translate idioms and subtle meanings from Korean. During Bruce's earlier Mormon missionary work in Korea he had become thoroughly fluent in Korean and Chinese—enough that he could translate and even write books in both languages.

In preparation for this meeting, Steve Bradner gave me a remarkable memorandum of conversation (memcon) between a former CINC, General Carter Magruder, and Lieutenant Colonel Kim Jong-pil. The latter, as mentioned earlier, had been the mastermind behind the coup staged in May 1961. It was not clear whether Kim had been summoned by Magruder or had come of his own volition. In any event Kim was there to explain the actions of the coup leaders, including Major General Park Chung-hee, who eventually dominated the coup group and became president. A feeling of *déjà vu* came over me as I read the memcon; virtually all of the reasons given for the coup in 1961 were reflected in what Chun and his associates said about their actions.

In the conversation, Kim apologized to Magruder for violating the chain of command by using ROK forces without CINC authority. Kim respectfully explained that the coup leaders had no political goals; their actions were to oust the corrupt, aging military leaders who blocked promotion opportunities of more able officers, and to "clean up" the government, which had grown so inefficient and corrupt that the people were not well served. Kim assured Magruder that after he and his associates had achieved their limited objectives, they would return promptly to the barracks. "Trust us," said Kim. The thought crossed my mind that I could change the date of Magruder's memcon and use it as a record of my discussion with Chun.

Chun's sole objective seemed to be to justify his actions on December 12. At the outset, he looked right at me and expressed his complete regret for any problems he had created for me and the other U.S. authorities. Bruce Grant later told me that Chun's language was flowery and effusively respectful. Then Chun began to paint himself as an authentic national hero who was simply trying his best to fulfill his difficult investigative duties for the benefit of the Korean people. He said he had been thwarted at every turn by an arrogant minister of defense and an unscrupulous army chief, and he had been maligned unjustly by the press and by U.S. authorities who really did not understand him or his objectives. His voice and face showed his bitterness.

Chun's explanation of General Chung's purported involvement in the assassination offered nothing new except for a few details about his strange behavior immediately afterward. Chun said that his team of investigators had strongly urged him to order Chung's arrest in the predawn hours of October 27, but he had refused to do so because he had not amassed enough incriminating evidence.

Chun looked straight at me again and repeated his regret over any misunderstandings that arose from the night of December 12. He said that he did not regret the actions themselves—since he was convinced they were fully justified—and that, "I have to press on with what I am doing, or else resign from the army, which I do not choose to do because the army is my whole life." He considered that his actions were having a therapeutic benefit, because his firm control over the military had opened up promotion opportunities for an officer corps that had been stultified by older, less able, and sometimes corrupt officers. He insisted that the officer corps largely applauded what had happened and dismissed the barracks talk about unrest in the officer corps on the basis that, as a Korean, he would know much better than me what was happening in the military. Moreover, he said, his extensive DSC spy apparatus throughout the armed forces and Korean institutions gave him both the knowledge and influence to maintain stability. Of course, there were always bound to be a few disgruntled individuals who were passed over for promotion and would invent rumors and grumble about his actions.

I asked Chun whether he had set a dangerous precedent. Wasn't there a chance that the next generation of younger generals might someday see Chun and his contemporaries as obstacles to their own promotions, and then seize upon the events of December 12 as justification for similar actions, again endangering national security? Chun obviously did not like this question, probably because I had categorized him as a younger general. He pointed out that he and many of the army's major generals were 49 or 50 years old and therefore not young at all. Chun said he had been promoted to major general at the age of 45 and was now 48. He said, "You are just 51 and a four-star general already. You have moved rapidly. We need opportunities like yours in the ROK army."

Chun had either missed or sidestepped my point, so I reminded him that the precedent for change set by the December 12 incident could be dangerous for the future, couldn't it? Might not today's field grade officers be tempted to follow his precedent if they should find their path blocked?

"No," said Chun, "the December incident would not be repeated without destroying the whole country." The circumstances involving an army chief of staff taking money from the president's assassin, as Chung had, were unique and could not serve as a precedent. Chung should have cooperated in the investigation instead of stonewalling and undermining the combat strength and morale of the army. Furthermore the incident could never be repeated, because Korean army officers were patriots, endowed with a strong tradition of Confucian values—loyalty, fealty, courtesy, comradeship. "We army officers are loyal to our country and our president," he insisted. "We are great leaders, and the comradeship between officers is of a higher nature than that known in Western countries. Thus the December 12 incident is no precedent in our Korean world. Please do not pay attention to rumor mongers or those who are dissatisfied. Please call me. I will be happy to come and discuss these issues with you. I want to be helpful."

Chun's reference to Confucian values was curious. He sounded even more Confucian than the "older generals" he and the other dissatisfied officers had branded as being hidebound by Confucianism and therefore unprogressive and unwilling to entertain new ideas.

Chun repeated several times his "absolute disinterest in political matters," saying that he would prove this by his actions. He told me I would be proud of what he had done after my tour of duty ended in Korea. "Trust me," he said. There was obvious bitterness in his comments about the "unjust rumors" about his intentions and he reaffirmed that there was "no plan at all or desire to go beyond what had spontaneously happened with the arrest of army Chief [of Staff] Chung." Once again, Chun dwelled on his desire to open up promotion opportunities in the army. He told me that he personally aspired to be the chief of staff, nothing more. As the meeting drew to a close, Chun expressed some frustration over what he regarded as repeated rejections of his efforts to establish direct contact and relations with me. He said it would be important for us to work closely together in the future.

I suggested that the controversy over the December 12 incident probably would persist for a long time but that what had happened was history and could not be turned back. Neither Chun nor I nor the Korean people wanted to see this sort of event repeated. To protect the strong ties between our countries, there must be no military involvement in politics, the country must remain under civilian authority, and political development must continue. I gave him a mini-lecture: the soldier must support his constitution and legal authorities and stay confined to his purpose of defending the nation. If this could be assured, I predicted there would be continued international economic assistance, improved national security, and close relations between our nations. Chun nodded, but I couldn't tell whether he agreed.

Finally, I asked Chun how those of us in uniform could ensure that the ROK army would face north during this dangerous year, instead of being concerned with political matters. Chun bristled at this, claiming that American officials must be victims of bad information if we were hearing that the military was involved in politics. He disavowed any such involvement and asserted that we would have ample opportunity to judge the DSC by its future actions. He pleaded, "I was new to this job when Park was assassinated and I have had a rough time of it as investigator, becoming suddenly famous and being described by foreign journalists as either number one or number two in the nation. But all of this was wrong. I seek no political future, only to do a good job as a soldier."

After our discussion I wrote a brief summary for my superiors, concluding:

> Chun impressed me as a ruthlessly ambitious, scheming and forceful man who believes he is destined to wear the purple. His manner was cocky and self-assured despite extreme nervousness in smoking almost a pack of cigarettes. I found him unsophisticated in his knowledge of the United States and of the international consequences that could result from instability in his country. There is a hint of anti-U.S. attitude in his intensely nationalistic and conservative views. Without lecturing him, I reaffirmed U.S. concerns over the December 12 incident and the fact that we would not tolerate further instability from any group. In addition, I made it clear that the best course of action for the ROK military would be to stay out of politics entirely and devote themselves to defending the nation. After reflecting carefully on the lengthy meeting I remain suspicious of Chun. He is on the make, has a taste for power, knows how to use it, and does not strike me as a man to be trusted. He recognizes that he will have to earn our trust by actions, not rhetoric.

Another Meeting with Chun

Within a month Chun came to see me again. The meeting was friendly, and Chun appeared more relaxed than before, perhaps because he now wore the three stars of a lieutenant general. From what we could discern he had consolidated his grip on the military and was moving behind the scenes to establish firm control over other institutions of the government. My impression was that Chun remained self-assured, articulate, and willing to express firm opinions on almost any subject, including economics and politics. There was no doubt that he was trying hard to establish closer relations with U.S. authorities. Clearly, he realized that U.S. support and understanding were central to his ambitions.

Chun described in detail his views on the North-South talks, concluding that while the North was simply trying to exploit weakness in the South, Seoul should nevertheless work toward limited initiatives as a basis for building trust. He told me that KCIA was the action agency on the current talks, but that agency views were not as strong as those of Chun. (Less than a month later, Chun installed himself as KCIA director. Chun, like Park, realized the agency's importance to the achievement of his objectives. Also, within the next few months, Chun was reported to have "accepted" a promotion to four-star general. Park had similarly promoted himself shortly after the coup in 1961.)

According to Chun, North Korea wanted the talks at that moment because it recognized that South Korea had a weak government and faced a difficult internal situation. The North Koreans were adjusting their approach to the talks to take advantage of the situation. Chun explained that, in the past, the North would press a demand for a congress of social representatives and would insist on holding the diplomatic sessions every two or three days, leaving the South inadequate time for internal consultation and preparation. Pyongyang would make demands that were impossible for the South to meet and then use propaganda organs to accuse Seoul of torpedoing the talks.

Chun's monologue on the politically charged issue of the North/South talks struck me as another manifestation of his political ambitions. I found it strange that virtually all of our two-hour talk dwelt on internal political matters, with hardly any mention of military matters, although I tried continually to steer the conversation into defense-related issues.

As to the internal ROK situation, Chun expressed optimism, despite American concerns about growing labor and student unrest. "Yes," he said, "demonstrations are likely but they could be contained by local authorities and the national police. Do not worry about them." He did not foresee the need to use military forces, even though they historically had been available to the national police. As for rumors of instability in the military, Chun saw no trouble at all. "Do not be worried on this count." Acknowledging his views, I emphasized once again the importance of maintaining military cohesiveness and political neutrality because of the threat from the North. I urged that we work harder at establishing closer working relations and cooperation between our military establishments;

there was too much secrecy and suspicion and not enough trust. Chun agreed with these views, including the comment about building trust.

I had made the point about secrecy and suspicion because Chun had some weeks earlier ordered a tightening of security procedures throughout the ROK military. New procedures had been put into effect, procedures that prohibited any unauthorized contact between ROK officers and foreigners, including U.S. military officers. In order to meet with their American counterparts, ROK officers had to request an authorization. Even if the authorization was granted, only approved topics could be discussed, and a transcript of the conversation had to be submitted afterward to Chun's DSC. Chun was trying to stop leaks of politically sensitive information to the Americans. The directive was also an indication of how paranoid he had become about the possibility of a countercoup that might have American support. Secretary of Defense Brown had already told me that he was very concerned about the new security restrictions. They obviously made the whole notion of a combined defense impossibly awkward.

Chun seemed to listen closely as I noted that mid-1980 to mid–1981 would be a particularly difficult year. In 1981, there would be a reassessment of the troop withdrawal issue that was likely to be based on the state of tensions and the military balance on the peninsula. However, the decision would also depend on the stability and political neutrality of the ROK military and the extent of cooperation between our military establishments. To the extent that progress continued in those areas, U.S./ROK relations should improve.

Chun visibly stiffened over the troop withdrawal issue. His reaction surprised me. Rather than become defensive, he attacked. He said that ROK confidence in the durability of the American mutual security commitment had been shaken badly by troop withdrawals during the Carter administration. Then he asked how, in light of the increased North Korean threat and the domestic unrest in the South, I could in good conscience raise anew the issue of troop withdrawals. Before I could answer, he urged that everything possible be done to avoid the resumption of withdrawals. In his opinion, the morale of the Korean people would suffer immeasurably if there were more withdrawals.

His response was proof of his naivete. He was completely oblivious to the fact that the troop withdrawal issue was a political matter, and that, although I would have a voice in the decision, ultimately the decision would be made by the political authorities elected by the American people. Nor did Chun accept that his own actions were placing the security of his nation at greater risk. But given the depth of his emotion on this issue, I chose not to explain further why the matter might be reviewed in 1981. Besides, U.S. presidential elections would be held in 1980, so the troop issue might not come up.

Turning to another subject, Chun expressed his deep concern about the emerging relations between the United States and China, sensing that the United States might be led to abandon the ROK. As Chun related this concern I was reminded that the Koreans, particularly the military who had served with valor alongside American forces in Vietnam, had developed grave doubts about the reliability of the United States after our tragic abandonment of South Vietnam just five years earlier. The recent troop withdrawals from Korea had aggravated those doubts. I replied that our security interests were tied to peace and stability of South Korea and that I could not foresee any way that our relations with China would proceed in such a manner as to require severing American relations with his country.

During our lengthy discussion, Chun again repeated his assurances about the political neutrality and internal stability of the army. Once again, he came across as strong-willed, assured of his power base, and biding his time as he accumulated more power and influence. He apparently had resigned himself to moving slowly so as not to further alarm the Korean people or American policymakers. However, it was clear from the nature of the subjects he chose to broach—great power politics, the broader relations between our two nations, the issue of troop withdrawals—that he no longer saw himself as a general leading a command concerned only with the internal stability of the ROK army, but rather as a national leader of great stature and importance.

Chun Takes Control of KCIA

The next time I met with Chun was on May 13, days before the Kwangju tragedy. We met at his office in KCIA headquarters. For this occasion, I had asked to meet with him in keeping with our mutual desire to have regular contact. Once again, our discussion was very frank and cordial. It lasted more than two and a half hours. Chun did most of the talking, seemed very self-confident, and was manifestly comfortable with the trappings of his new position as KCIA director. Instead of a uniform he was wearing expensive civilian clothing. Korean protocol governed the seating; Chun occupied the leader's chair. Photographers spent several minutes before the meeting taking our pictures. Cameras were never used during my frequent visits to other officials in the ROK Government.

The thought crossed my mind that it was almost like a visit with the president in the Blue House, and I wondered if the photographic recordings of my presence would be employed for some future ulterior purpose. In Chun's lavish office, my seated position was that of a foreign visitor to a top, if not the top, official in the ROK Government. I understood enough Korean to detect in Chun's language that he no longer included any of the honorifics he had previously used in addressing me or in referring to the U.S. Ambassador or other senior U.S. officials.

Chun lectured me with two messages. First, he said the rumor that he was anti-American was absolutely false and that he fully recognized that the ROK could not survive without U.S. support. He said he believed there was little or no misunderstanding among ROK and U.S. officials and that it was important to avoid misunderstandings and to foster warm relations, as he had been attempting to do on a personal level. Second, he was deeply concerned with the potential for instability as a result of the wide-scale student unrest. He said he was convinced that the unrest was being orchestrated by the Communists and that there was a distinct possibility that the North Koreans were instigating the problems in order to justify an intervention. That was why he had taken on the responsibilities as KCIA director.

In Chun's view, KCIA had been paralyzed since President Park's assassination. Virtually every responsibility of the agency had been neglected, including the important task of monitoring the ominous North Korean threat and the growing Communist influence in the South. He described the current student situation as quite different from that which existed after President Park assumed power in 1961 or in any of the years that followed. The basic demands of the students included the announcement of a political development timetable, the immediate lifting of martial law, and the removal of all remnants of Park's *Yushin* administration, including the firing of every official currently in the government. Chun sadly concluded that the government had no long-term plan for dealing with the student unrest, because officials had no idea the situation would deteriorate this far. He said the first mistake of the government was the release and restoration of students and professors who had been held in prison. Chun told me that he had recommended against releasing the prisoners, because he believed there were Communists among them, and that he had accurately predicted that, once free, they would become the catalysts of campus unrest.

Unlike 1961, the National Police had solid evidence that "impure" elements were behind the situation on the campuses; unfortunately, the police "dare not make arrests because doing so would hopelessly inflame the schools." Students demanded the overthrow of the government, using such Communist phrases as "Let us raise high the flag of mass struggle" and "class struggle." Even Chun's son was telling him that the peer pressure was so strong that he had no choice but to join the protests. Beyond the student unrest, Chun said that there were three million or more criminal offenders living in Seoul, many of them unemployed lower class, who had suffered discrimination since the Korean War. These people were disaffected from the government. If they were to make common cause with the students then there could be "mass rebellion," with an enormous loss of life and property in Seoul and other urban areas. Current government leaders were unable to decide how to cope with the desperate situation. More force was going to be needed, Chun told me.

I thought his lengthy, somewhat emotional harangue about the Communist threat reflected his growing personal anxiety over this challenge to the government's ability to maintain law and order. He felt the threat personally, although he obviously could not admit that. Chun emphasized that it was his own philosophy to react moderately toward the students, but he concluded emphatically, that there was nothing more the government could do to cool off the situation and no more leeway could be given.

It did not escape my notice that he was speaking for the government. He lowered his voice for effect as he said that South Korea was very close to the "decisive moment that North Korea has waited patiently for since the armistice in 1953." He noted that a May 12 report from a reliable agent carried in the *Chosun Soren*, a Korean-language newspaper published in Japan that was often used by Pyongyang as a propaganda outlet, stated that there will be a "shocking incident" in the South perpetrated by the North. The intent would be to provoke the students and laborers into violent action to topple the ROK Government. The model for this provocation stretched back to spring 1960 when, under similar circumstances, a student had been killed by the police and the discovery caused mass demonstrations. It was that incident that led to the overthrow of President Syngman Rhee's government.

I told Chun that U.S. authorities had checked into the Japanese report and found no corroborating evidence. And while we did have some intelligence that an invasion of the South could occur in May or fall 1980, the Chinese had assured us that they had no knowledge of such reports. Chun sourly dismissed the Chinese assurances, saying that the Chinese were too close to the United States and were not paying enough attention to the expressed wants of North Korea. As a result, North Korea was moving quickly toward closer relations with the Soviet Union.

I wondered whether Chun was using these allegations to accelerate his timetable for movement into the Blue House, or, alternatively, whether he was trying to frighten the populace into restraining its behavior while Chun and the military cracked down on the protests. Unfortunately, I did not ask Chun what he might do to quell demonstrations. In hindsight, maybe I should have. Not that Chun would have answered truthfully, but perhaps I could have detected something in his manner. As it was, I had no warning that he was planning to use military force to quell student unrest.

Before departing, I gave Chun two messages. First, I reassured him that the U.S. commitment to South Korea remained steadfast and affirmed the ability of the U.S.–ROK military establishments to work together effectively. Second, I pointed out that the United States did not seek to interfere or meddle in the sovereign affairs of his country and that America's interest was to ensure deterrence, but deterrence obviously was a function of military preparedness and internal stability. Hence, "We want to see orderly political progress consistent with the will of the people." Chun smiled for a moment and then expressed full agreement with these points. He seemed to have heard them before.

Within four months Chun would become president based on formal election by a council of 5,000 elders, the National Conference for Unification. Because of the fast pace of events subsequent to our meeting at the KCIA headquarters, Chun and I did not meet formally again until after his election, although we did have informal discussions from time to time, and he did meet with Bill Gleysteen and Bob Brewster. Chun had moved into lofty political circles. As noted earlier, the position Bill Gleysteen and I took with regard to Chun and his associates sought to establish a dialogue because of the reality that they had seized complete military power and faced no overt opposition. Our national security interests were overriding. At the same time, Bill and I did not want to convey to Chun or the Korean people any impression of approving Chun's seizure of control, because the U.S. Government supported the official government of President Choi and sought restoration of political progress in Korea. Although we did not say so in any public manner or to Chun himself, our view was that if he were to make an overt move to become president, it would have to be done in a "legitimate constitutional" manner, reflecting support of the Korean people and assuring domestic stability as well as political progress. In short, Chun needed to be "legal" to garner support from the U.S. Government. These factors eventually became conditions in the late summer for American tolerance of Chun's final moves to become president.

On May 14, I returned to the United States for scheduled consultations concerning the defense of the peninsula and developments in the domestic situation, and to attend my son's college graduation. Neither I nor other American officials saw anything abnormal in North Korean belligerence or activities. Neither did we anticipate the tragedy that would befall the Korean people in the next few days.

Map 4. **Korean Peninsula**

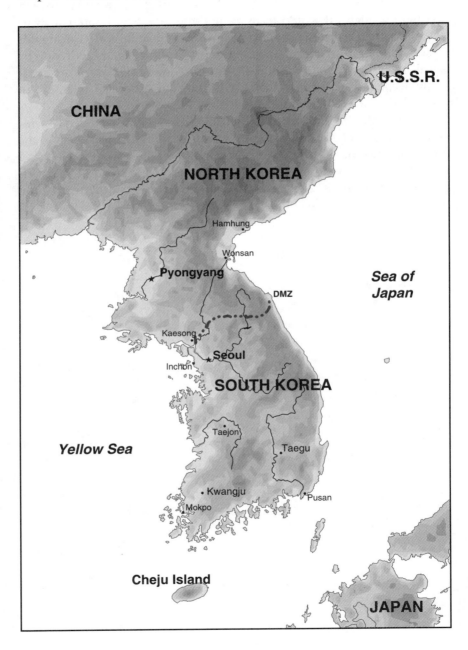

Chapter Seven

The Kwangju Tragedy

Full Martial Law Imposed

South Cholla province carves out the southwestern corner of the Korean peninsula. Historically, it was mostly agrarian countryside and poor, and for centuries its impoverished farmers and artisans had resented the country's wealthy provinces. That resentment was strongest toward the two domineering Kyongsang provinces to the east, especially the city of Taegu, which produced many of the country's political and military leaders. The first seven graduates of the four-year course at the Korean Military Academy who achieved early promotions to brigadier general rank, including Chun Doo-hwan and Roh Tae-woo, were from Taegu. They became known as the "Taegu Seven Stars."

The ancient city of Kwangju, with some 750,000 residents, lies in the heart of South Cholla Province. During Japan's colonization of Korea, from 1910 to 1945, there was a great deal of unrest as the Korean people chafed for independence. Student nationalist organizations, particularly in Seoul and Kwangju, often erupted into vigorous demonstrations. Thus, there were strong historic precedents for student unrest throughout Korea, particularly in the Cholla region, where the residents continued to feel deprived and discriminated against by the national government. In May 1980, the rebellious student movements—coupled with severe labor unrest in urban areas such as Masan, Pusan, Inchon, and Seoul—threatened to degenerate into massive, violent demonstrations or, worse, into anarchy.

Chun and his associates sensed that their grip on power could be lost completely if the rising tide of unrest got out of hand. On May 17, demonstrators in Seoul demanded an end to martial law, and that panicked Chun and the other governmental authorities. In their view absolutely no more concessions could be made, because the government was already on the edge of an abyss.

Consequently, on May 17, Chun arranged for the government to impose full martial law and to make wide-scale arrests of radical leaders and opposition political leaders on charges of corruption. Also, at Chun's direction, President Choi issued an extraordinary national emergency declaration that was carried by television, radio, and newspapers throughout the country. The statement set the stage for the armed forces to smash demonstrations and prevent them from spreading throughout the nation. A key extract of that statement offered the justification for what was to follow:

> When we review the situation at home, the maneuvers of the North Korean Communists have been stepped up with each passing day to communize the South by taking advantage of continuous social disturbances. . . . They are maneuvering to create a decisive moment for a southward invasion by inspiring and agitating disturbances on the campuses.

> At this critical moment the irresponsible rash attempts and blind behavior of some politicians, students, and workers have converted this society into a lawless one of chaos, disorder, agitation and subversion. Moreover, the aftermath of social disturbances has resulted in slowing down of exports and creating an economic depression, thus increasing labor disputes and unemployment and further increasing social unrest. Our country is faced with a grave crisis.

In response to the ROK Government's imposition of full martial law, the U.S. State Department issued from Washington the following public statement on May 18 and 19, which I'm sure Bill Gleysteen drafted, as he had done on previous occasions:

> We are deeply disturbed by the extension of martial law throughout the ROK, the closing of the universities, and the arrest of a number of political and student leaders. Progress toward political liberalization must be accompanied by respect for the law. However, we are concerned that the actions which the government has now taken will exacerbate problems in the ROK. We have made clear the seriousness of our concern to Korean leaders, and we have stressed our belief that progress toward constitutional reform and the election of a broadly based civilian government, as earlier outlined by President Choi, should be resumed promptly.

We urge all elements in Korean society to act with restraint at this difficult time. As we affirmed on October 26, 1979, the U.S. Government will react strongly in accordance with its treaty obligations to any external attempt to exploit the situation in the ROK.

And to emphasize the U.S. Government's growing concern, the new Secretary of State, Edmund Muskie, said on May 20:

My reaction to the Korean situation is one of deep concern that it is moving away from liberalization policies, which I think are essential to its long-term political health. I would hope that all elements of the society would exercise restraint in this transition period.

On my return to Korea, I visited Defense Minister Chu and JCS Chairman Rhu on May 19. I wanted to get their sense of the situation. Bill Gleysteen and I were, of course, aware of the demonstrations that had already occurred in various urban areas, but we had no inkling of the trouble in Kwangju or the fact that the ROK Government had sent ROK Special Forces troops to crack down on the unrest in the city. Because the ROK Special Forces were not under CFC OPCON, we were blind to their plans.

Smoking one cigarette after another, Chu nervously explained that the student scene was really unraveling even though he, martial law commander General Lee Hee-sung, and Chun had argued for moderation in dealing with the students. However, firm evidence existed that there was Communist influence within the student and labor movements and that certain political leaders, such as Kim Dae-jung, had irresponsibly agitated the people for their own interests. The students' demands could never be satisfied, because they were demanding the total overthrow of the government. During a May 17 cabinet debate over the imposition of full martial law, the ministers concluded that strong action had to be taken immediately. Chu said that the cabinet unanimously recommended the imposition of full martial law, the arrests of opposition political leaders and radicals, and the closure of the National Assembly. The intent was to deal firmly and swiftly with the crisis.

As an aside, Chu mentioned a secret meeting he held with more than 40 senior generals and admirals on May 17. These officers had voiced bitterness over the "drift in the Korean society and the absence of effective leadership in the government." They had been very critical of efforts to foster political liberalization. In their words:

> Democratic values cannot be achieved all at once, and we have been trying to go too fast, partly by pressure from the United States.

In their view, the military was the only organized body which was capable of providing crisis leadership, and it was time to take strong measures to preclude instability.

Rhu suggested that the arrests of Kim Dae-jung and a number of other dissident political leaders were clearly warranted because of charges that they were involved in corruption. He told me that this action should not be seen as a setback for political liberalization; rather, it was necessary for the ROK Government to begin a cleansing of society and the development of future political leaders with solid, ethical backgrounds. He said that everyone knew that rampant corruption existed throughout society, but those who were grossly corrupt in misusing their public office to gain personal wealth should be punished. The Korean people wanted this kind of cleansing activity to occur. Chun had made a public promise, right after the December 12 incident, that he intended to begin cleaning up the government.

As I listened to their arguments, I was still convinced that the arrests of Kim Dae-jung, Kim Jong-pil, and other opposition political leaders were simply a way for Chun and his associates to rid themselves of potential presidential candidates. I noted that Kim Young-sam had not been imprisoned and suspected that it was because an opposition political leader, even a token one, would be necessary in the election process, and Kim Young-sam posed the least threat to the military.

By secure phone, on May 19, Secretary Brown asked for my personal assessment of the declaration of martial law, the arrests of political leaders, and the domestic situation. Intelligence reports suggested to him that the situation was going from bad to worse and he wanted my view. In response, I sent him a message:

> Officials cite the evidence of Communist influence in student demonstrations and escalating demands which could not be satisfied by a moderate response. The ultimate demand called for overthrow of the government, which understandably was rejected by the cabinet and acting president. Moreover, military officials, including Chun, saw in the student movement the rejection of certain Confucian values, such as respect for

elders, institutions, individual rights, and law and order. This was more than youthful rebelliousness. The military felt that such rejection tore at the very fiber of Korean society. They sensed also that most of the people did not sympathize with the actions of the student movement.

The military leaders and cabinet officials concluded that martial law had to be strengthened by an emergency decree and the presence of regular military forces in urban areas. Moreover, the closure of campuses and arrests of radical student leaders as well as those agitating and funding them, such as Kim Dae-jung, could head off serious demonstrations in the future. In addition, it was decided to initiate the investigation of political figures who had abused positions of authority to amass personal fortunes, such as Kim Jong-pil. In short, officials justify their actions on the basis of patriotism and concern for national security. They do not want another Vietnam and they believe that they know best how to protect the nation as well as to lead it into a period of greater political and economic freedom.

As a consequence, ROK leaders have grown deeply concerned about political and economic drift in the society. While many recognize the need for some political liberalization, particularly after Park's death, there is a belief, especially in the military, that too much liberalization is underway and at too fast a pace. What we are beginning to see now is a reversion to a more conservative approach to political development. The military under Chun's firm control are convinced that they are the guardians of conservative values and the only organized force capable of maintaining the nation's safety and assuring its future. Military leaders are absolutely convinced they are on the right track in protecting their homeland and in leading Koreans into the Fourth Republic. They will do what they believe is right for Korea, and if necessary, disregard U.S. concerns. While they express deep gratitude for the stalwart U.S. stand in protecting Korea, they also display some contempt for what they describe as the unrealistic moralizing policy objectives of the United States, and an apparent inability of the United States to achieve success in such foreign areas as Vietnam, Iran, and Afghanistan.

Given this brief description of the current situation and the attitudes of military leaders, I posed the question: what are the broad policy implications for the United States? I recommended that:

> We must recognize the reality of control by Chun and his associates. It is clear now that the group's ultimate objective is total power. The only issues are the speed of consolidating power and the form in which it takes place. The form could be the facade of a civilian government and controlled elections, or it could be a military council chaired by Chun. We have to accept this reality of control by Chun and work with it because we are in no position to unhorse Chun and his group.
>
> While we can work with Chun in shaping political development that is minimally acceptable to the United States, we must recognize the limitations on our leverage and therefore resist adopting actions which could jeopardize fundamental U.S. security interests in the ROK. We of course know that it is in the U.S. interest to maintain peace and stability in the region, hence we must continue to improve our combined military capability in the face of a North Korean threat which is growing qualitatively. War must be deterred. As a consequence, our leverage with Chun and his group must be largely in areas other than the military. Even so, we must be careful not to take punitive actions in the economic area, which could be counterproductive by contributing to further economic difficulty and defense spending cutbacks. In short, then, our leverage is relatively limited and we must take care how it is used, lest we undermine our ability to communicate openly and effectively with Chun who today controls power, and tomorrow may overtly run Korea.
>
> Consequently, we must broaden and deepen our communication with the power structure so that we can increase our mutual understanding of acceptable courses of action and retain an ability to influence developments. I believe there is an art to this process, because if we aren't careful we shall poison the atmosphere by too much bad news and lecturing. This is not to say that we cannot express grave reservations and objections to major policy actions such as the detention of opposition political leaders.

Fighting Reported

Reports of fighting in Kwangju began to trickle into CFC and the U.S. Embassy from a variety of sources on May 21, including frantic telephone calls from American residents in the city. I went to see General Rhu to find out what was happening. He had just returned from a meeting with Chun, Defense Minister Chu, and others. ROK military reports confirmed the serious nature of developments in the rebellious city. Out of a population of some 750,000 residents, it was believed that more than 150,000 had joined in mass riots since May 18. Special Forces soldiers had been sent into the city to support the police force. Rhu told me that the number of casualties was still unknown, but that the number of fatalities should be low because the soldiers had avoided shooting. He said that rioters had broken into homeland defense force armories and explosive storage bunkers and were in possession of more than 2,000 military weapons as well as a supply of demolitions. Considerable destruction had already occurred, and mobs were directing particular violence against Special Forces soldiers, whom the mobs were mocking as "Chun Doo-hwan's troops."

Neither Bill Gleysteen nor I knew that the Special Forces brigades had been ordered into Kwangju on May 18. We did know, however, that the ROK 20th and 30th Infantry Divisions, both of which had special training for riot control duty, were being withdrawn by Defense Minister Chu from CFC operational control. My permission to withdraw these units was neither sought nor required under the terms of the CFC agreement. Rhu told me that some units from the 20th Division were being dispatched by ROK authorities to the Kwangju area, but that the 20th Division's troops had not yet been involved in suppressing the riots.

Rhu told me that the mobs in Kwangju were out of control and that there was grave danger that the violence could spread to other areas, including Seoul, because the rioters planned to send convoys of trucks north. Rhu described the situation as the worst he had seen in two decades, and he told me that what happened that night would be critical if the government's troops were to ease the situation.

Amplifying on his meeting with Chu and Chun, Rhu said he had tried to moderate their panic and dampen what he described as their instinctive reaction to take swift, harsh military action to suppress the uprising. Rhu told me that he had urged them to support, for at least the next 48 hours, his plan for responding to the riots with moderation. Once the soldiers began shooting, the situation would rapidly deteriorate, and there would be many casualties on both sides. Rhu's preference was to try to work out a ceasefire whereby the demands of the dissidents could be discussed and some give and take could occur. But part of the difficulty army commanders on the scene were facing was in trying to identify the dissident leaders and to communicate this plan to them. So far the dissident leaders had demanded apologies from the martial law commander and the provincial governor, the release of captured civilians, the removal of the martial law forces, and freedom for Kim Dae-jung, who was a Cholla resident.

Rhu's plan was to withdraw nearly all of the military units from the city by nightfall. He told me that Chu and Chun had given their approval and he said that withdrawing the units during daylight would minimize the confusion that would result from darkness and prevent bloodshed. The only facilities that would still be protected by troops would be the combined arms center and the national prison, which housed more than 2,000 leftist prisoners. Kwangju Air Base also would be protected by army troops, however, the rest of the units would take up roadblock positions outside the city to prevent convoys from entering or leaving.

In addition, Rhu said he had upgraded the alert status of ROK forces throughout the nation to *Chin Do Kae II*, almost the highest counterinfiltration readiness state. He then asked me to deploy U.S. airborne warning and control system (AWACS) aircraft to help deter the North Koreans. I told Rhu I would request the deployment of our AWACS and that CFC would take additional measures to increase our intelligence collection efforts against the North Koreans. I added that CFC was examining the feasibility of mobilizing one or two of the ROK ready reserve or rear area security divisions to take the place of the 20th and 30th Infantry Divisions that had been removed by the ROK Government to deal with the crisis.

Efforts to Defuse the Crisis

The next morning, May 22, I met again with Rhu concerning Kwangju. Rhu said things were settling down. He told me that there was evidence of civil unrest in towns south of Kwangju, including the large urban area of Mokpo, where the rioters had taken control. Mokpo was the headquarters of the ROK Third Naval Sea Sector. It was also Kim Dae-jung's hometown.

Rhu did not seem worried about the rioting in these smaller towns, because he felt that once the Kwangju situation became settled the rest of the province would follow suit. His plan for moderation seemed to be working, although Kwangju was still in the hands of local residents, and there had been some shooting and property destruction during the night. He told me that eyewitnesses had been reporting shooting by youngsters and drunken men, and that large crowds and vehicle movement were also jamming the streets. Army troops were manning the road blocks outside the city and continuing their guard of the combined arms center and prison. There had been some civilian casualties near the prison as a group of rioters attempted to storm the gate, but the total number of casualties was unclear. Rhu estimated that as many as 60 civilians were dead and more than 400 seriously injured and said the numbers could rise. Four soldiers and four policeman had also been killed. Meanwhile, a dialogue had begun between Lieutenant General Yoon Hung-jong, who was the senior commander on the scene, and 14 representatives from the various groups inside the city, including the university students and a cross section of religious and political groups.

Rhu then confided to me that the martial law command was developing a contingency plan to assault the city with several infantry regiments, in the event that the violence could not be contained. He told me that Chun and his group wanted such a plan, just in case events turned sour. We discussed the concept of an assault on the city, reviewing the dangers peculiar to urban hostilities, where block-to-block fighting inevitably would result in many casualties on both sides. Snipers and booby traps would be difficult to root out and could wreak havoc. Any plan to undertake such a high-risk operation would have to be carefully organized in terms of command and control and detailed instructions to small unit leaders, and the troops would have to be equipped with specialized equipment, such as loudspeakers, stun grenades, and protective gear.

Rhu agreed with me that all of this detailed preparation would take time and acknowledged the wisdom of delaying an assault on the city. He also agreed that such an operation would require great restraint to avoid a major confrontation between the army and Korean citizens. I told Rhu that a large number of casualties would have serious implications for the rest of the country, and that Bill Gleysteen and I strongly urged a restrained approach.

While Rhu agreed with my comments about careful planning and restraint, he reminded me that the government was intensely concerned that the violence could spread and lead to nationwide anarchy. Nonetheless, he and martial law commander General Lee Hee-sung had decided that a military assault on the city would not take place that night or on the 23rd, provided that Rhu's plan for moderate actions continued to produce positive results. I urged Rhu to discuss this entire matter with Chun and his associates and to make sure they were fully aware of the serious risks inherent in street fighting and the use of regular army troops against Korean civilians. Casualties could be enormous, particularly among civilians. Rhu called me later that day to report that he had discussed the matter with Chun and he had been assured that the moderate approach would be continued. President Choi also agreed and promised to underscore that point in a public address the next day.

Before leaving the meeting with Rhu, I again emphasized the solid U.S. commitment to South Korea's security and reviewed the actions already underway to improve our readiness posture, to include a swift response on the AWACS deployment he had requested the previous day. Rhu was gratified and thanked me for American support while he focused his efforts on dealing with the "insurrection in Kwangju." He told me that in response to the CFC request to activate two homeland defense divisions—to replace the two active army divisions that had been withdrawn from CFC control—the army had begun mobilizing two divisions north of Seoul. We quickly compared notes and ended up agreeing that there was no conclusive evidence that North Korea was preparing to attack, but that the potential remained quite high for increased infiltration to aid and abet unrest in the South.

In reports to my superiors I urged that two additional actions should be taken. First, diplomatic initiatives should be taken with Beijing and Moscow to ensure they fully understood the strength of America's commitment to South Korea's security. Second, the United States should issue a public statement that emphasized America's concern over the civil strife in Korea, urged the conflicting parties to rely on dialogue to end it, and warned North Korea against any intervention. Bill Gleysteen agreed with these actions and decided to send a draft statement to the State Department.

My report summary read:

> The Kwangju situation for the time being has cooled and that voices of moderation seem to have prevailed over Chun and his group. Rhu demonstrates a good relationship with martial law commander Lee who is a contemporary and is a highly respected elder in the military community. Also, Chun and his generals appear willing to heed Rhu's advice, at least for now. This is encouraging. Naturally Chun and his group feel very threatened by the Kwangju situation which could escalate and unseat them so they need all the seasoned help they can get. Fear is one reason why they have been arguing for hawkish,

swift solutions. Minister Chu told me that he too is trying to emphasize the rule of reason and moderation. But Chu does not inspire confidence for he seems emotionally distraught, probably reflecting Blue House and Chun's anxiety. Rhu on the other hand appears cool and confident and is exercising thoughtful initiative in a reasoned, moderate way. Bill Gleysteen and I have been trying to reinforce Rhu in this restraining role.

Good News Before Bad

I met again with Rhu on May 23. He reported that the situation in Cholla was very favorable. His plan for moderation appeared to be working, and the dialogue with the leaders from Kwangju was continuing. Arms were being collected, and more than half of the 2,000 weapons had been turned in voluntarily to the local military hospital. The provincial government had been reestablished in its offices, and the city hall was back in operation. Some national police had returned to duty. While events in the city were relatively quiet, there appeared to be some friction between the radical and moderate groups in the city. Some of the radicals were escaping. In one instance, a truck filled with weapons and explosives ran into a military roadblock, 17 civilians were killed as a result. In the city itself, citizens were organizing restoration committees, and cleanup work was already underway. Some small units of the homeland defense reserve force were back in uniform and protecting government buildings. The martial law command estimated that about half of the towns and villages in the province that had been "lost" were now restored to government control, including Mokpo.

Rhu beamed with satisfaction as he told me that the situation was turning dramatically in favor of the government and that, as a result, President Choi intended to delay his radio and television statement. In view of this delay, I urged Rhu to recommend that Choi's statement address broader issues than those in Kwangju. The timing was right for Choi to take the initiative and head off further unrest in the nation. These broader issues should deal with the political timetable for the election of the president and members of the National Assembly. I called Rhu's attention to the just released U.S. Government statement, which touched on these broader issues.

To my superiors I reported:

> . . . rule of reason and moderation appears to be yielding re-
> sults for a variety of reasons. Clearly many people throughout
> the nation are shocked and sobered by the violence as well as
> the physical destruction of the Kwangju episode. Older citi-
> zens, with the most to lose by violence, appear to be counsel-
> ing the restoration of law and order in Cholla and urging pa-
> tience elsewhere in the country, provided of course that the
> government demonstrates a sensitivity to popular concerns for
> political progress. Naturally, for most Koreans the threat of
> North Korean invasion which they have lived with all of their
> lives continues to push them in the direction of solving do-
> mestic problems as peacefully as possible. While the prospect
> for continued violence throughout the country remains high,
> the starkness of the Kwangju tragedy may encourage re-
> strained behavior on the part of all sides in the ROK. Chair-
> man Rhu's role has been statesmanlike in achieving goals con-
> sistent with the long term interests of the Korean people and
> with maintaining solid U.S.–ROK relations. We may have
> strengthened his influence with Chun and his associates.

On May 24, I went again to the Ministry of Defense to meet with
Chu, Chairman Rhu, and martial law commander General Lee. They were
very upbeat. Virtually all provincial and city officials were back in their
offices restoring administrative services. The dialogue with various
groups in Kwangju also continued to be productive; by late morning,
more than 1,000 weapons had been returned to the military with another
3,000 weapons under the custody of the local citizens committee. Nevertheless, there still remained some radical activity in the city, principally in
the industrial area, where the labor unions were concentrated. There were
still demonstrations, one involving more than 30,000 people gathered in
front of the provincial capitol to demand the lifting of martial law, the release of Kim Dae-jung, no punishment for offenders, and the removal of
Chun Doo-hwan. I had not heard of this last demand before.

Lee briefed his plan for reentering Kwangju with infantry regiments to assist in the restoration of law and order. But he told me that,
in his view, the likelihood of actually executing the plan remained low
because of the success being achieved by the current policy of moderation and reliance on the local citizens to assist with weapon turn-in and
clean up. Lee assured me that he would not allow any army troops to

reenter the city without letting me know his intentions. In his view, the current situation did not warrant any military presence in the city. Noting that the decision to use force in domestic matters rested solely with the martial law commander and constitutional authorities, rather than CFC, I complimented Lee on the policy of moderation and predicted that it would permit a more fruitful opportunity for settling major differences later on.

Turning to the North Korean issue, I reviewed CFC actions to bolster the availability of reserves to replace the two units that had been withdrawn for riot control duty. General Lee assured me that the 20th Infantry Division could be returned to its operational position north of Seoul in a matter of hours, if needed. The division's heavy artillery had been left up north when the division's infantry regiments moved to the vicinity of Kwangju.

Adding a bit of humor, Rhu told a story about the 60th and 71st Training Groups, which had been mobilized. Virtually everyone showed up at the mobilization station, including some individuals from Cholla who had respectfully requested to be excused so that they could continue demonstrating in Kwangju.

Preliminary Assessment

The Kwangju episode understandably drew many questions from my superiors. Based on discussions with General Rhu and other senior officials, including Bill Gleysteen, I responded on May 24 with a brief analysis of Chun's status:

> It appears unlikely that the Kwangju disorders will bring about in the near future Chun's downfall or disruption in military unity. Like most Koreans, the military have been alarmed by the scale of Kwangju activity and are in the process of trying to put it into perspective. While some dissatisfaction undoubtedly exists with recent actions by Chun, we are not likely to see overt moves to oust him at this stage. Chun, of course, because of his prominence seems to be a lightning rod for dissatisfaction among all Koreans who are angered with the martial law command and tough governmental policies. But it would be highly dangerous for individual officers outside of Chun's core group to express disagreement with him, let alone attempt to organize against him. Chun's internal security apparatus with the KCIA and Defense Security Command enable him to de-

tect and suppress dissension. Concern for the unity of the army as an institution also would tend to militate against opposition to Chun so long as he appears to be trying to settle the Kwangju situation and other unrest with minimum damage to social harmony. As a consequence, for the near term, Chun's position and military unity seem assured. However, because of his popular image problem Chun probably has been weakened in his ability to move quickly into the Blue House. Nevertheless he retains power to influence events behind the scenes and will continue to do so.

In the mid to long range, Chun's position seems less secure. The Kwangju uprising is almost unprecedented since the Korean War. The only comparable developments, those in the spring of 1960, caused the downfall of the Rhee government. The principal differences are that regional bitterness played a greater role in the Kwangju riots and that fighting in the city involved actual combat between army troops and local folk. This use of the army to fight against Korean citizens is totally unprecedented in modern Korean history, and has the potential for further damage to public trust and support as well as respect for the army. Thus it is conceivable that over time the officer corps will conclude that a change in top leadership is needed to salvage the army's public image and its role as the guarantor of security.

In any case the potential for domestic trouble is serious and will remain so for some time not only in view of Kwangju but also because of other political issues which were evident prior to Kwangju and will continue to pose difficulties. Should the internal situation deteriorate seriously, such as might occur with mass demonstrations in Seoul, the officer corps could turn against Chun, forcing him to step down. Recognizing this possibility, Chun surely will take whatever actions are necessary to squash unrest before it reaches a danger point.

In short, it remains unclear what impact the Kwangju episode will have on Chun's power although for the time being Bill Gleysteen and I see no change at all. Whatever changes do occur should evolve gradually, Korean-style. As a consequence we must continue working carefully with Chun without building him up or cutting him down. We cannot and should not try to unhorse him because it would lead to serious disunity in the military with risk of North Korean intervention, and probably would beget us only another Chun and the black eye of meddling in Korean affairs.

The Bad News

Unfortunately, the news from Kwangju on May 25 was very bad. General Rhu reported that the critical point occurred on May 24 when citizens were to turn in government weapons. Late on the 24th, more than 10,000 rioters had demonstrated near the capitol and radical elements forcibly turned away citizens trying to turn in weapons. The radical group now consisted of student leaders, including some from Seoul, criminals, and poor people who had little to lose. The hardcore radical group was estimated to number about 500. They were wearing army fatigues, were heavily armed, and were quite willing to shoot.

The group had begun to organize a city-wide control mechanism and were employing intimidation, in the form of kangaroo courts and quick sentences, to force innocent people into complying with their directives. Rhu said the police were hopelessly inadequate against the rioters. The capitol had been occupied by the radicals, and provincial leaders had fled for their lives. It was estimated that some 5,600 weapons and more than 350,000 rounds of small arms ammunition were unaccounted for, so a dangerous situation existed. Rhu summarized the scene in few words: bad and getting worse. The radical group was engaged in a life or death struggle and appeared to be gaining strength. Rhu told me that local citizens were clamoring for the government to return with superior military force to restore law and order.

While the rest of the nation appeared to be quiet, Chun and the martial law command were worried that, unless they settled the Kwangju situation quickly, radical elements could slip out and contaminate other provinces. In fact, all of the access bridges into Seoul had military checks of all vehicles entering the city.

The afternoon of May 24, a secret meeting had been held by student leaders of Seoul's numerous high schools who had agreed to organize student demonstrations on May 26 in sympathy with their brothers in Kwangju. The government was going to attempt to head off the demonstrations by appealing to teachers and school authorities, but the military was very apprehensive about trouble from high school youths, because of their large numbers and innocence.

Rhu outlined the latest martial law command plan for military intervention. Since the military forces were already in place, the plan could be executed quickly. It required a continued effort to negotiate with the citizen leaders for a peaceful settlement, but, if those talks failed, the military would use loudspeakers, radio, and leaflets to announce that the troops would be moving in to restore law and order. The soldiers had been instructed to support the local authorities and to avoid any direct engagements with moderate citizens, but were authorized to return fire if the city's more radical elements attempted to engage the military. Lieutenant General So Joon-yul, who had replaced General Yoon on May 22 as the onsite commander, had been given the flexibility to negotiate or to pick the propitious time for the military option. So estimated that he could carry out the option with perhaps a 70 percent chance of avoiding bloodshed.

I didn't see how he could be so optimistic, since the intelligence reports indicated that the radicals were well armed, and events had already shown that it was a life-and-death struggle. While Rhu nodded in agreement, he said General So anticipated that an overwhelming show of military power would incite the radicals to surrender or flee. In view of the probability of executing the military option, the government had urged the evacuation of all foreign nationals from Kwangju.

After listening to Rhu's explanation of the assault plan, I acknowledged the basic responsibility of the ROK authorities, including the martial law command, to take whatever actions they considered best for the maintenance of internal law and order. As the CFC commander in chief, I had no responsibility in this area. I told him, however, that American officials were pleased with the restrained approach taken so far by the Korean authorities and that we strongly urged them to maintain their moderation. Rhu agreed with this view.

We then discussed the potential dangers of employing troops to restore law and order in a major city. The negative impact of soldiers killing civilians would erode popular support for the military and even lead to mutinous conditions within some units, as a result of provincial loyalties and animosities. Moreover, the use of military force in an attempt to settle what were essentially political issues could easily aggravate rather than solve the original source of unrest. Of course, both of us recognized that a time might come when force was the only resort.

I told him that, for what it was worth, my advice was to delay as long as useful negotiations continued, and that, if the military option were used, it should be executed cautiously, with well-trained, disciplined troops, and with restraint on how lethal fire was to be applied. Rhu nodded. He said he believed that restraint would be exercised but admitted that Chun and his associates were losing patience with the moderate handling of the situation and had grown fearful that unrest would get out of hand.

In the summary report I sent to Washington that day, I noted that the turn of events illustrated the fluidity of the Korean domestic situation and that we were far from being through this crisis. That leaders were losing patience with the moderate approach was evident when Chun, in a meeting with a group of Korean news editors on the evening of May 24, had said that force would soon be needed to restore the government's prestige and law and order in the city. While he and the younger generals appeared willing to listen to voices of moderation, they had become very impatient and fearful. They were surely aware that if the situation unraveled to the point that they lost power, that could mean courts-martial or worse. Rhu was much more somber than I had ever seen him, although he was calm and his thoughts were ordered and logical. I knew he was under great stress and had probably had little sleep, I also sensed that he was very uneasy and troubled by Chun's rejection of moderation in solving the Kwangju problem.

Chairman Mun of the Defense Committee made an urgent request to see me on May 26. He had returned the night before from Kwangju, which was his constituency and wanted to share his concerns about the situation. While he had supported the moderate policy, he now believed that any further delay in reestablishing law and order would lead to the spread of unrest. In Mun's view, the "Kwangju radicals are definitely under Communist control either within the city or from an external source." He said he was shocked that, "for the past eight days a major urban area of the nation has been controlled overtly by Communists or sympathizers." This was outrageous for Koreans, he told me, and it could not be tolerated any longer. He confirmed that the military would reenter Kwangju early the next morning and he said that it was none too soon. He admitted that the assault inevitably would involve considerable casualties. In his view, though, that could become a blessing in disguise, as it would symbolize the invidiousness of North Korean subversion and the necessity for self-restraint by the county's citizens, as well as the need for firm military action to deal with the Communist-inspired insurrection. After the assault, the government could demonstrate its magnanimity by making reparations, granting amnesty to the offenders, making rapid efforts to rebuild, and using the army to provide social services.

As a parting comment I told Mun, "My interest in ROK military cohesion arises solely from the standpoint of deterrence. None of us can afford to have any further unrest within the military and the United States would not support any dissident elements that might come to us for an endorsement. The present power structure is a reality with which we are working. Any change to it would have to be totally a Korean affair." Mun gave me a smile and a firm handshake and said that my views "were very reassuring."

Wrapping up the Tragedy

In my May 26 update, I reported that there had been no significant change in the Kwangju situation, but that indications were ominous. President Choi had visited Kwangju, spoken with the local citizen leaders, and made a broadcast, but so far there had been no results from his visit. ROK authorities, however, had not expected the radical elements to respond favorably, despite an offer of full amnesty made by the president.

A rally was to be held in Kwangju late on May 26, and the scale of attendance would offer some indication of the effect of the president's speech. A substantial turnout would be a negative vote. Unfortunately, the country's political leaders were expecting just that outcome. Despite heavy rains, some 50,000 of Kwangju's citizens had demonstrated against the government on May 25. The city's civilian authorities and police had reported that they were barely operating because the radical elements had insisted on a combined management whereby all civil offices would be shared and all civil policies had to be jointly agreed. The local committee for the restoration of law and order was now in the hands of radicals, who had expelled all moderates. Evidence existed that the radicals were organizing "do-or-die" armed teams to fight against ROK military intervention, and citizens with criminal records were joining the radical cause. Elsewhere in the province and nation things seemed quiet. The high school demonstrations in Seoul had failed to materialize, although some college demonstrations were expected.

In the face of the adamant radical opposition in Kwangju, and operating under the belief that the revolt had been instigated by the Communists, ROK political authorities and Chun felt they had exhausted all peaceable measures. They had become convinced that any further delay would demonstrate a lack of resolve and could lead to spillover into other areas of the nation. Consequently, orders had been issued to General So, the local commander in Kwangju, to reenter the city and restore law and order. So estimated that the operation would kick off between midnight and dawn on May 27.

So's concept was to move rapidly and with surprise to seize the city's key installations and then, with police assistance, apprehend the radicals and recover the stolen weapons. Four regiments of the 20th Infantry Division, each with about 3,000 soldiers, were to be the main assault force. Because the Special Force brigades had inflicted most of the earlier brutalities, they were to be used only as reserves. Each battalion of the assault regiments was to have national police guides and was ordered to assist with police functions, once they were inside the city. The instructions to the infantry commanders were to avoid unnecessary bloodshed, but the soldiers' weapons would be loaded and they could shoot in self defense. The key installations to be seized included the capitol and some nearby hotels the radicals were using for housing. In fact, early that morning, one of the radical guard posts on the edge of the city had been captured without casualties by the 20th Division, and General So had used that example to claim that the plan could be executed smoothly and without serious casualties.

General So executed his plan on May 27, restoring order and government control, recovering the stolen weapons, and making many arrests. Unfortunately, some resistance, especially around the capitol, had to be resolved with deadly force.

The Kwangju story itself was both tragic and complex. Even today the story remains shrouded in myth. Some Koreans still believe that U.S. authorities, particularly the ambassador and I, condoned the abuses by ROK soldiers in Kwangju. There were several hundred deaths and many more injuries, not to mention significant damage to property. It was the worst domestic tragedy in modern Korean history, and it badly tarnished the illustrious history of the ROK army and its leaders, who had served with honor and courage as the guardians of the nation's security.

The Special Committee

The ROK Government notified Bill Gleysteen and me on May 27 that President Choi would announce the formation of a Special Committee for National Security Measures, which he would chair. We were told that the committee was being formed to provide "more effective management of governmental affairs in view of the total martial law situation in the country." General Rhu explained that the committee would serve simply to assist the president in carrying out his national security responsibilities. (In fact, it was controlled by Chun in his capacity as chairman of the Special Standing Committee.) Rhu compared this committee to the one formed by Park after his seizure of power in 1961, and it occurred to me that Chun was following his mentor's script rather well.

Rhu acknowledged that the committee could be construed as a super cabinet, but that its size and composition would make it cumbersome. He predicted that a small number of the members might exercise power, but he did not elaborate on who those members might be. When I asked how this committee would differ from the current National Security Council (the internal, or executive, cabinet), Rhu explained that the new committee would have a permanent staff and would include all officials with direct responsibilities for national security affairs. Elaborating a bit, Rhu confided that "the president needs such an organization because his administration has not demonstrated strength and a sound basis for transitioning to the next government." Moreover, the president had little experience with security matters, and his halting leadership during the Kwangju crisis made the case for stronger direction, a goal that had been strongly endorsed by Chun and his associates. On the upside, Rhu was convinced that "the committee concept is sound because it is entirely constitutional and will provide a coherent, strong mechanism for helping the president to coordinate security policy."

On May 30, I provided a final wrap-up on the Kwangju tragedy and the new security committee. Both Minister Chu and General Rhu had told me that the situation had grown quiet and stable. The government estimate on casualties from the Kwangju episode included at least 152 dead and 588 wounded. Almost 90 percent of the weapons and hand grenades had been recovered, and almost 1,800 people had been arrested. Most of the army troops had been withdrawn from the city, and most of the units withdrawn from CFC had been returned. As for North Korea, our intelligence had shown no firm evidence of preparations for military intervention, although North Korea's forces had just completed extensive field training and a series of major exercises, so their readiness level was high. It was our mutual view that the North Koreans probably had adopted a wait-and-see attitude toward events in the ROK, while keeping their forces at a high readiness level to intervene at propitious times with infiltrators and commando-type units.

In my report, I concluded that the new committee seemed to be the next step in the consolidation of total power by Chun and his associates. Cosmetically, they were following the constitutional route, but it was abundantly clear that the military had lost patience with what they viewed as the indecisive leadership of Choi's government. In addition, they were understandably fearful that unrest, unless checked by strong governmental action, could grow to such a point that Chun and his group would be unseated. In part, Chun's motive was entirely self-serving. However, there was no question that most ROK military officers were convinced that the best interests of the Korean people were served by strong leaders and a disciplined political structure, particularly in the face of the dangerous threat evidenced in Kwangju. Moreover, I felt that Chun and his associates genuinely believed that the field of potential political leaders who were seeking the presidency lacked any strong leadership talent.

My initial reaction was to wait and see how the Korean people accepted this development, in light of Kwangju. The American mission was over a barrel, because our basic objective was to protect the ROK from invasion. That left us obliged to accept the realities of the Korean political apparatus, with all of its warts, and to work with it as best we could. Our leverage was limited because of our security commitment, and because the Koreans, particularly the military, were increasingly intolerant of U.S. intervention in their domestic affairs.

Chu and Rhu went into great detail about the government's appraisal of the Kwangju episode and the reasons for the formation of the Special Committee for National Security Measures. I sensed from the tenor of their explanation that Chun believed the Americans were skeptical about the purported motives behind the formation of the committee. Chu and Rhu described a lengthy national security committee meeting that had occurred the day before, which had dwelt in some detail on the origins of the problems that began with student demonstrations on May 13 and culminated in the Kwangju uprising.

The security committee laid much of the blame on the government's policies for dealing with the campus problems. The policies had been too moderate and too amenable to the students' demands for greater self-government and the autonomy of student leadership. The government misjudged, believing that its concessions would appeal to mature leaders. However the election of student leaders had introduced influences from various off-campus political forces, such as Kim Dae-jung and his supporters. The elected radical leaders then had pushed for even greater government concessions, including the extreme demand that the government be overthrown. Moreover, because the government had agreed in advance to demonstrations on campus, it had created the conditions for riots to spill over into the streets. Thus, in Chu's words, the misguided policy of concessions and temporizing with student demands had contributed to confrontation rather than avoiding it. I looked over to see if Rhu agreed with this conclusion. He did.

Coupled with the student problems was the unrest between labor and management. Because labor unions were a relatively recent phenomenon in Korea, the activities of labor organizations tended to be unruly and feisty. In addition, Chu believed that North Korea was behind some of the labor and student unrest. Both Chu and Rhu agreed that most Koreans regarded the current situation as the most dangerous and difficult time since the Korean War; how Korea came out of this transition period would set the stage for the next generation or two of Korean economic and political history. Chu looked at me long and hard after this statement, as though he wanted to be sure I realized the seriousness of his concern.

What all of this meant to the military was that strong action had to be taken to preserve national unity and the authority of the government, if for no other reason than to prevent intervention by the North Koreans. As a result, Chu said, the military insisted upon the imposition of full martial law and strong action to prevent the Kwangju crisis from escalating. According to Chu, the president had no alternative but to agree to these adamant recommendations from the military. I asked if Chun were a key player in these discussions. Chu said nothing, but Rhu nodded yes.

Chu claimed that the formation of the Special Committee for National Security Measures had nothing to do with a "grab for political power," because the committee structure and mission remained consistent with the constitution. The committee would only coordinate actions between the separate martial law command and the various cabinet departments, so the President could receive integrated and focused advice. Chu explained that under the constitution the martial law commander controlled all of the cabinet, including the prime minister, but that would be impractical over a prolonged period. Chun, as director of the KCIA, of course would occupy a key position in the committee, but he would still be serving under the president. In response to my question about how the committee differed from the one President Park had established in 1961, both Chu and Rhu answered that while the functions of the two committees were similar, the essential difference lay in the fact that the current committee was "totally within the ROK constitution." Rhu stressed that point and the fact that he had played a key role in recommending how the committee should be formed.

Both men expressed extreme uneasiness about the potential for further unrest in the nation. They were still convinced that the North Koreans were capable of exploiting the nation's unrest, and I knew that the American intelligence community had reached the same conclusion. Chu and Rhu insisted that the Korean people earnestly wanted strong leadership to ensure the maintenance of law and order and to protect the nation from the Communists. As Rhu put it: "We are worried about drift in all sectors of national activity. The damage from this drift is inestimable in the areas of economics, trade, vitality, and human interests." Chu chimed in with his cautionary view that "the military cannot and never will control the nation in the future because the Korean people will not allow this to happen. . . . And the next government definitely will be popularly elected." I had heard Chu as well as Chun roll out this litany many times before, but I knew it was just talk, and that Chun and his associates were still accumulating power.

Speaking alone to me, Rhu said that his greatest usefulness continued to be in broadening Chun's understanding of the complexity of the international situation, the limits of Chun's actions, and the absolute necessity of respecting the authority of the constitution. Rhu believed that Chun and his group could be educated. They were constantly seeking Rhu's advice on how to deal with the Americans, and Chun was deeply appreciative of America's steps during the crisis to strengthen deterrence. According to Rhu, this sort of "favorable impression by Chun would assist in establishing a basis for future influence and cooperation."

Driving away from the MND, I wondered about Rhu's parting comment concerning future influence. I quickly concluded that it was an empty promise. We probably had little if any real influence over ROK internal developments, and we were little more than helpless bystanders as Chun shrewdly maneuvered toward total power.

An abiding bitterness continues to poison the attitudes of Cholla's residents toward the ROK Government and the United States. They remain angry that U.S. authorities failed to prevent the ROK army's brutality, and they believe the myth that I contributed to the horror by allowing the deployment of the ROK Special Forces brigades that were blamed for most of the brutalities.

Chapter Eight

Chun and the Presidency

Breakfast with Chun

At Chun's request, we met informally on August 8 for a 2–hour breakfast at the classy Silla Hotel in downtown Seoul. Chun's staff made all the arrangements, including a Western-style breakfast with scrambled eggs, bacon, fried potatoes, and pastries. Chun, however, smoked more than he ate. The room's name, the Royal Suite, seemed apt, given Chun's increasingly powerful position and his promotion to full general a few days earlier.

Chun had elevated himself to full general in about as many months as it took President Park to pin on four stars. Military rank was important for status in Korean society, but Chun did not wear his uniform, choosing instead a well-tailored business suit. We were alone in the room except for two interpreters—Bruce Grant from my headquarters and a Korean interpreter for Chun. I was surprised by the number of plainclothes bodyguards in the hallway and by the evident subservience shown to Chun by his aides and the hotel staff alike. Chun was very cordial toward me. He seemed relaxed, very self-assured, tough-minded on every issue we discussed, and he spoke as though he were the "boss." (As a matter of fact, he would be elected President in less than three weeks.)

I began by noting that Ambassador Gleysteen and I had been working hard to explain the events in Korea in a positive light to American audiences. However, our explanations aside, there were still grave concerns. These concerns were borne out by congressional actions that restrained American economic assistance and Foreign Military Assistance and by letters from various congressional officials to President Choi. I had previously sent copies of some of these letters to Chun, and he remarked that he had read some of the extracts. I suggested that certain developments in the ROK might be helpful in allaying some of these concerns. There should be continued progress on the political timetable, and the election of the new government should proceed in accordance with the constitutional process. Second, the government in power in the ROK must demonstrate a broad base of support from the Korean people. Third, the government should foster an atmosphere of openness within South Korean society and reduce repression. Kim Dae-jung's imprisonment had become a lightning rod of international criticism, and Koreans should be clever enough to figure out how to handle the issue in an open and fair way. Fourth, the governing authorities must avoid actions that led to instability and thereby threatened national security. Chun listened carefully and simply said: "thanks for good advice."

Then he turned abruptly to the domestic situation. In his view, stability was the number one concern of the Korean people and the senior leaders in the government. The people wanted economic progress to be resumed and were anxious to avoid any further episodes like Kwangju. With a wave of his arms, Chun said: "There will be no more demonstrations or riots, because they will be blocked," and "There will be economic recovery and the ROK defense effort will have the highest priority." It sounded to me almost as if Chun were issuing orders from the Blue House.

After lighting another cigarette, he said he wanted to clarify the term "political development." He said he disliked the term and it did not have a clear Korean equivalent. Chun said he preferred to talk about the political schedule for elections, although it would be "tough to accomplish in view of the time constraints and the complexity of the task involved." For example, the revision of the constitution was just one step, and it had to be done properly to avoid confusion and discord. Also, at least six basic laws had to be redrafted and legislated. Nevertheless, Chun expressed confidence that the schedule of constitutional revision and national elections would be followed. "Trust us in this regard, we know what we're doing."

Referring to Kim Dae-jung's arrest and upcoming trial, Chun said that the matter had been blown out of proportion by the media: "So much criticism is now leveled at the ROK and me, as to be deeply offensive and to connote to my people that outside interference is being applied to ROK domestic affairs." He added, "The legal community as well as many other Koreans feel as I do. We are not a race of barbarians, and Kim Dae-jung will be handled according to our laws, which are different than yours."

I noted that, his explanations aside, American concerns were being reflected in decisions to cut Foreign Military Sales (FMS) credits and to delay the annual Security Consultative Meeting. I asked Chun how he viewed these matters. He said it was essential to hold the SCM, not only for substantive military reasons, but also because the failure to do so would create the wrong impression with the North Koreans about the solidarity of relations between the ROK and the United States.

Knowing of Chun's interest in military preparedness issues, I asked him how familiar he was with the Ministry of National Defense Force Improvement Plan (FIP) and its priorities for the much needed acquisition of modern equipment. Chun regretted that he knew little about the FIP but said he would do more homework on the details. He asked me to review the important priorities for weapon modernization. I answered that these included artillery expansion, improvements in antitank capabilities, and ground mobility. These would be needed to defend against North Korea's increased offensive capabilities. I also noted that the aging ROK F–86 fighters needed to be replaced with F–5s, and ultimately by F–16s. Chun was surprised because he considered the F–86 to be superior to the North Korean MiG–19. I assured him it was not. Also, the ROK air force needed air-to-air missiles and more ample ground support equipment and spares. In the naval area, priority had to be placed on improved antisubmarine and antimine capabilities, and eventually the fleet would have to be upgraded with Korean-manufactured corvettes and frigates. After listening intently to my brief review of his country's defense needs, Chun commented, "Force modernization will cost a great deal, and the challenge for the government will be how to pay for it all."

As a final comment, Chun explained the difficulties of getting things done in the current bureaucracy. He said that President Choi, "while a good man, is a poor administrator, and policy papers, as well as decisions which ordinarily should take a few hours, frequently consume several days or longer." For this reason, various special committees had been organized to "get things moving in an efficient, decisive way and to shore up the government." Roughly 25 percent of each committee were officers, but he said most of them were technical soldiers, not combat types. I mentioned the rumor that President Choi would resign in the near future and expressed the hope that, for reasons of stability, this would not occur. Chun looked away from me and tersely replied, "Well, that's a rumor." His abruptness suggested it was more than a rumor.

After our meeting, I reported back to Washington that Chun's endeavors seemed complicated. He had told me that he was exploiting opportunities as they arose, distilling advice from a wide variety of sources, and assessing the domestic as well as international situations. He had insisted that he found it "difficult to see as far as a week in advance," as though he and his associates had no plan to usurp political power. I doubted that Chun was merely muddling along, looking for opportunities and taking advantage of whatever chance threw into his lap. That would have been foolhardy, and Chun was no fool. I believed that he had a plan, but he had to pioneer each step. His lack of familiarity with defense matters struck me as understandable, since he was completely preoccupied with gaining power. Nevertheless, his willingness to listen suggested an open-minded approach and the possibility that he would become knowledgeable on force improvement matters. I also thought he had an inquiring mind and a fairly good perspective on strategic issues. On the Kim Dae-jung matter, it was clear that Chun understood U.S. and international concerns, but those concerns left him angry over what he considered to be offensive interference in domestic affairs.

Martial Law and Censorship

Chun's imposition of full martial law gave military censors a field day. They were able to control print and broadcast information throughout Korea and did not shirk from the task. As an illustration of how far this control and manipulation went, the local government radio in Kwangju incredibly reported during the crisis, "The United States had approved the dispatch of ROK Special Forces troops into Kwangju." It was untrue, but it promulgated the myth that the United States supported the actions of the Special Forces Command in Kwangju. When Bill Gleysteen protested the gross disinformation and demanded an official retraction, nothing happened. He was not even granted the courtesy of a reply.

On another occasion, an official U.S. statement issued on May 22 called for an open dialogue between the opposing sides in Kwangju. The statement, prepared by a Washington policy review committee chaired by Secretary of State Edmund Muskie, had concluded that the United States must "advise the ROK Government to restore order through dialogue and the minimum use of force, in order to avoid sowing the seeds of wide disorder, and to continue pressure for responsive political structures and a broadly based civilian government." The Department of State warned:

> We are deeply concerned by civil strife in Kwangju. We urge all parties involved to exercise maximum restraint and undertake a dialogue in search of a peaceful solution. Continued unrest and an escalation of violence could risk dangerous miscalculation by external forces. When calm has been restored, we will urge all parties to seek means to resume a pro-

gram of political development as outlined by President Choi. We reiterate that the U.S. Government will react strongly in accordance with its treaty obligations to any external attempt to exploit the situation in the ROK.

Throughout the Kwangju crisis, Bill Gleysteen and I had already been articulating this exact policy to our ROK counterparts. Thus, the statement from Washington came as no surprise to Chun or the rest of the ROK Government. Bill and I were assured by ROK Government authorities that the U.S. statement, printed on leaflets in Hangul (the Korean language), would be airdropped over Kwangju. To our dismay, the leaflets stayed in the warehouse and were never distributed. Chun did not allow the statement to be broadcast or printed in ROK media. He alone knew best what was needed, and he refused to tolerate anything that appeared to be meddling by the United States, or American encouragement of the radicals.

Ambassador Gleysteen and I were convinced that something needed to be done. The tight censorship not only allowed Chun to manipulate the media, it also kept Western journalists from reporting on Korean developments, such as the upcoming trial of Kim Dae-jung. Reporters had virtually no access to ROK officials, unless the government wanted a particular story revealed. Chun periodically granted on-the-record interviews, but only if he thought it would help his popularity. Few other officials were permitted to meet with Western reporters. Instead, grossly biased, government-approved handouts were given to the press.

Media Troubles

Bill Gleysteen had decided to start giving interviews with Western media representatives in Seoul and urged me to do the same. Our goal was to help the reporters acquire appropriate knowledge so they could develop reasonably objective articles about ongoing developments in Korea. Over the next several months, I had a series of off-the-record interviews with reporters from the *Far Eastern Economic Review, The Asian Wall Street Journal*, and the *Los Angeles Times*.

On August 8, after my breakfast meeting with Chun Doo-hwan, I granted an afternoon interview with Terry Anderson of the *Associated Press,* and Sam Jameson of the *Los Angeles Times*. The ground rules for the interview stipulated that it was a background briefing only, with no attribution to me, by name or position. Both reporters said they fully understood the rule and would abide by it. Although the reporters could not use my name, they could refer to me in their reporting as a senior military official. My public affairs officer, Colonel John Klose, tape recorded the entire interview, as did both reporters. The session lasted about an hour. When it ended, Anderson rose and asked if he could have an answer to one last question. He said the question was on the minds of virtually every journalist in Seoul. I knew enough to be wary of the "one last question" routine, and I should have declined to answer.

As Terry stood near the door of my office, he asked whether the U.S. Government would support Chun, were he to successfully consolidate his power and become president of the ROK? It was a crucial question and I reflected on it for a moment. It was the same question Bill Gleysteen and I had discussed countless times. Finally, I answered, "The United States would support Chun provided he comes to power legitimately, demonstrates over time a broad base of support from the Korean people, and he does not jeopardize security of the situation here."

Although the United States had maintained the firm position of distancing itself from Chun, Bill Gleysteen and I had come to the conclusion that were Chun to become president, then the United States would have little choice but to support him. For months we had been warning Chun and his associates that if he sought his country's highest political office, he would have to achieve that goal through constitutional procedures, that he would have to demonstrate wide popular support, and that the security situation must not be threatened. What I told the reporters was consistent with internal American policy, and I wanted to be candid and straightforward. Of course, it was not my place as a military official to announce U.S. Government foreign policy, and I did not do so in a for-the-record interview.

Unfortunately, the interview remained off-the-record fewer than 24 hours. In their hotel that night, Anderson and Jameson allowed Henry Scott Stokes of *The New York Times* either to hear their tape of the interview or to read excerpts from Anderson's AP wire story. At least, that was what I gathered afterward from various sources. Anderson and Jameson told Stokes about the nonattribution ground rule, but all three reporters recognized that they might well have a headline story on their hands.

Stokes told the other two he would be meeting with Chun on August 9 and he asked if he could borrow the tape or extracts from it, so he could ask Chun to identify the speaker. Apparently, Anderson and Jameson agreed. In the interview with Stokes, Chun eagerly identified me as the source of the statement. With a laugh, "Chun welcomed support from his friend, General Wickham." As a result, the entire tape of my interview with Anderson and Jameson became public information and was circulated widely throughout Korea.

I was appalled at the breach of journalistic ethics by these three reporters. To his credit, though, Terry Anderson sought to apologize to me several weeks later at a diplomatic reception, but it was an inopportune time to talk at length with him, and I have never seen him since.

For Chun, it was an opportunity to exploit. He saw to it that the censor-controlled media ran numerous front page articles trumpeting Chun for president on the basis that the United States now would support him. The three conditions for support that I explicitly outlined in the interview were totally omitted, as were the criticisms of Chun's repressive policies. The Korean media reported simply that Chun was a good guy and that the United States would support him unconditionally.

To illustrate how the Korean media manipulated my remarks, an editorial in the English-language newspaper, *The Korea Herald,* on August 10 said:

> Citizens of this Republic are increasingly trusting [of] and admire General Chun as the new leader needed for the new age. And we note with a sense of encouragement that a top U.S. military official in Seoul (General Wickham) shares our view about General Chun and asserts that the U.S. would support him if the Korean people elect him the next president. Although Americans have no right to interfere in our internal political affairs, a close accord of opinion is welcome for cooperative relationship between the two allies.

An August 12 editorial in *The Korea Times* concluded:

> We have heard voices (General Wickham) from the U.S., our traditional ally, predicting General Chun as the incoming national leader of this country, foreseeing overwhelming support for him from the Korean people in choosing their supreme leader through lawful procedures. General Chun has implanted a strong image as a sincere and capable leader among his brethren, displaying impressive leadership as well as undertaking sweeping reforms leading to the revitalized social climate. A new era appears to call for such a leader as General Chun.

The Korean media barrage continued for days and understandably angered officials back in Washington. They were outraged that a military officer appeared to be announcing official foreign policy in an interview, and that the Korean-controlled media blatantly manipulated my remarks to Chun's benefit. The Carter administration disliked Chun a great deal, and the fact that all of this occurred just a few months before the U.S. presidential election probably added to the consternation. Washington moved swiftly to disavow my remarks:

> [*The Washington Post* on August 10] The U.S. military commander in South Korea said the U.S. would support strongman Chun if as expected he consolidates his already near-total power by taking over the presidency. General Wickham's view differs from State Department officials in Washington who have said Chun has not yet demonstrated broad-based support in the country.

> [The *Los Angeles Times* on August 12] A general speaks out of turn. An American military commander in South Korea has embarrassed his government by appearing to give not only his own but also official U.S. blessing to the military dictatorship imposed by General Chun. Chun loved it.

> [*The New York Times* on August 13] Mr. Muskie and other State Department officials were startled by an interview quoting a highly placed U.S. military official as saying Washington had decided to support Chun. The source of the interview was General Wickham, who had taken part in the review of American policy toward Seoul with Mr. Muskie and Ambassador Gleysteen at the end of June in Tokyo. Because of concern that South Korea might interpret the interview as signaling acceptance of Chun, the State Department disavowed the interview. The Defense Department, which said it had no differences with the State Department on Korean policy, said that General Wickham had been quoted out of context. Pentagon officials said General Wickham maintains that he said the U.S. would only support General Chun if he met the criteria that have already been conveyed to South Korean officials. One State Department official said that, even if General Wickham's remarks were misinterpreted, he should not have been giving an interview touching on delicate political matters.

In Limbo

On August 9, I departed Korea to attend a worldwide CINCs conference hosted by JCS Chairman General Jones in Norfolk, Virginia. Secretary of Defense Brown and the Joint Chiefs of Staff also participated. The agenda and frank discussions were of great interest, but I was distracted by the reports of the growing uproar over my interview. Curiously, no one in the government chided me over the matter, although a few colleagues poked fun at my apparent case of "hoof in mouth disease." I headed back to Korea after the conference ended on August 13.

While in flight, I received urgent phone calls from General Jones and Assistant Secretary of State Dick Holbrooke. Both of them voiced concern over the continuing manipulation of my remarks by the Korean media and the fact that a prompt return to Seoul could be misread by the Korean authorities as tangible U.S. Government support for Chun's presidential candidacy. It was a valid point.

Events were moving fast in Korea. Intelligence reports concluded that President Choi would resign very soon. On August 16 he in fact announced his resignation because, in his words, he had "failed to fulfill satisfactorily the presidential duties, and because several political decisions have been made where results had a destabilizing influence on the nation." At the same time, President Choi praised General Chun as "an unselfish man full of confidence and ability to put theory into practice. In a country like South Korea, which faces a special security situation, the nation's leader should be a man who is widely supported by the military." The Defense Ministry echoed the president's praise by announcing that the nation's military "shared the view that General Chun is exceptionally highly qualified for the presidency as well as the top military leader who cannot be matched by anybody." Chun's public relations campaign was in full swing.

As a result of Choi's surprise resignation, Chun made preparations to retire from his 25–year army career. His retirement would be a necessary precondition, as the ROK constitution required that the president be a civilian. Chun, of course, knew that if he ever hoped to attract U.S. support he would have to comply with constitutional procedures. After his retirement, Chun would run as the only candidate before the national assembly of 5,000 electors from all over South Korea, which was ready to convene before the end of August.

Because of all these considerations, Jones and Holbrooke instructed me to divert my flight to Hawaii and remain there until "things cooled off," whatever that meant. Holbrooke and Jones believed that holding up my return would cause South Korean authorities to realize that the U.S. Government was extremely unhappy with ongoing developments. Dick Holbrooke also mentioned that a few senior officials in Washington, including the President and Secretary of State Muskie, were really upset over my interview and its implications for U.S. policy. Holbrooke and General Jones promised to do their best to get things back on track, but they made it quite clear that they couldn't promise anything.

I was on the hook. Of course, I was partly to blame for the situation, but my superiors gave me the impression that the fault was wholly mine, notwithstanding the ground rules for the interview or the fact that the Korean media had unscrupulously manipulated my remarks.

Under ordinary conditions, a forced stay on Hawaii's beautiful beaches would be the kind of penal condition for which most people pray. Of course, these were not ordinary conditions. Ann and I were worried. We had no idea of what was being said back in Washington, or whether my career in the Army would be cut short after 30 years in uniform. I made periodic phone calls to General Jones and Dick Holbrooke, but they were not very reassuring. I was particularly troubled that no one in authority had asked about the ground rules for the interview, or even for a transcript. Ann and I talked about it often. Ignorant of what was happening back in Washington, I was concerned that I had been judged guilty by the White House and State Department without any opportunity to present my side of the story.

Finally, in distress I went to see my long-time friend, Admiral Bob Long, the Commander in Chief of U.S. Pacific Command. I said, "Bob, I'm ready to submit my retirement papers from the Army. I know you'll agree with me that this is no way to treat a senior military officer." Fortunately, Bob gave me good advice, as he always did. He told me to "cool it a bit longer." He asked for a copy of the interview transcript and had his staff review it, and then he sent a personal message on August 19 to Secretary Brown, Assistant Secretary Holbrooke, and General Jones.

His message concluded that the "established ground rules for the interview were violated by both news services, and that [Wickham's] comments were generally consistent with U.S. Government policy." I am sure his message helped. However, it was also fortunate that Bill Gleysteen was in the United States on home leave. I am convinced he played a major role in arguing my case, as did a few other senior officials, including my friends Mike Armacost and Nick Platt. Without doubt, my relationship with Secretary of Defense Brown also was helpful.

At a Pentagon meeting of the Joint Chiefs with the unified and specified commanders, I am seated at the left front. To my left (clockwise) are General Edward Meyer, Army Chief of Staff; General Bernard Rogers, U.S. European Command; Admiral Thomas Hayward, Chief of Naval Operations; General Donn Starry, U.S. Readiness Command; Admiral Robert Long, U.S. Pacific Command; General Robert Barrow, Commandant of the Marine Corps; Lieutenant General James Hartinger, Aerospace Defense Command; General Lew Allen, Air Force Chief of Staff; Admiral Harry Train, U.S. Atlantic Command; General David Jones, Chairman of the Joint Chiefs of Staff; General James Allen, Strategic Airlift Command; General Bennie Davis, Strategic Air Command; and Lieutenant General Robert Kingston, Rapid Deployment Joint Task Force.

On August 22 welcome news arrived. I was authorized to return to my military duties in Korea. In phone calls and messages, including the one below, Dick Holbrooke told me:

> I'm glad you are now returning. What broke this sticky issue open was your comment in our telephone conversation about the need for you to participate in the U.S.–ROK military exercise (Ulchi-Focus Lens). This enabled us to find a valid justification for your return, earlier rather than later. I am pleased this has worked out and I appreciate your waiting in

Hawaii. In recent discussions with Choi Kwang-soo, chief secretary of the Blue House, I spent much time on the fact that the Koreans misused you, and said that this was going to create great problems for the United States if it continued. Your responsibilities included the safety of tens of thousands of Americans, and if anti-Americanism were to arise as a result of ROKG misrepresentations of our actions or statements, it would be a major and unprecedented problem. I have also stressed that your position (in the interview) is consistent with the rest of the U.S. Government, if read in context and properly understood. We must now look forward to the period after your return, in which your every move will become a potential public and political issue both here and in Korea. One reporter has already indicated that he will try to misinterpret your return before Chun's inauguration as a sign of official U.S. Government benediction. That is of course not the case. We are, in fact, trying to walk a tightrope between two equally unattractive extremes in this situation. My suggestion is therefore to stress in every way your role as commander during the period after your return. It would be best to try to prevent Koreans from abusing your role through symbolic actions or photographic opportunities. In any case, these are just some personal and unofficial thoughts. You have a tough job; I am in the easy position of the back-home kibitzer. But also your friend and supporter. Dick

That same day, probably based on an interview with Holbrooke, *The Washington Post* reported:

The Carter administration, in what is likely to be interpreted as a signal of approval of the South Korean strongman, General Chun, has decided to permit the return to Seoul of the U.S. military commander there, General John Wickham. The decision to permit Wickham to return was made at the general's request after a lengthy telephone conversation between him and Assistant Secretary of State Holbrooke. Wickham is reported to have been anxious to participate in a previously planned U.S.-Korean command post exercise. While seeking to avoid conveying an endorsement of Chun, the administration has sought to avoid any sign of lessening U.S. military support for South Korea where 40,000 American troops and a long standing security commitment remains. Failure to permit Wickham to return, especially in view of his own recommendation that he participate, could have generated criticism on grounds that security was taking second place to political considerations.

Dick Holbrooke and General Jones continued to work on my behalf. During hearings before the House Foreign Affairs Committee on August 28, they provided testimony that, in their words "laid to rest, or at least sharply reduced for the Committee members questions about your interview." Holbrooke said he took a "very strong line about my role as an integral part of the policy making and implementing team in whom everyone had the fullest confidence." He also pointed out that the ROK Government had deliberately distorted my statement as part of their campaign to misrepresent the U.S. Government position. As a result of this supportive testimony, Holbrooke said, the Committee abandoned further questioning about my interview.

However, the Carter administration continued to have grave doubts about President Chun, and this attitude complicated my relationships with my Korean counterparts. During a August 21 press conference, President Carter said;

> We have been deeply concerned about Chun and some of the policies he's put forward. I understand now he might step down as general to become president. We also are concerned about the upcoming trial of Kim Dae-jung. Under the new leaders in Korea our influence is limited, and we've got the option of expressing our extreme displeasure by withdrawing our forces, which might destabilize that whole region of Asia, or accepting some political development of which we disapprove. We would like to have a complete democracy with full and open debate, free press and elected leaders. The Koreans are not ready for that, according to their own judgment, and I don't know how to it explain it any better.

Return to Seoul

After returning to Seoul, I immersed myself in the U.S.–ROK military exercise, ULCHI-FOCUS LENS, which was largely a command post exercise. There also was some ROK Government participation from their extensive underground command post south of Seoul. During a lull in the exercise I had a long private meeting with General Rhu, who wanted to talk about recent developments. Given Dick Holbrooke's suggestions to avoid any discussions about political matters, I listened to Rhu but remained reserved.

Rhu said that Kwangju had made Chun's rise virtually inevitable. He said he did not want to criticize former President Choi, but he felt it necessary to explain that Choi had performed miserably during and after the Kwangju tragedy. His indecisiveness and his penchant for avoiding complex situations made it difficult to reach decisions. Cabinet meetings tended to drag on and on, with little action. As a consequence, there was almost universal agreement in the ROK hierarchy that Choi, while a nice man who had a distinguished diplomatic career, could not govern the nation effectively. In order to preclude another potentially dangerous incident, such as Kwangju, it was decided that Choi should retire in August, just prior to the reopening of the universities. That decision had been "made many weeks ago and the plan to submit Chun's name for election was also decided then."

Rhu then confided, "[Your] press remarks did not accelerate or have any effect on the timetable for Choi's retirement and Chun's election." I did not view his comment as patronizing, because he was a trusted friend and because he said he was privy to the internal discussions about the political timetable for Chun's election. Rhu elaborated that there had been gross misrepresentations of my remarks by the press. He said that he and other senior military officers had read the full text of the interview, and he understood and agreed with the three preconditions that had to be met before the United States would support Chun's presidency. I told Rhu that the misrepresentation of my remarks by the local media was not at all helpful. The views I expressed were obviously my own. The background nature of the interview had been violated, and it was unfortunate that General Chun had identified me by name. Rhu said he regretted all of this.

As a final comment, Rhu believed that the military were fully behind President Chun, and that the Korean Military Academy graduates, particularly, provided a strong base of support. Rhu said that he sensed high morale and esprit in the armed forces and that the relationships between the ROK and U.S. military were becoming the best he had seen in years.

Toward the end of August, Defense Minister Chu suddenly summoned me to his office. Speaking in English, without any interpreter present, he asked when "you, as CFC commander, intend to pay a courtesy call on President [elect] Chun?" I was surprised by the directness of Chu's question, but I also sensed that the question emanated directly from the Blue House. Any personal feelings aside, I knew that as a matter of protocol and courtesy I had better get over to the Blue House pretty soon. I already had been approached by my CFC deputy, General Baek, and he had urged me to co-host a dinner with him in honor of President Chun, before he was formally inaugurated. In fact, Baek had already taken the liberty of making the arrangements, to include securing a date from the Blue House. I had told Baek, as graciously as I could, that the dinner could not occur at this time. Baek was very disappointed, and we both knew that his ROK superiors would not like my answer.

The combination of Baek's proposal and Chu's blunt question clearly indicated that the ROK military anxiously wanted to arrange a meeting between me and Chun, without delay. I had no doubts that such a meeting would be publicized in the Korean media as tacit American support for Chun. I also recalled Dick Holbrooke's guidance for me to avoid any symbolic actions, including photos, that might convey a U.S. Government benediction of Chun.

After thinking it over, I told Chu that it would be inappropriate for me to call on President Chun until Ambassador Gleysteen's home leave had ended, and he had returned to Seoul. I told him that the ambassador would be back in a few days; however, if President [elect] Chun summoned me, then of course I would go to see him, although my preference was to await Bill Gleysteen's return. Chu clearly was upset with my answer, but he dropped the discussion and ended the meeting. Chu's irritation did not particularly trouble me, since I had become accustomed to his abrupt manner when things did not go the way he wanted. After leaving Chu's office I repeated my views to Chu's official interpreter, Lieutenant Colonel Hong. I wanted to make sure that I avoided any misunderstanding, because I suspected that my response would be passed to the Blue House.

Shortly after this meeting, General Mun, the chairman of the National Assembly Defense Committee, came to give me his perspective. He began by expressing his sincere regret over the misrepresentations of my views from the interview with Anderson and Jameson. He confirmed General Rhu's comment that the distortion of my views had little, if any, bearing on political developments in the ROK.

Before leaving, Mun urged me to meet with Lieutenant General Roh, Chun's military academy classmate and currently the DSC commander. Mun described Roh as "the man most powerful next to the president." I told him that we would be meeting in a day or so.

A Visit with Roh

On September 4, General Roh Tae-woo came to see me at the CFC head-quarters. Roh intended it as a courtesy call, but we had serious discussions that lasted nearly two hours.

Of the three military academy classmates who were involved in the December 12 coup (Chun, Roh, and Chung Ho-young), Roh impressed most people as being the brightest and least personally aggressive of the three. He was soft spoken, thoughtful, mild-mannered, and somewhat retiring in attitude. Nevertheless, beneath this manner I detected a willingness to adhere to hardline positions and to tough it out. That willingness had been evident in his rock solid support of Chun during the night of December 12 and during the Kwangju episode.

At the outset, Roh stated that the ominous North Korean threat and ROK internal stability had been problems of great concern for all Koreans over the past months. While the situation had been extremely difficult and might continue to be so, "We can overcome our problems by mutual effort." Then he thanked me for my efforts to assure peace and stability on the peninsula and particularly for my role in "allowing Koreans to solve their own internal difficulties." I did not comment.

Much of our conversation then focused on the need to achieve a better understanding of each nation's viewpoints and to share our concerns about developments in the ROK. Even though Roh was not in the CFC chain of command, he urged that we meet more frequently to exchange views. It was an unusual request, because the CFC and the DSC normally maintained a great distance. In fact, Roh and I would meet often in the future, including in tennis matches that he usually won.

Roh then launched into a long, impassioned explanation of why the ROK army in general, and KMA graduates in particular, best understood the United States and its values. He was clearly trying to justify the seizure of power as he pointed out, "Due to training over many years by the United States, the establishment of KMA along the lines of West Point, and the presence of a substantial number of instructors at KMA who attained higher education in the United States, KMA graduates believe they have developed from U.S. values their view of self, life, and fundamental convictions about duty, honor, and service to the nation." Since they paralleled West Point's motto of "duty, honor, country," Roh knew that I would relate to these convictions. And I knew it would have been useless to point out that West Point taught its graduates to respect and protect the country's political institutions.

Roh then described the Vietnam War—where he and Chun had served together in combat—as a tragic misfortune that the ROK army would never allow to occur in South Korea. Given the great potential for insurrection and invasion, the army had to be the nation's guardian and it must remain vigilant. He considered it unfortunate that the Western media had misrepresented the situation, particularly during the Kwangju episode, when the press had failed to report on the extreme danger of insurrection spreading throughout the nation and leading to a civil war. He said, "If Kwangju-type upheavals were to have occurred in Taegu, Pusan and other major urban areas, the very existence of Korean society as we know it would have been imperiled."

Roh told me that the army had no alternative but to stop the disturbances from spreading. The press had not only failed to sense the danger of widespread social unrest, but also the corruption that existed throughout Korean society. All this dissatisfaction could have allowed radical elements to ignite a countrywide insurrection. Because of these circumstances, Roh emphasized that the "first order of business for our new government must be internal stability and cleaning house." South Korea was unlike the United States in size and stage of political development; hence, internal difficulties required different solutions. "Democracy in our nation has not been successful, thus my government must build a climate that would support movement toward democracy. But first our leaders must clean up political and business corruption before they can push for more democratic development." Unfortunately, the "United States holds the Korean people and its leadership to too fine a standard of democracy and does not give us enough maneuver room."

Roh concluded his philosophical explanation by suggesting that the "leadership values of KMA graduates now headed by President Chun imbue all four-year KMA classes with values that clearly are correct for ROK society in the 1980s, and these graduates, in a sense, are chosen leaders of the nation." As he spoke, his voice rose in emotion and he glanced directly into my eyes, and I was struck by the impression that he and his KMA classmates really believed that destiny was on their side. He said that Korean leaders from President Chun on down would be "true and honest in all we do and that the United States should simply watch our actions as proof of our sincerity. I am sure that democracy will come to my country. Please, good friend, be assured of this."

Secretary of Defense Caspar Weinburger during his first official visit to South Korea in 1981.

The Blue House

Shortly after his inauguration as President, Chun summoned me to the Blue House. The compound included both the President's residence and his official offices set off by beautiful landscaping. I noticed extensive construction on one side of the imposing central building. Apparently, the main visitor entrance was being moved to another side of the building. I learned later that Korean geomancers had suggested that the omens for Chun's regime would be far better if the main entrance were shifted from the south to a western location. Chun immediately ordered the change.

President Park also had made changes in the Blue House compound. As the story went, after scrutinizing aerial photos of the layout, geomancers had concluded that the location of several buildings in the presidential compound revealed bad signs, connoting "fire and wood." Such signs obviously would not be auspicious for the wellbeing of Park's regime or his personal situation, so he changed the location of the buildings.

After a brief wait, I was ushered into one of the meeting rooms. My last visit to the Blue House had been a courtesy call with President Park, almost a year ago. A few minutes passed and then President Chun strode in.

I was startled when he dismissed everyone except his official interpreter. Then he greeted me with surprising warmth. He looked very relaxed and sure of himself, almost as though he had occupied this office for a long time. I was also surprised that there were no photographers present, since it was routine to have a few pictures taken before presidential meetings. I had no idea why Chun wished to see me, but I was prepared to provide him with an update on military matters, including CFC operations and the North Korean threat situation.

While the traditional ginseng tea with pine nuts was being served, Chun began by reviewing many of the difficulties we had experienced during recent months. He didn't cover them in any detail, because he knew that I was well aware of them. He said that the threat of North Korean intervention had worried him most after the assassination of President Park. Like millions of other Koreans, he had lived through the searing Korean War, and he worried every day about the dangerous threat posed by North Korean forces deployed in attack formations just 30 miles to the north of Seoul and its almost 12 million inhabitants. The risk of war was always on the minds of most Koreans, and ROK soldiers in particular. Yes, he said, U.S. and ROK forces had kept the peace since the armistice in 1953, but the threat of renewed hostilities remained high, particularly during crises in the South.

Chun then pointed to an original calligraphy on the wall. I had seen replicas of it in many public buildings throughout Korea. It was a Korean proverb that had been brushed in ink by President Park himself, and it served as the national defense slogan. It read *yu pi mu hwan*, which translates roughly as, "Be prepared and have no anxiety." Chun said that he lived by this maxim.

He then repeated something I had heard before. He had not sought a political role for himself, but after Park's death, it had been thrust on him. Perhaps it was destiny and he had been chosen, but he felt there were several compelling reasons behind it. Among these were the real threat of Communist-inspired insurrection, the ever present potential that North Korea might exploit ROK domestic unrest, the serious ROK social problems of labor unrest, rampant corruption and immorality, the worsening economy, and the abuses of authority.

Chun said he had found it absolutely essential to revitalize the military by realigning the promotion and assignment systems to reward merit, youth, and true patriotism. To do this, he had to retire many older and less capable officers. Chun told me that he reluctantly shouldered all of these political and military responsibilities because "no one else with solid support from the military was capable of doing so, and former President Choi unfortunately seemed unable to accomplish the executive tasks in an effective manner."

Chun seemed to be leading up to something, so I merely nodded and stayed silent. As one of his first actions as president, Chun said, he wanted to thank the United States for the military support and strong diplomatic statements provided during the difficulties of recent months. In his view, this support had been invaluable in deterring the North Koreans. He said that the Korean people deeply appreciated America's friendship and the strong military relationships, including those in Korea, between our two nations. He said he personally considered these "relationships as good or better than at any time in recent years." He also commended the CFC for its "very effective leadership at every level and direction of operational forces from both nations."

After pausing for a moment, Chun looked at me closely and spoke very slowly. "I want to thank you very much for your role in my country. I personally appreciate everything you've done, as do all of the senior military in my country. All of us understand how difficult your task has been here. You have helped to keep the peace, and to allow Koreans to solve their own internal problems." Our meeting ended shortly after these comments. I'm sure that in his own way Chun also thanked Bill Gleysteen for his efforts.

Driving away from the Blue House on this beautiful fall day, I reflected on Chun's expression of gratitude and his apparent warmth toward me. During our recent meeting, General Roh had conveyed similar sentiments. But why did the men who had led the December coup consider it necessary to thank me? They had accomplished their goal of achieving political power, and they had done it their way. And why didn't their words of appreciation provide me any comfort?

Given all that had happened—the misuse of CFC forces, the attempt to undermine me, the distortion of my comments to the press, the jeopardy to my career—Chun and his associates must have assumed that I harbored some resentment, if not some bitterness toward them. They would recognize that my latent anger would not be helpful, as Chun and

Being congratulated by President Chun Doo-hwan, who had just decorated me with the Taegeug, *South Korea's highest military medal, with Ambassador Richard Walker and General Kim Yoon-ho in the background.*

his colleagues now embarked on restoring a close and harmonious U.S.–ROK relationship, which would be absolutely essential for their country's economic, military, and political development. Chun probably had concluded that it would be essential to dissipate my possible resentment. That would be the Korean way. Chun's gratitude was probably genuine, and he would go on to show it in a variety of ways. When I departed Korea in June 1982 to become the U.S. Army Vice Chief of Staff, he personally decorated me with Korea's highest military honor, the *Taegeug* Medal, an honor that was awarded to only a few U.S. or Korean military leaders.

Still, I took no comfort. Throughout the difficult period after Park's death, Chun and his associates had been consistently dishonest with me and Bill Gleysteen. As military professionals, they knew full well the implications of violating the chain of command, and yet they were willing to weaken my legitimate authority and jeopardize their nation's security in the face of a clearly recognized North Korean threat. Further, knowing full well that I did not support him or his goals, Chun had tried his best to undermine me, if not have me relieved as commander of forces in Korea. He had very nearly succeeded. The manipulation of my interview remarks for Chun's electoral benefit had come within a thread of destroying my Army career.

A soldier's misfortunes are not suffered alone, but are shared with their families, and my wife Ann had suffered greatly through these painful episodes. She could not forgive what had been done to her husband. Thus, I took no comfort from the expressions of appreciation by Chun and his associates, nor could I bring myself to believe they were sincere. Instead of gratitude, I would have expected apologies. They never came. I eventually came to recognize that it would have been too much to expect proud Koreans, particularly senior military leaders, to apologize for actions that they believed were absolutely essential to their own self-preservation and for the security of their Korean brothers and sisters. It was just one more sign of how difficult it was to span the cultural chasm between Koreans and Americans.

I still had two years of service to fulfill in Korea, and that made it necessary that I put all of these feelings and scars behind me. I turned my wholehearted attention to my military duties and fully expected that at the end of my tour, and 32 years of service, I would wind up my Army career. I did not anticipate that I would be offered any further assignments, as Chun's efforts to have me removed could have poisoned whatever support I might have enjoyed among my seniors in Washington. Meanwhile, I had to do my best to keep the peace. And there would be at least one more dangerous episode with the North Koreans, when they tried to shoot down one of our SR–71 reconnaissance aircraft with SA–2 missiles fired from the remote North Korean peninsula of Choktori.

Moreover, the Carter administration was over, and President Ronald Reagan was bringing a new team to office. The new president had appointed an extraordinarily able Secretary of Defense, Caspar

Weinberger, and an equally able deputy, Frank Carlucci. I had to assist them, as well as a new U.S. Ambassador, Richard L. "Dixie" Walker, on Korean defense matters. I looked forward to my association with these new friends and to the challenges ahead.

Chapter Nine

Reflections

As the events I have described in this volume unfolded, I tried to identify key lessons and develop general conclusions about American policy toward South Korea. The intervening years have given me time to reflect further and have yielded additional information on that turbulent period. With these advantages, I would like to offer a few observations from the perspective of a military commander.

The most important lesson was the humbling discovery of how little I really knew about the complex Korean culture. Of course I had been immersed in it since June of 1979 and had been exposed to it during 14 months spent on the DMZ in the tumultuous period of 1961–62. But, apparently, I knew a lot less than I had thought.

Ann and I had been studying the Korean language for several months, until the tension and the rapid pace of events after Park's death interrupted our efforts. Still, I had learned enough Korean to understand the gist of basic military conversations and to read out loud the texts of short speeches. My shallow linguistic ability, however, did not lend me a deep understanding of the culture. For that, I had to turn to my valuable assistants, Steve Bradner, who had married a Korean Olympic athlete, and Bruce Grant, who was fluent in Korean and Chinese. They had spent much of their adult lives in Korea, and Bruce was author of several books on Korean culture.

After the assassination, I was surprised by the coup. With my American background, I really expected the Korean people to show more visible outrage at their loss of freedoms. Surely there were Korean leaders who could have seized the initiative and organized an effort to counter the coup. There had been widespread student demonstrations, and of course the uprising in Kwangju, but for the most part, I was amazed by the passivity of the Korean people.

From December 12 onward, the Koreans tolerated the illegal seizure of political power and the loss of freedoms that resulted from the imposition of full martial law. This tolerance of oppression, or their resignation in the face of it, was a both a surprise and disappointment to me. It complicated my role as military commander.

My predecessor General Vessey had given me a perceptive book—*Korean Patterns*, by Paul Crane. Jack's handwritten inscription read: "This book is an absolute must for anyone taking this job." Crane describes a revealing aspect of Korean culture to which I should have paid more attention the first time I read it:

> One of the great virtues of Koreans is their ability to endure hardship. Korea is the land of those who have learned to endure in order to survive. If it cannot be escaped, one endures oppression, corruption, injustice, and physical torture with stoic calm. One dreams of the day when he will be liberated. In Korea there is no set of ethical or religious teachings in the culture that tend to bind anyone to abstract principles. Anything that one must do to survive is usually right.

Some critics might argue that the author tended to oversimplify Korean culture, or that his observations were based more on the oppressive periods of Japan's occupation and the savagery of the Korean War, than on modern times. Clearly, economic prosperity, the growth of freedom, and the widespread aspirations for a better life among all Koreans had altered South Korea's society. Still, I am convinced that Crane's observations held grains of truth. From my perspective, the Korean people appeared to be willing to "endure." American officials who were familiar with Korea's culture perhaps should have expected that Koreans would not rise up as a whole against the coup leaders and the repressive actions they imposed on society. If I had understood this better, then my frustrations would have been lessened, and American policy might have been better focused and more tolerant of the politico-military realities in Korean society.

U.S. authorities might have pursued more vigorous economic penalties, such as restricting Korean imports to the United States and imposing restraints on credit and economic aid. To be sure, these measures would have hurt average Koreans, but that anger might have led the people to protest against what was happening.

On the military side, we had pushed back the timing of the Security Consultative Meeting and withheld Foreign Military Sales credits and the sale of some modern weapons that we knew were needed by the

ROK armed forces. These actions obviously failed to accomplish their intended purpose of forcing Chun and his associates to toe the constitutional line. Nor did they elicit protests among the Korean people, since the military censors made sure that their countrymen knew little of what the United States was doing.

What these military penalties did accomplish was to irritate Chun and the rest of the ROK military. Coming on the heels of the Vietnam War and the withdrawal of some of our forces from Korea, our actions only fueled further doubts among Korean military leaders about the reliability of the United States as a strategic partner. That, of course, complicated my professional relationships with my ROK counterparts. They let me know in very pointed terms that they wished I had been more effective in persuading my American superiors to be more tolerant of the politico-military realities in Korea and in contributing to the enhancement of our combined defenses against a growing threat. They viewed the delay of the SCM and the withholding of military sales as inconsistent with our mutual goal of strengthening defenses. I heard quite a few such angry opinions from my Korean military friends.

None of this is to say that the United States should have tolerated undemocratic developments in Korea. We were quite right in protesting the loss of freedoms for the Korean people and the illegal behavior of Chun and his associates. We were on sound ground in urging Chun to support the rule of law and to comply with the constitutional process. The American people would expect no less, and I fully agreed with the official U.S. protests. I conveyed them in unvarnished terms to my ROK counterparts, even though I knew that I sounded like a broken phonograph record. But in retrospect, the United States was not prepared to take an active role in overthrowing Chun, with all its attendant risks of bloodshed and North Korean intervention. Chun's seizure of power was irreversible, and the Korean people ultimately came to accept this reality. Therefore, the limited policy tools we applied served only to alienate the Koreans and did nothing to reverse Chun's seizure of power or to force him to comply wholly with the constitutional process.

The Korean people expected the American authorities to protest any loss of freedoms as well as human rights abuses in their country, even as they were quick to criticize any direct interference in their domestic affairs. It was a curious attitude—a discordant note—that resulted from the disparities between the two nations and the overwhelming U.S. role as the protector of ROK sovereignty. America's officials did vigorously protest

the events that followed Park's death, although we did not actively encourage the Koreans to rise up, as that would have violated the sovereign
ties between our countries. The line between acts of influence and outright interference always was difficult to identify.

Also, there were practical reasons why Koreans accepted the oppression, instead of violently attempting to overthrow the coup leaders.
Koreans knew that their military leaders had seized control over the army
and the national police forces, and that these leaders could crush any resistance. For many months, Chun and his associates retained the facade of
a civilian government headed by President Choi, and repeatedly claimed
that they sought no political power. "Trust us," they said, and that tended
to lull Koreans and Americans alike. These shrewd actions muted the in-
tensity of criticism. But another factor ultimately muted criticism. Every
Korean over the age of 25 recalled the horror of the war that had ravaged
South Korea and would do nearly anything to keep it from happening
again. Virtually every family had a son approaching draft age or perform-
ing military service and was willing to accept the oppression as the lesser
evil, while they "dreamed of better days."

In retrospect, it was inevitable that a prolonged period of domestic turmoil would follow President Park's death. Fearing challenges to his
regime, Park had ingeniously prevented the development of a robust political structure, and his country suddenly found itself plunged into a vacuum with splintered, weak political parties and virtually no popular leaders who could command wide support from the populace or the army.
The "three Kims"—Kim Dae-jung, Kim Young-sam, and Kim Jong-pil—
were well known, but at least two of them were unlikely candidates for
president. Kim Jong-pil suffered from allegations of corruption, and Kim
Dae-jung was accused of having Communist ties. None of the three Kims
enjoyed strong support from the ROK army. Moreover, were they to have
been the principal contenders for president, their fractious campaigning
could have provoked widespread unrest in the countryside. At least, that
was the charge frequently heard from ROK military leaders and many
members of the National Assembly.

Thus, given political candidates who were unpalatable to the
ROK military, coupled with the potential for serious domestic unrest,
something like a military coup was at least probable, if not inevitable.
Nevertheless, not only American policymakers, but most Koreans as well,
were surprised when the coup came.

Should American authorities have tried to prevent a coup, or alternatively, should we have been more tolerant of Chun than we were?

When I heard the rumors that trouble was brewing among some of the junior generals, I reported them to my ROK counterparts, including the minister of defense and my deputy, General Rhu, who dismissed my information as empty rumors. Perhaps if they had acted on my report, the minister of defense and the army chief of staff could have arrested Chun and his associates, heading off the coup which occurred on December 12.

Should I have acted on my own? If so, how? Chun's DSC had agents in every unit from battalion up, so he would have sensed immediately that I was making trouble. Besides, the ROK officer corps was well aware that the CFC CINC only had operational control over those ROK forces designated by the Korean government, and absolutely no authority over national forces. Essentially, I was powerless to prevent a military coup.

As to the question of American attitudes toward Chun after he seized power, in good conscience, I could never have tolerated his actions. Even after all these years, I still consider his actions immoral and harmful. No matter how often he and his associates claimed they were acting out of patriotism, I remain convinced that they were motivated almost completely by personal gain. Chun's actions undermined the CFC chain of command and set in motion a chain of events that could have precipitated a war. Although it's impossible to know what North Korea's leaders were thinking during that difficult period, I remain convinced that a war was prevented by U.S. military and diplomatic actions, and also by the heightened readiness and resolute leadership throughout every level of the CFC.

In America we had experienced constitutional transitions of power after the assassination of President John F. Kennedy and the resignation of President Richard M. Nixon. Throughout American history, even during the infancy of our nation, the threat of a military coup has never surfaced. I consider Chun's claim that his country was too politically immature and unsophisticated to accept democracy to be an empty fabrication.

I believe the U.S. policy of keeping Chun at a distance and pressuring him to abide by his country's constitutional process was fundamentally sound. At times, the U.S. authorities might have hectored too much over human rights abuses and the repression of freedoms, but our emphasis was right on target. Our arms-length policy no doubt irritated Chun and his supporters, but I am convinced it obliged him to accumulate

Presenting a five-star helmet to Ambassador Gleysteen at the Hill Top House on his departure from Korea.

power very cautiously, and it forced him to tolerate the constitutional process in order to become the president of the Fifth Republic.

Should American authorities have supported the counter-coup that was proffered by ROK military officers? On three counts, the answer is no. First, we knew little about the counter-coup faction or what they expected by way of support from the United States. If they desired substantial U.S. military support, and they probably did, then we almost certainly would have been drawn into a domestic conflict. Second, we might have replaced the "devil we knew" for one we did not know. Third, a countercoup inevitably would have led to fighting between ROK military units, and the resulting civil conflict could have attracted North Korean intervention.

Finally, what conclusions might be drawn about my role? Should I have stayed focused on military affairs and been less concerned with ROK domestic affairs? Since I was the combined commander, should I have tried to balance or offset U.S. policy guidance with policy direction from the ROK authorities? And should I have been less responsive to the U.S. Ambassador?

Some officers, including my CFC deputy, General Baek, and the Combined Field Army commander, General Eugene Forrester, believed strongly that I should have established harmonious relations and worked more closely with Chun and his associates. Baek and Forrester assured me that Chun could be trusted and that he meant well for his countrymen and for U.S.–ROK relations.

I recall a strange lunch discussion on this topic with Forrester at his CFA quarters. Gene was a good friend and a National War College classmate, so I was surprised when he blurted out that I had poor and ineffective relations with Chun and his associates. He was very serious as he told me that I did not relate well to my Korean counterparts. Over the years since that conversation I have often wondered whether Gene's criticism was intended as confidential advice, or whether he was indirectly disclosing what he had discussed with his senior military friends back in Washington, perhaps in an effort to have me recalled. He had just returned from a trip to Washington, and the timing of our conversation

My departure ceremony on June 4, 1982, with (from left) Admiral Robert Long, General Kim Yoon-ho, and General Robert Sennewald.

corresponded with Chun's efforts to have me replaced. I thought Gene was a superb field commander—I'm sure he considered himself fully qualified to replace me as CINC—but his apparent lack of loyalty undermined my confidence in him.

If American authorities had sensed that I was ignoring their guidance, or that I was pursuing a course of action that was at variance with U.S. policy, they would have unhesitatingly replaced me with a commander who would abide by instructions. Vital American security interests were at stake in Korea, and I believed that my responsibilities as the commander of both the U.S. and combined forces were to abide fully with the direction from my government. As America's senior officer, I also had to work harmoniously with the President's representative, Ambassador Gleysteen.

Developing a closer relationship with Chun would have violated my instructions from Washington. Even if I could conscionably have allied myself with Chun, I would have created vulnerabilities for other American policymakers that a man with Chun's shrewd cunning unquestionably would have exploited. The damage that could have caused is inestimable.

As to devoting all of my energies to military matters and ignoring domestic affairs, the situation made that impossible. Some in Washington, particularly the readers of my numerous personal messages reporting on ROK internal developments, might have thought that I was spending too much time on domestic matters, though no one ever said so to me. Moreover, I knew that I had unique access through my extensive professional and personal contacts with the ROK military and was convinced that my reporting was valuable to Washington analysts and policymakers. Many senior Koreans came to see me on their own, and I could not turn them away or ignore what they said. Moreover, I believed that the better informed Washington officials stayed, the more supportive they would be of our work in the military field.

As it was, anyone who really understood Korea would have recognized the virtual impossibility of separating military from political affairs. In view of the ominous North Korean threat and the preeminent role played by the army under the ROK constitution, not to mention under President Park's 18–year regime, the two were inextricably linked. It would have been a fool's errand for me to have ignored or attempted to separate ROK domestic issues from my military responsibilities, particularly after the coup, when ROK army officers intruded deeply into every aspect of political affairs.

In *Korea Patterns*, Crane observed that the Korean military, though traditionally rated low in the Confucian order, wielded the power needed to propel Korea's rural economy into the modern, technologically advanced nation it is today. President Park's era was seminal. The military drew from and developed some of the best trained and dedicated leadership in the nation. After it became a four-year institution, the Korean Military Academy attracted the country's top high school students, who graduated as first-rate professionals with solid undergraduate educations. Perhaps more importantly, the military services fostered a unifying sense of purpose, vision, and national pride. Its leaders believed that the military fulfilled a vital, perhaps historic, role as the "guardian of the nation's security and future." One consequence of this attitude is that some military leaders, even today, tend to disdain politicians as self-serving, sometimes corrupt, and unwilling to sacrifice for the greater good of the Korean people.

My political superiors told me that both the close personal and professional relationships I enjoyed with ROK military officials provided invaluable leverage for American policy and the efforts to persuade Chun to abide by constitutional processes and to be less repressive. An example was the relative moderation shown by the ROK army the second time it entered Kwangju. I had repeatedly urged moderation upon General Rhu and others and was later told by several senior ROK officers that my efforts helped lead to the decision to delay the second assault. Moreover, some of my suggestions about how to use the 20th Infantry Division troops helped minimize the number of casualties, in contrast with the earlier assault by the ROK Special Forces. Of course, American authorities had no prior knowledge and therefore no influence over the Special Forces assault.

In summer 1988, lingering bitterness over the Kwangju massacre motivated the ROK National Assembly to establish a Special Committee on Investigation to look into the May 18th Kwangju Democratization Movement. The United States agreed to cooperate with the ongoing investigation by the National Assembly. In November the Special Committee formally invited Ambassador Gleysteen and me to testify in Seoul.

After careful consideration of diplomatic precedents and the legalities of former U.S. officials testifying before a foreign government's legislature, the U.S. Department of State determined that it would be inappropriate for Bill and me to appear before the Committee on any matters related to our official duties in Korea. Bill and I therefore did not testify, but the State Department agreed to provide written answers to questions prepared by the Special Committee and to make available a detailed statement by the U.S. Government concerning the events in Kwangju. Bill Gleysteen and I assisted in the preparation of the statement and the answers to the questions. The official document (see appendix) was released to the ROK Government and the media on June 19, 1989.

Subsequent to the issuance of this official document, numerous meetings took place with the ROK press and the representatives of various groups in Korea. The purpose was to help clarify any misunderstandings and to answer questions. I attended several of these meetings, including a long interview with a dozen Korean journalists who were very sharp in their questioning.

These meetings may have helped some to better understand the American role, but there are still myths that somehow or other Washington "allowed" Chun to come to power, that the United States "tolerated" Chun's abuse of power and suppression of freedoms, and that our military leaders, specifically me, either "looked the other way" or in fact "authorized" the use of ROK army forces to engage in domestic law-and-order missions that ultimately led to the massacre of protestors in Kwangju. Many Koreans understandably remain bitter over the Kwangju incident, and they seek justice by punishing the officials responsible for the tragedy.

Epilogue

During late 1995, in an extraordinary development, ROK Government prosecutors arrested former Presidents Chun Doo-hwan and Roh Tae-woo on charges of mutiny, treason, and accumulating hundreds of millions of dollars in bribes from Korean industrialists. Chun was arrested on December 3 in his hometown of Hapchon in North Kyongsang province, and immediately taken to Anyang Prison. Some 19 other Koreans, including prominent businessmen, members of the National Assembly, and several retired generals—all of whom had been associated with the two ex-presidents—also were arrested on related charges. I was shocked by the arrests, because I knew virtually all these individuals and their families and had worked closely with most of the South Korean military leadership during my three years in that country.

The arrests were the result of a special law, named for the May 18 Kwangju massacre, that was enacted by the National Assembly in December 1995. President Kim Young-sam had initially announced that he would not support such a law but had changed his mind, announcing, "The coup of 17 May 1980 tarnished the honor of the state and people as well as the pride of the nation, to the grief of all of us. . . . I will show the people that justice and law are still alive in this land." The law overrode a 15–year statute of limitations to allow charges to be brought against Chun, Roh, and those who aided them in their 1979 takeover of the government and the bloody suppression in Kwangju.

Roh was the first ex-president to be investigated, on the charge of having received more than $500 million in bribes from commercial firms. The investigation grew out of revelations made on October 19, 1995, in the National Assembly by an opposition assemblyman, Park Kye-dong. At his trial, Roh claimed he never took bribes while in office. Rather the money he accumulated was reputedly contributed by "businessmen during my private meetings with them, but not in return for favors. The money was routine contributions that I received as part of my ruling fund." In response to questioning on whether he had contributed any money to candidates for the presidency in 1992, particularly Kim Young-sam, who eventually was elected, Roh said "I cannot disclose it because if I do, it would bring great confusion to the nation!" This curious statement fueled speculation among many Koreans that Kim may have received funds, and that to deflect criticism, he had reversed his position and decided to support the May 18 special law. His motive would have been to create a vehicle to focus public attention on the prosecutions of Chun and Roh.

During the Roh investigation, prosecutors also examined the allegations of payoffs received by Chun. As a result, on December 21, 1995, both Chun and Roh were indicted on charges of graft and military rebellion in connection with the "12/12 Incident". The historic trials of 16 individuals began on March 11, 1996 at the Seoul District Criminal Court. Like Roh, Chun claimed that any monies he received while in office were only for purposes of election campaigning and had not influenced any government contracts. Furthermore, Chun and Roh asserted that they were innocent of all charges, including those relating to mutiny and treason. They said they had been merely doing their duty to protect the nation and to lead it into a new era of prosperity.

In opening the trial, prosecutors told the court that "the incidents (December 12 and May 18) significantly altered the course of history of the Republic of Korea. It is hoped that during this trial, hidden truths will be uncovered and that it will serve as an occasion to bring genuine justice to the land." The prosecutors accused Chun of being responsible for the massacre of the demonstrators in Kwangju by army troops who used the inherent right of self-defense as an order to fire on unarmed civilians. They said, "Chun gave the instructions that led to the invocation of the self-defense right."

In addition to Chun and Roh, the defendants included retired Generals Chu Yong-bok, a former air force chief of staff and minister of defense during most of my tour; Chung Ho-young, a former army chief of staff who also had been minister of home affairs and a member of the National Assembly; Yoo Hak-sung, assistant minister of defense logistics during the "12/12 Incident"; Hwang Yung-si, a former army chief of staff, devout Christian, and personal friend; Lee Hee-sung, former army chief of staff; and Cha Kyu-hun, former transportation minister and commander of the Second ROK Army. Indictments against three other army

With South Korean officers along the demilitarized zone.

officers were suspended because they had escaped abroad. They were re-tired generals: Park Hee-do, Chang Ki-oh, and Cho Hong.

After extensive testimony and a lengthy trial the prosecutors de-manded severe sentences: death for Chun; life in prison for Roh, Hwang, and Chung; 15 years imprisonment for Yoo, Cha, Lee, and Chu. In an im-passioned conclusion the prosecution claimed, "It is the call of the times for our generation to liquidate the mistaken legacy of the past lest those criminal acts should be repeated, which disrupt the constitutional order and suppress the people's freedom or which generally corrupt the na-tional economy through bribery," Chun and Roh claimed that their in-dictments amounted to a political circus created by President Kim Young-sam in an effort to bolster his low esteem with the public and to divert attention from the fact that Kim had received substantial campaign funds from both Chun and Roh.

In his final statement before the judges, Chun concluded:

I alone was responsible for all things and I am ready to go to prison, or even to die, if the people so wish. From the date I returned home alone after losing so many important figures in Burma (where North Korean terrorists exploded a bomb in an attempt to assassinate Chun), I have been living with the belief that heaven had given me an extra life and dictated me to better serve the nation. I therefore am not afraid of any punishment. All I wish is that the punishment would prevent any split of public opinion and the waste of national energy. Lastly, I sincerely wish that the practice of trying the leaders of a former regime in political reprisal would come to an end with the case of myself.

Roh, who appeared very contrite with his head bowed and voice barely audible, made the following admission:

As a man who once assumed unbounded responsibility toward the people, I have no intent of shunning any responsibility. All histories have both dark and bright sides and it is unreasonable to judge things that took place under past conditions with today's yardstick. I still believe that I had done my best under the then social and political conditions following the assassination of President Park Chung-hee. But, I feel sorry for failing to rectify ill political practices and to honorably dispose of large funds. I looked back over myself in the past 10 months of imprisonment. The conclusion I reached was that I never received any bribe or took money for my personal fortune building. And I never thought of using the money for personal purposes after my retirement. Today's trial will not end in the trial of Roh Tae-woo himself but will remain an issue of our history.

Both Hwang Yung-si and Chung Ho-young, for whom the prosecutors demanded life imprisonment, closed their final statements with the following emotional remarks:

[General Hwang] I had been working with the sense of mission that I, as a soldier, was helping defend the homeland. If there still was any sin on my part, I would humbly accept punishment. I hope this trial will serve to console the souls of victims and help promote national harmony.

[General Chung] I first wish to say I am sorry to the bereaved families of Kwangju's victims. I haven't been living a life with lies, excuses, or nasty tricks. The statements I made during the trial were all true. I couldn't say fully because if I did, it could give the impression that I was shifting blame to my subordinates. I was shocked to hear the prosecution demand life imprisonment for me. I hope the court will give a verdict based on facts. I thank the prosecution for not taking legal actions against field army commanders in Kwangju at that time. If my sacrifice is needed, I think it is my fate. I repeat that we had no intent of seizing power or causing rebellion through the Kwangju incident.

Toward the end of August, the Seoul district panel of three judges found the two ex-presidents guilty of mounting a coup in 1979, and also of the May 1980 massacre in Kwangju.

In plain prison garb, holding each other's hands as military academy classmates and close friends, Chun and Roh stood solemnly before the judges, awaiting their sentences. Millions of Koreans viewed the historic scene on television and in the media. Roh appeared contrite, his head slightly bowed. Chun's manner showed no remorse. Some Koreans who saw Chun's face must have recalled the ancient saying, *chol myon pi*, or "iron face skin." The saying was used to refer to someone so tough and shameless that his skin would be more than just thick, it would be like iron.

Chun received a death sentence and Roh was given twenty-two and a half years in prison. Twelve other generals were sentenced to varying prison terms ranging from four to ten years. Subsequent verdicts were handed down for other generals, former presidential aides, and business executives. The death sentence was automatically appealed to the next higher court, and court-appointed defense attorneys appealed sentences for the remaining defendants. In addition to prison sentences, Chun was fined $132 million and Roh $158 million. Although the size of these fines was unprecedented, they were substantially less than the fortunes accumulated by the ex-presidents while in office. Perhaps the judges took into account their disbursements for legal fees and political campaign donations in 1992.

In December of 1996, the appellate court reduced the sentences of the Seoul District Court. Chun's sentence was commuted from death to life imprisonment, and Roh's sentence to 17 years in prison. The fines were dramatically reduced as well. In rendering their opinion, the judges noted that the public service performed by Chun and Roh during their presidencies led to significant progress for the nation and deserved to be taken into account as mitigating factors.

On April 17, 1997, the Supreme Court addressed the cases of Chun and Roh and upheld the convictions by the lower courts. The justices concluded: "Military action that wounded and killed persons demonstrating during the Kwangju incident advanced the cause of treason. This rendered guilty those charged with murder in pursuit of treason."

Korean politics played a key role in the decision by President Kim Young-sam and President-elect Kim Dae-jung to pardon the ex-presidents and 23 accomplices in December 1997. In announcing the pardons, the Blue House spokesman stated that it was necessary to achieve a "grand national unity" to overcome the pressing economic difficulties facing the nation. Kim Young-sam recalled "how precious blood, sweat, and tears had to be shed in order to right the wrong of a history tainted by the seizure of power that disgraced the nation and the people. . . . Such things should not take place any more in our history."

Most Koreans are not vindictive. They believe that the pardons are acceptable, if not desirable, particularly in light of the ex-presidents' generally commendable public service while in office, the prison time already served, and the enormous shame that will be suffered by the ex-presidents and their families for the rest of their lives. Moreover, many Koreans viewed the trials and convictions as partisan because of the legal wrangling over the statute of limitations. Political pressure eventually forced Kim Young-sam's government to abandon its previously stated position of leaving the verdict to history and to take belated legal action against the two ex-presidents. Additionally, for many Koreans, the public trials and severe sentences symbolically went a long way toward assuaging their anger and bitterness. Of course, many citizens of Kwangju may never be entirely willing to forgive.

In the wake of these dramatic convictions and subsequent pardons, the Korean people have turned an important page in their postwar history. These actions called for courage and political maturity. The new page continues the process of institutionalizing South Korea's basic freedoms and civil rights. The new page also reveals that the Korean people will no longer tolerate or endure any revocation of their constitutional rights. Nor will they accept, as they have in the past, military dictatorships in place of a democratically elected president, a truly representative National Assembly, and an independent judiciary. Before the economic troubles in 1997, Korea's economy ranked 11th in the world. This monumental economic achievement reflects enormous credit on the thirst for education and the work ethic of the Korean people. But the achievement also pays tribute to the abiding, close friendship between Americans and Koreans. Most importantly, it is a monument to the military strength of the Combined Forces Command, which continues to maintain peace on the peninsula.

Si Chak i pan i ta—so goes the old Korean proverb which roughly translates as "Getting started is half the job." Closing the book in a resounding way on its repressive, totalitarian past, the people of South Korea have made an impressive start on the institutionalization of democratic freedoms, basic human rights, and respect for law. It remains in America's interest to support the Korean people as they make that journey.

Appendix: United States Government Statement on the Events in Kwangju, Republic of Korea, in May 1980 (June 19, 1989)

Introduction

The United States welcomes efforts to establish the facts about the events which occurred in Kwangju in May 1980. It recognizes that the lack of an accurate historical record has generated widespread misunderstanding. This statement presents the facts about what the U.S. did and why, in the belief that this is in the best interests of the close friendship which exists between the United States and the Republic of Korea.

A clear understanding of U.S. views and actions requires that they be viewed in the context of events from the assassination of President Park Chung Hee on October 26, 1979 to and beyond the actual events in May 1980 in Kwangju City. This statement therefore begins with the assassination of President Park.

When the Special Committee on Investigation of the May 18th Kwangju Democratization Movement was established by the National Assembly of the Republic of Korea in the summer of 1988, the U.S. agreed to cooperate with its investigation. On November 23, 1988, the Ministry of Foreign Affairs of the Republic of Korea delivered to our Embassy in Seoul letters from the Committee addressed to Ambassador William Gleysteen and General John Wickham inviting their testimony before the Committee.

On December 2, 1988, after careful consideration of the relevant diplomatic precedents and legal principles with regard to such testimony, the Department determined that it would be inappropriate for Ambassador Gleysteen or General Wickham to testify before the Committee on matters related to their official duties as U.S. officials in the Republic of Korea. They were so advised and they concurred in this view. However, the Department agreed to answer written questions from the Committee. On March 17, 1989, the Embassy of the Republic of Korea in Washington conveyed to the Department of State forty-eight questions prepared by the Special Committee. This statement reflects those relevant events and actions as known to the U.S. Government, as can best be determined at this time. Answers to the Committee's questions are incorporated in the Appendix to this Statement, with references to the pertinent paragraphs in the Statement and, as appropriate, clarifying comment.

Summary

- The United States had no prior knowledge of the assassination of President Park Chung Hee on October 26, 1979. The United States was shocked by the assassination and alarmed that the North might see it as an opportunity to attack the South. The United States was also concerned that the prospects for democratization in the ROK might be undermined.

- The United States had no advance warning of the December 12 (12/12) incident, in which a group of ROK army officers led by Major General Chun Doo Hwan seized control of the military.

- The United States was angered by the generals' use on December 12, without proper notification, of units under the Operational Control (OPCON) of the Combined Forces Command (CFC), deeply concerned over the use of force to usurp power, and troubled at the prospect of instability if the principle of civilian authority was not quickly and firmly reasserted.

- The United States protested repeatedly and vigorously to the Korean government, to Major General Chun, and to the Korean military about the misuse of forces under CFC OPCON.

- The United States was deeply disturbed by the evidence, gradually accumulating after the 12/12 incident, that Korean military leaders did not intend to relinquish de facto control or set a timetable for democratization.

- The United States repeatedly urged the Korean civilian and military authorities to resume the democratization process, warned against the repression—specifically that any actions against politicians, such as arresting Kim Dae Jung, would prove "incendiary"—and forcefully protested when leading opposition figures were arrested.

- The Korean authorities gave the United States two hours' advance notice of the declaration of full martial law, which began at 0001 on May 18. The United States had no prior knowledge of the Korean military authorities' intentions to arrest political leaders and close the universities and National Assembly. On May 18, in both Seoul and Washington, the United States sharply and vigorously protested the implementation of martial law.

- The United States did not initially know the full extent of the violence in Kwangju. When it became aware of the seriousness of the situation the United States repeatedly urged restraint by ROK military forces and issued a public statement on May 22 expressing concern over the civil strife in Kwangju and calling for dialogue between the opposing sides.

- The United States was assured by Korean authorities that its May 22 statement calling for dialogue would be broadcast and distributed in the city. This never happened. Instead, official radio reports in Kwangju falsely asserted that the U.S. had approved the dispatch of Special Warfare Command (SWC) troops into the city.

- Neither troops of the SWC nor elements of the 20th Division, employed by the Martial Law Command in Kwangju, were under CFC OPCON, either at the time they were deployed to the city or while operating there. None of the Korean forces deployed at Kwangju were, during that time, under the control of any American authorities. The United States had neither prior knowledge of the deployment of SWC forces to Kwangju nor responsibility for their actions there.

- The 1978 Agreement establishing the Combined Forces Command preserved the sovereign right of both the United States and the Republic of Korea to assert OPCON over their respective forces at any time, without the consent of the other party. The United States could neither approve nor disapprove the movements of elements of the 20th Division which had been removed from OPCON.

- The United States was informed that Korean military authorities were considering the use of elements of the 20th Division—one of the few regular army units trained in riot control—to reenter Kwangju. United States officials, who had pressed for a political rather than military solution and continued to caution against the use of military force to solve political problems, reluctantly accepted that, if negotiations failed, it would be preferable to replace SWC units with elements of the 20th Division.

- The United States protested to the Korean government and Korean media over public distortions of United States' actions and policy which included claims that the U.S. knew in advance of the December 12 incident, of Chun's appointment to the KCIA, of the government's actions of May 17 and that the U.S. approved the SWC actions in Kwangju.

- No information indicating a North Korean intention to attack was received by the United States during the period covered by this statement, nor did United States officials regard the domestic situation in the South as being so serious as to justify either Full Martial Law or harsh repressive measures.

- Throughout this period, however, the United States was concerned that the North might miscalculate the situation in the South and warned Pyongyang against trying to exploit it. Also, as a precaution, the United States deployed air and naval units to the area to demonstrate to North Korea the United States' resolve to stand by its security commitment to the ROK.

- Despite strenuous efforts, the United States failed to persuade Major General Chun to restore civilian authority and to institute a timetable for democratization. The United States, however, was successful in drawing international attention to the charges against Kim Dae Jung, which it characterized as "far-fetched," and in obtaining a commutation of his death sentence.

Statement

The Combined Forces Command and Operational Control

1. To understand the responsibilities of the Combined Forces Commander, it is necessary to review the nature of the Combined Forces Command (CFC). The CFC is a binational military command comprised of both Korean and American officers. The CFC was established in 1978 by joint agreement between the governments of the Republic of Korea and the United States to deter external aggression against the Republic of Korea and, if deterrence fails, to defeat the attack. Its sole mission is defense against external attack. The CFC, whose Commander is an American officer and whose Deputy Commander is a Korean officer, is subordinate to a binational Military Committee headed by the Chairmen of the Joint Chiefs of Staff of the Republic of Korea and the United States. Each nation places certain selected units under the Operational Control (OPCON) of the Commander-in-Chief (CINC/CFC), but retains the national right of command, including the right to remove units from CFC OPCON upon notification. In the event of notification, the CFC Commander can neither approve nor disapprove, but can only point out the effect such removal might have on the CFC's mission of external defense. Once forces are removed from CFC OPCON, the CFC Commander no longer has authority over them.

The Assassination of Park Chung-Hee

2. The United States Government (USG) was surprised and shocked by the assassination of Park Chung Hee on October 26, 1979. In light of the possible military threat from North Korea, the USG immediately warned Pyongyang not to try to take advantage of the assassination and issued the following statement:

> "The United States Government wishes to make it clear that it will react
> strongly in accordance with its treaty obligations to the Republic of Korea to
> any external attempt to exploit the situation in the Republic of Korea."

The United States followed up this statement by dispatching an aircraft carrier to the waters off the Korean coast and sent airborne warning and control aircraft to the region.

3. Immediately following the assassination, Korean military authorities, following appropriate agreed upon procedures, notified the CINC/CFC that the Korean army would assume OPCON of a number of units, including the 20th Infantry Division, for deployment to Seoul as a precaution against possible disorders in the wake of the assassination. OPCON of the 20th Division artillery and its three regiments reverted from CFC to the Korean army at 0230 hours on October 27. The Korean army returned the division artillery to CFC OPCON on 30 October and one of its three regiments on November 28. (There is no record that the other two regiments of the 20th Division were ever returned to CFC OPCON.)

4. Concerned about the domestic political situation in Korea, Secretary of State Cyrus Vance, at a press conference on October 31 prior to his departure for President Park's funeral, stated:

> "We hope that political growth in the Republic of Korea will be commensurate with economic and social progress."

While in Seoul Secretary Vance met with President Choi Kyu Ha and urged him to release political prisoners and to consult with the National Assembly and the political opposition in drafting a new constitution that provided for direct election of the president.

The December 12, 1979 Incident (The "12/12 Incident")

5. The United States had no advance warning of the December 12 incident, when a group of ROK army officers led by Major General Chun Doo Hwan forcibly removed the ROK military leadership. In late November 1979, Gen. Wickham became aware of some "unrest" among senior members of Korea Military Academy (KMA) classes 11 and 12. When he informed CFC Deputy Commander Gen. Lew Byong Hion and ROK Defense Minister Ro Jae Hyun, they regarded the reports as mere rumor.

American officials first became aware of the incident early the evening of December 12 when the Eighth Army Command Post at the Yongsan U.S. garrison (the "bunker") began to report unusual troop movements. General Wickham and Ambassador Gleysteen went immediately to the bunker where they began to piece together fragmentary but alarming reports of troops moving around the city and of shots being fired. Almost from the beginning they suspected that a coup of some sort was underway. Later, they were joined by Defense minister Ro and Kim Chong Hwan, Chairman of the ROK Joint Chiefs of Staff, who established radio and telephone contact with some elements of the ROK military.

6. During that night, units under CFC OPCON were moved by their commanders without proper retrieval of OPCON or even the knowledge of the CFC. Seeing this as a weakening of the CFC's defensive capability, General Wickham that same night formally protested to Korean military leaders and urged the Ministry of National Defense (MND) to suspend until dawn movement of forces loyal to the MND to avoid clashes between army units. At the same time, word was sent to Chun Doo Hwan warning him of the dangerous implications of a conflict within the South Korean forces.

7. U.S. officials were concerned over the possibility of serious armed clashes between Korean army units and the possibility that such a conflict could be seen by North Korea as an opportunity to attack. Ambassador Gleysteen sought to telephone President Choi to express his concern but was unable to reach him. The Ambassador was told that the fighting involved troops sent to arrest Army Chief of Staff General Chung Sung Hwa. Gen. Chung had refused an "invitation" by Maj. Gen. Chun Doo Hwan, principal investigator of Park's assassination, to come in for questioning about the assassination. Amb. Gleysteen also tried to contact the forces headed by Maj. Gen. Chun to warn them of the danger from North Korea of fighting within the ROK army and the threat to political stability posed by their actions. They refused direct contact with USG officials until they had established effective control.

8. The U.S. Government was very concerned that the December 12 seizure of power would lead to an interruption of the democratization process, to which it attached great importance. Wanting both to caution North Korea and to deter civil conflict, the U.S. decided to issue a statement of warning to all concerned. The substance of this statement was brought to the attention of Blue House Secretary General Choi Kwang Soo and at least indirectly to the rebellious officers. The U.S. Department of State issued the following statement the next day:

> "During the past few weeks we had been encouraged by the orderly procedures adopted in the Republic of Korea to develop a broadly based government following the assassination of President Park. As a result of events today in Korea we have instructed our Ambassador and the Commander of U.S. Forces in Korea to point out to all concerned that any forces within the Republic of Korea which disrupt this progress should bear in mind the seriously adverse impact their actions would have on the ROK's relations with the United States. At the same time, any forces outside the ROK which might seek to exploit the current situation in Seoul should bear in mind our warning of October 27."

The statement was written in Seoul on the night of December 12, 1979, but—as a practical matter—had to be issued from Washington because the Embassy lacked access to the government controlled public media to disseminate it to the Korean people.

9. On December 13, Ambassador Gleysteen met with President Choi. He stressed that it was the view of the United States that Korea needed civilian control of the military and continuation of the program of political liberalization. Gleysteen concluded from his meeting, however, that it was unlikely that the weak administration under President Choi would ever be able to gain effective control of the army. Assistant Secretary of State for East Asian and Pacific Affairs Richard Holbrooke also that day, December 13, in Washington, underscored U.S. concern in a meeting with the Korean Ambassador.

10. On December 14, Ambassador Gleysteen met with Major General Chun Doo Hwan. The Ambassador strongly warned that disunity in the Korean army invited North Korean attack and noted that the United States was very concerned. He also stressed to Chun the importance of maintaining constitutional order and of making progress towards political liberalization. Chun replied that the 12/12 incident was an accidental outgrowth of a legitimate effort to carry out his investigation of the assassination of President Park. Chun said that he had no personal ambitions, that he supported President Choi's liberalization program, and that he expected unity in the military to be strengthened as a result of his changes in the command structure.

11. To demonstrate U.S. anger over the December 12 seizure of power, General Wickham refused to meet with Chun on the advice of the Ambassador. Instead, Wickham met with the Prime Minister, the new Defense Minister, and other officials; his message was stark and strong—the movement of ROK Army troops under CFC OPCON without prior notification to CFC ran an unacceptable risk that the CFC would not be able to defend against a North Korean attack. Gen. Wickham also conveyed this point in writing and emphasized it in numerous discussions with senior ROK military officers.

12. To deliver to the ROKG the message of U.S. displeasure with the events of December 12 as strongly as possible, President Jimmy Carter wrote a personal letter to President Choi on January 4, 1980. The U.S. Embassy disseminated the contents of this letter throughout the Korean government and military. President Carter applauded President Choi's plans for political reconciliation and constitutional change. He noted he was "deeply distressed" by the events of December 12 and warned that similar occurrences in the future "would have serious consequences for our close cooperation."

U.S. Policy following 12/12

13. The White House, Department of State, and Department of Defense reviewed U.S. policy toward Korea following the 12/12 incident and reaffirmed U.S. objectives:

- attempt to preserve momentum toward a broadly based democratic government under civilian leadership;
- continue to deter North Korean aggression;
- strive to keep the new ROK military leadership focused on its primary role of defending the country against attack".

14. USG officials recognized that their options were limited. Threats to lessen or remove U.S. military support would lack credibility and risk encouraging North Korean adventurism. Economic sanctions might aggravate South Korea's already serious economic situation, cause social unrest, and play into the hands of those advocating strongly authoritarian policies in the South.

15. The U.S. understood that U.S. actions would not be decisive in affecting the direction of Korea's domestic politics, although it hoped to promote democracy to the degree possible. U.S. officials believed that despite whatever actions were undertaken by the U.S., the outcome of Korea's political transition would ultimately be decided by how the system itself reconciled conflicting pressure.

16. From the beginning there was strong suspicion both in Washington and among U.S. officials in Seoul that the political trend was away from democracy toward authoritarian rule. Nevertheless, the U.S. did not accept as inevitable that General Chun's ascendency in the army would preclude democratization in Korea. With few illusions about where the real locus of power lay or about Chun's ultimate objectives, the U.S. decided that its best and only feasible course would be to continue to express support for President Choi's civilian government while advocating, at every opportunity, that it implement a timetable for democratization. Also, the U.S. recognized the need to continue urging the young generals who had seized control of the army on December 12 to refocus their attention away from intervention in politics and back to legitimate defense matters.

17. Thus, over the next few weeks, the U.S. coupled expressions of support for President Choi and for setting a timetable for democratization with warnings to military leaders of the dangers of upsetting the democratization process and of failing to focus on the continuing, genuine security threat posed by North Korea.

18. On February 14, 1980, General Wickham met with General Chun. This was their first meeting since the December 12 incident. The CFC commander emphasized the importance of civilian government, democratization, and adhering to CFC OPCON procedures. Afterwards, Wickham reported to Washington that he was not certain he had been able to make any impression on Chun.

19. Still, there had been some favorable developments. The formal constitutional order was preserved, Kim Dae Jung's civil rights were fully restored, political prisoners were released, media censorship slackened, and there was a significant relaxation of constraints on student political activity on campus.

20. However, economic conditions continued to deteriorate. In March and April the military began to talk of "instability." Partial martial law and selective media censorship continued. USG officials were concerned that the ROK Government had still not committed itself to a specific timetable for democratization, including the lifting of martial law. Large-scale, but generally non-violent student protests reemerged over this issue.

21. Especially disturbing and surprising to the U.S. was Chun Doo Hwan's sudden appointment as KCIA Director on April 14, 1980. To show its disapproval, the United States announced to senior Korean officials the indefinite postponement of the Security Consultative Meeting (SCM), which is held annually between the ROK Defense Minister and the U.S. Secretary of Defense. The U.S. hoped that this would signal that Chun's move to consolidate his position could impair ROK-U.S. relations.

22. Among American officials in Washington as well as in Seoul, concern grew that Gen. Chun was seeking to manipulate the political situation to further increase his power. Senior officials of the State Department, Department of Defense, and White House met in Washington on May 2 and reaffirmed U.S. policy to do what it could to promote constitutional reform and to encourage a political outcome, acceptable to the Korean people.

23. U.S. officials were alarmed by reports of plans to use military units to back up the police in dealing with student demonstrations. On May 8 Ambassador Gleysteen was instructed to stress these U.S. concerns to Korean government officials. On May 9 Ambassador Gleysteen met with General Chun Doo Hwan, who blamed the unrest on "a small number" of student radicals, professors, and ambitious politicians. He said the situation was not critical, however, and that military force would be used only as a last resort. Ambassador Gleysteen expressed the U.S. view that real stability in Korea required that the people recognize that orderly progress was being made toward political liberalization. He added that it was important not to alienate moderate students and the populace in general; he specifically cautioned against repression of opposition politicians. Afterwards, amidst widespread speculation that martial law would be lifted and a political democratization schedule announced, Ambassador Gleysteen reported to Washington that there seemed a good possibility that upcoming student demonstrations would be treated with moderation.

24. Also on May 9, General Wickham met with the ROK Defense Minister and the Chairman of the Joint Chiefs of Staff to point out the dangers of escalation if troops were used against civilians. General Wickham told them that he was obliged to stress the importance of coordination with CFC before movement of any troops under CFC OPCON so as not to impair the ability of the CFC to fulfill its mission of deterring North Korean aggression.

Toward Full Martial Law

25. Within days, however, this optimism began to fade. During the second week of May, numerous reports began reaching the Embassy that hardline elements were calling for a crackdown on students. The Blue House informed Ambassador Gleysteen and the Korean army informed General Wickham that the Korean Government might take back OPCON of some units from the CFC.

26. General Wickham met Chun Doo Hwan on May 13. In contrast to what he had told Ambassador Gleysteen previously, General Chun now told General Wickham that North Korea was the hidden hand behind the student demonstrations and that the decisive moment for an attack on the South might be at hand. Wickham replied that the U.S. as always stood ready to defend Korea, but that there was no sign that a North Korean invasion was imminent. General Wickham asserted the U.S. view that movement toward political liberalization would bring stability to South Korea and that stability was the principal means of deterring North Korea. General Wickham reported that Chun's pessimistic assessment of the domestic situation and his stress on the North Korean threat seemed only a pretext for a move into the Blue House.

27. On May 13, Washington reacted to reports from Ambassador Gleysteen and General Wickham and to rumors of North Korean activity then circulating in Seoul. The State Department press spokesman stated:

> "From our information we see no movement of troops in North Korea out of the usual and we see no movement which would lead us to believe that some sort of attack upon the South is imminent."

28. On May 14, Ambassador Gleysteen met with Blue House Secretary General Choi Kwang Soo and urged restraint. General Wickham was absent from Korea. Lieutenant General Rosencrans, Deputy Commander of U.S. Forces Korea, delivered the same message to the Defense Minister. Ambassador Gleysteen also appealed to Kim Dae Jung, Kim Young Sam and other politicians to make every effort to head off confrontation. Although opposition leaders were clearly reluctant to appear to be serving the government's purpose by calling for restraint, the Ambassador reported that they were beginning to do what they could in this regard. He also told Washington that the censored press was not reporting calls for moderation by opposition politicians.

29. Although the student demonstrations had grown to massive proportions, the police, without the military, were able to contain them. U.S. observers reported that given the tremendous political tension and the numbers of those involved in the protests, there was considerable restraint from violence on both sides. However, Embassy officers were concerned that troops had been deployed in some areas to back up the police.

Events of May 16–17

30. There were no demonstrations in Seoul on May 16, and student leaders announced a suspension of further demonstrations until after a National Assembly session scheduled for May 20. The U.S. noted a widespread perception that the demonstrations had sobered the government, and that the National Assembly would demand the lifting of martial law and the publication of a timetable for democratization. ROK officials reinforced this impression by announcing that President Choi was cutting short his Middle East trip. He returned to Seoul on May 17.

31. Also on May 16, military authorities notified CFC officials of their intent to remove the 20th Division's artillery and its 60th Regiment from CFC OPCON. The CFC received the Martial Law Command's OPCON retrieval notification while General Wickham was in the United States on official duties. CFC Deputy Commander, Korean four-star General Baek Sok Chu, responded for the CFC, acknowledging the OPCON release notification, but requesting that other forces be provided to replace the 20th Division troops being transferred to control of the Martial Law Command.

(See Para 3 above for account of removal of three of the Division's regiments plus artillery on October 27 and return to CFC OPCON of the artillery on October 30 and one of the three regiments on November 28.)

32. The discernible lull in demonstrations continued through Saturday, May 17. However, concerned over the hardline stance being taken within the government, Ambassador Gleysteen met Blue House Secretary General Choi Kwang Soo. Ambassador Gleysteen urged the Korean government not to let the military dictate hardline policies and specifically warned that any actions against politicians, such as arresting Kim Dae Jung, would prove "incendiary." The Ambassador was not told by Choi of the imminent decision to impose full martial law.

Full Martial Law

33. Early in the evening of May 17, U.S. officials learned of the arrests of student leaders on one campus. The U.S. had no information about the impending arrests of opposition politicians or other repressive measures. Around 9:30 P.M. that night, U.S. officials were informed by the Blue House that full martial law was to be imposed at 0001 hours on May 18. By then, reports of the arrests of Kim Dae Jung, Kim Young Sam, Kim Jong Pil, and other political leaders were making clear the sweeping nature of the government's actions. Acting on instructions from Washington, Ambassador Gleysteen called on President Choi on May 18 to deliver a sharp U.S. protest, stating that the U.S. found the May 17 crackdown and the move to full martial law, "shocking and astounding." President Choi responded that his government had been forced to declare full martial law because it feared it would be toppled by uncontrollable student demonstrations. Ambassador Gleysteen, acting on instructions, also called for the release of opposition leaders including Kim Dae Jung. He also made a forceful protest to martial law commander Lee Hui-Seung.

34. At the Ambassador's instruction, his special adviser delivered the same strong U.S. protest directly to General Chun Doo Hwan. General Chun responded with the same argument as President Choi about uncontrollable demonstrations by students. He added that leadership of the demonstrations had been taken over by "radical" elements. Ambassador Gleysteen reported to Washington that he did not believe that justification. He felt the full martial law order, the accompanying arrests, and the suspension of the National Assembly meant that "the military (had) all but formally taken over the country."

35. When Korean Ambassador Kim Yong Shik called upon Assistant Secretary of State for East Asian and Pacific Affairs Richard Holbrooke on Sunday morning, May 18, Holbrooke informed the Ambassador that the Department of State was issuing a public statement at 1 P.M. that day deploring the extension of complete martial law throughout Korea. Kim protested the U.S. statement, but Holbrooke said future statements would be even more critical if events "continued down the present path." He warned that relations between the U.S. and Korea would be endangered.

36. The State Department issued the following public statement in Washington on May 18 and again on May 19:

> "We are deeply disturbed by the extension of martial law throughout the Republic of Korea, the closing of universities, and the arrest of a number of political and student leaders. Progress toward political liberalization must be accompanied by respect for the law. However, we are concerned that the actions which the government has now taken will exacerbate problems in the Republic of Korea. We have made clear the seriousness of our concern to Korean leaders, and we have stressed our belief that progress toward constitutional reform and the election of a broadly based civilian government, as earlier outlined by President Choi, should be resumed promptly.

We urge all elements in Korean society to act with restraint at this difficult time. As we affirmed on October 26, 1979, the U.S. Government will react strongly in accordance with its treaty obligations to any external attempt to exploit the situation in the Republic of Korea."

37. On May 20, the new Secretary of State, Edmund Muskie, addressed the situation in Korea in a press conference, stating:

"I must say that my reaction to the Korean situation is one of deep concern that it is moving away from liberalization policies, which I think are essential to its long-term political health. I would hope that all elements of the society would exercise restraint in this transition period, and that those in authority will find it expedient and appropriate to move in the direction of political liberalization."

38. On May 21, the Department's spokesman stated, in response to a press inquiry:

"The reports of escalating confrontation in Kwangju are most disturbing. The United States repeats its urgent call to all parties to exercise restraint. We have seen reports that military security forces are pulling out of the city to establish a cordon around it."

"We have also been informed that efforts are underway to develop a conciliatory dialogue, but it is not clear at all whether this effort is going to be successful."

Events in Kwangju

39. To recapitulate, the Korean authorities gave the U.S. two hours' advance notice of the declaration of full martial law. Neither the CFC Commander nor the Ambassador anticipated the subsequent closing of campuses and the National Assembly, the arrests of political leaders and journalists or the intrusion of military officers into various civilian areas, including the media.

40. The Korean military units used for full martial law fell into two categories—those which had never been under CFC OPCON at the normal alert status prevailing in May, 1980, and those which had been removed from CFC OPCON. The brigades mobilized from the Special Warfare Command (SWC) and the 31st Division, based in Kwangju under the 2nd ROK Army, had not been under CFC OPCON. Elements of the 20th Infantry Division had been removed from CFC OPCON (see paras 3 and 31). None of the forces deployed at Kwangju were, during that time, under the control of any American authorities.

41. U.S. officials were caught up in a maelstrom of activity Sunday morning May 18, as they protested the imposition of full martial law and attempted to ascertain its scope and meaning, especially the arrests of Kim Dae Jung, Kim Young Sam, Kim Jong Pil and other political leaders. U.S. observers reported that armed martial law troops were occupying college campuses and guarding key facilities throughout Seoul, but were unaware of any reports of significant clashes.

42. Embassy officials did not know the situation in Kwangju was starkly different from that in Seoul. It was not until the morning of Monday, May 19, that the U.S. received its first fragmentary information on violence in Kwangju, when David Miller, American Cultural Center Director there, telephoned the Embassy. Miller said Kwangju citizens told him that serious rioting was taking place in the city and that Special Warfare troops were responsible for numerous casualties and even some deaths. A U.S. military official in Seoul received a similar telephone call on May 19 from an acquaintance in Kwangju.

43. Since the situation in Kwangju which these reports described contrasted so greatly with the sullen, repressed but non-violent atmosphere in Seoul, it was at first difficult for the Embassy to understand their full significance. It was believed that any disturbances in Kwangju would be brought under control without the loss of life, as had been generally the case with earlier demonstrations.

44. Korean media, strictly controlled by martial law censors, also reported nothing Sunday, May 18 or Monday, May 19 about the events in Kwangju. The U.S. Embassy's fragmentary knowledge of developments in Kwangju during May 19 and 20 was based on bits of information from American Cultural Center Director David Miller; on limited observations from U.S. Air Force officials at an air base some 12 miles outside the city; and, increasingly, on the reports of foreign journalists. However, Miller's information was scanty as he had been ordered by the Embassy to remain indoors for security reasons. Official Korean sources either denied there was any particular problem in Kwangju or downplayed the seriousness of events there.

45. General Wickham returned to Seoul from the United States on May 19. He realized that he would need continuous and accurate information on the serious situation in Kwangju, which could affect his mission of defending the Republic of Korea against external aggression.

46. All available channels were used to urge moderation and patience. The key channel was military, through General Wickham, whose primary contacts were General Lew Byong Hion and the ROK Joint Chiefs of Staff. Gen. Wickham also remained in constant touch with Ambassador Gleysteen. The Ambassador urged civilian officials, including the President and Prime Minister, to work for restraint, to seek contact with the citizens of Kwangju and to seriously consider apologizing or expressing regret for the excessive use of military force. Ambassador Gleysteen also made contact with leaders of the Catholic Church, who were urging the same thing.

Troop Deployments: Special Warfare Units and the 20th Division

47. The U.S. had neither authority over nor prior knowledge of the movement of the Special Warfare Command (SWC) units to Kwangju. SWC forces were not under CFC OPCON. When the U.S. had finally pieced together a picture of what had happened in Kwangju, Ambassador Gleysteen concluded that overreaction by Special Warfare troops was the basic cause of the tragedy.

48. By May 20, U.S. officials had become aware that the ROK military authorities were considering use of 20th Division units in Kwangju. The 20th Division was one of the few regular army units trained in riot control. The Korean authorities asserted that the 20th Division would be perceived by the populace of Kwangju as less confrontational than the Special Warfare troops then in the city.

49. U.S. officials in Seoul agreed that use of the specially trained 20th Division—if negotiations to bring about a peaceful resolution of the crisis failed—would be preferable to continued deployment of the SWC against the citizens of Kwangju. General Wickham and Ambassador Gleysteen therefore responded to a query from the ROK authorities—after consulting with their own superiors in Washington—that they reluctantly accepted that it would be preferable to replace SWC units with elements of the 20th Division. (General Wickham asked that the 20th Division's heavy artillery remain near Seoul so it would be available in view of the continuing threat from the North, and this was done.)

50. Although the martial law command was not required to notify the CFC of the movement to Kwangju of elements of the 20th Division as it was no longer under CFC OPCON, it did so on May 20. U.S. officials assumed this was done because following the unnotified movement of units under CFC OPCON on December 12, Gen. Wickham had protested repeatedly and forcefully. It was also a fact that the movement of the division from its normal area of operations near Seoul would lessen its availability in case of a military emergency.

51. In subsequent publications and interviews Ambassador Gleysteen has stated that the U.S. "approved" the movement of the 20th Division, and a U.S. Department of Defense spokesman on May 23, 1980 stated that the U.S. had "agreed" to release from OPCON of the troops sent to Kwangju. Irrespective of the terminology, under the rights of national sovereignty the ROKG had the authority to deploy the 20th Division as it saw fit, once it had OPCON, regardless of the views of the U.S. Government.

52. By the time the special forces were withdrawn to the perimeter of Kwangju on May 21, the U.S. Government was well aware of the extreme seriousness of the situation. The Korean Government asked the U.S. Government to help deter North Korea from taking military advantage of unrest in the South. In response, the U.S. on May 21 dispatched two E–3A Early Warning Aircraft to the Far East to watch for any signs of North Korean activity. Some major U.S. Naval units were also deployed near the peninsula.

53. On May 22, the U.S. made a public announcement, on Ambassador Gleysteen's advice, which both warned North Korea and called for dialogue between opposing sides in Kwangju:

> "We are deeply concerned by the civil strife in the southern city of Kwangju."

> "We urge all parties involved to exercise maximum restraint and undertake a dialogue in search of a peaceful settlement."

> "Continued unrest and an escalation of violence would risk dangerous miscalculation by external forces."

> "When calm has been restored, we will urge all parties to seek means to resume a program of political development as outlined by President Choi."

> "We reiterate that the U.S. Government will react strongly in accordance with its treaty obligations to any external attempt to exploit the situation in the R.O.K."

Although this statement and subsequent ones were broadcast by the Voice of America, they were not carried by the Korean media. Ambassador Gleysteen and General Wickham were assured by Korean military authorities that the May 22 U.S. statement would be broadcast and airdropped into Kwangju. Leaflets containing the statement were printed, but U.S. authorities discovered later that they were never dropped or distributed. U.S. officials also discovered later that, on the contrary, the local government-controlled radio in Kwangju was reporting that the U.S. had approved the dispatch of the SWC forces into Kwangju. Ambassador Gleysteen protested this disinformation to the Korean government and demanded an official retraction. It was never given.

54. On May 22 at a high level policy review meeting on Korea chaired by the Secretary of State, it was decided that U.S. policy toward Korea in the face of the Kwangju incident was to:
- advise the Korean government to restore order in Kwangju through dialogue and minimum use of force in order to avoid sowing the seeds of wide disorder;
- after resolution of the problem in Kwangju, continue pressure for "responsive political structures and broadly based civilian government";
- continue signals that the U.S. would defend South Korea from North Korean attack.

55. On May 23, Ambassador Gleysteen met with Acting Prime Minister Park Choong Hoon. Gleysteen told Park that the policy decisions of May 17 had staggered the U.S. The U.S. agreed that the ROKG had an obligation to maintain public order, but the accompanying political crackdown was political folly and clearly had contributed to the serious breakdown of order in Kwangju. Gleysteen stressed that political progress must resume when calm was restored; the situation would not stabilize unless the people had hope for the future. The same day, Ambassador Gleysteen had lunch with a bipartisan group of National Assemblymen and discussed U.S. views on Korea. The Korean language press reported that the Ambassador had expressed "understanding" or "approval" of the events of May 17. However, this was not true. At the luncheon, Gleysteen had expressed strong disapproval of the arrest of political leaders, the closing of the National Assembly and of the general political clampdown that began May 17.

The Kwangju Lull and Negotiations

56. As for Kwangju, both Wickham and Gleysteen encouraged martial law officials to enter into a dialogue with citizen groups in Kwangju to seek a non-violent end to the confrontation. Ambassador Gleysteen urged Korean authorities to talk to an ad hoc, informal citizens' committee comprised of concerned civic and religious leaders who were trying to restore peace to Kwangju. Gleysteen also maintained contact with the Catholic Church to support its efforts to promote dialogue. When David Miller, the Director of the American Cultural Center in Kwangju, left the city for Seoul on May 24, he carried a message from Bishop Yun in Kwangju for Cardinal Kim which stated that the ROK Government would have to apologize for the SWC's actions in order to defuse tensions in the city. Ambassador Gleysteen endorsed the concept of an official apology for the misconduct of the Special Warfare units in Kwangju.

57. On May 24, General Lew Byong Hion told General Wickham that the martial law command had finalized plans to reenter and retake Kwangju. General Wickham acknowledged he could not dictate to the martial law command, but he pointed out to General Lew that using military force to solve political problems usually made the situation worse. Use of the military could erode popular support for the government and might raise the possibility of mutiny within the army. Gen. Wickham forcefully argued for restraint. He also urged that, if military units were sent to reoccupy the city, operational plans be carefully worked out to minimize the use of force and prevent needless casualties. Lew promised restraint. Wickham reported to Washington that the likelihood of martial law command forces having to reenter Kwangju was low because both he and Gleysteen believed that the Citizens' Committee was having some success at calming the situation.

58. On May 25, however, the U.S. Government began receiving ominous signals. The Korean Foreign Ministry asked all foreigners to leave Kwangju, a step presumed to presage further military action and potential violence. The U.S. Embassy and other embassies collected the names of their nationals who had not yet left Kwangju. The U.S. Air Force unit at Kwangju Air Base, which was able to make local phone calls into the city, tried to contact the citizens of various countries. Ninety-one nationals of the United States, Canada, Italy, Great Britain and South Africa gathered at Kwangju Air Base. Twenty-three of them were evacuated by the U.S. Air force on May 26; the rest stayed at the base. Several U.S. and other non-Korean citizens, including Peace Corps volunteers and missionaries, elected to stay in Kwangju.

59. Korean military authorities also began to tell the U.S. on May 25 that hard-core radical students had taken-over the city, that their demands were excessive, and that they did not seem interested in good faith negotiations.

The Retaking of Kwangju

60. The next day, May 26, Blue House Secretary General Choi Kwang Soo informed Ambassador Gleysteen that the local ROK military commander in Kwangju had been given discretionary authority to reenter the city and the operation would begin soon. Gleysteen said he realized the Korean government wanted the incident ended, but suggested that all non-military options be exhausted first. He also specifically said that it would be a mistake for the Special Warfare forces to be involved in the reoccupation of the city.

61. It was only a few hours before the beginning of the operation to retake Kwangju, when it was already common knowledge that an attack was imminent, that someone in the provincial capital building asked a journalist to relay to Ambassador Gleysteen a request that he act as a mediator. Gleysteen declined a telephoned request to mediate with the Martial Law Command because he believed such a role was inappropriate for the U. S. Ambassador and would not be accepted by the ROK authorities.

62. After martial law forces entered the city in the early morning hours of May 27, the Martial Law Command informed the CFC commander that the operation had been well-conducted and that, except for 30 persons killed after refusing to surrender their arms, casualties had been "light."

63. The bulk of forces used were from the 20th Division, not the SWC, which had provoked the incident. However, SWC troops, wearing regular army uniforms to disguise their identity, had conducted the final-assault on the provincial capital building and other places in Kwangju and, only after the end of fighting, had turned over their responsibilities to 20th Division forces.

Kwangju Aftermath: U.S. Policy

64. In a May 28 evaluation for Washington, Ambassador Gleysteen concluded that a group of army officers had taken power step by step and that an atmosphere of military occupation now permeated the country. The United States had been "demonstrably unsuccessful in trying to stop the march of these self-appointed leaders or even to slow them down." He concluded that, in essence, these leaders had discounted U.S. reactions because they thought that Washington had no option but to acquiesce. Gleysteen predicted that if Chun Doo Hwan and his group continued on their course there was the definite possibility of long-term instability in Korea.

65. On May 31, a high-level meeting in Washington considered the next steps the United States should take. Further meetings were held throughout June. To avoid signaling U.S. acceptance of the young generals, it was decided to take a "cool and aloof" public stance toward them. It was also decided to seek ways to encourage the new ROK power structure toward resumption of constitutional reform and elections. USG officials hoped that the generals, in the first stages of consolidating their power, would modify their actions to avoid public confrontation with the United States.

66. The United States decided not to threaten disruption of the ROK-U.S. security relationship (as opposed to taking political steps to demonstrate our displeasure, which was done) because of the North Korean military threat. U.S. policy makers, however, noted that dictatorship and instability in South Korea would eventually erode public and congressional support in the United States for the security relationship. In a May 31 TV interview, President Carter declared that the two considerations that underlay U.S. policy in Korea—South Korean security and human rights—had not changed. Carter stated firmly that the security commitment had not been shaken, but he also noted that democratization had been "given a setback" and that the U.S. was urging the Koreans "to move as rapidly as possible toward a completely democratic government."

67. Upon instructions from Secretary of State Muskie, Ambassador Gleysteen met with Chun Doo Hwan on June 4 and told him that recent events in Korea since May 17 had caused serious concern in the USG. Gleysteen told Chun it was unfortunate that ROK Special Forces had been used in Kwangju. They had been very rough and were not intended for crowd control, but for use on North Korean invaders. They were too tough ever to be used against South Koreans. The Ambassador hoped this tragic aspect of the incident could be publicly acknowledged. Chun told Gleysteen that he regretted that they had to be used, but that they were used as a last resort to control the situation.

68. In a June 26 meeting with Chun, Ambassador Gleysteen laid out U.S. views. Gleysteen stressed the need for overall progress toward political liberalization and the difficulty of sustaining the basic security and economic relationship in the absence of such an evolution. He urged an end to martial law. Gleysteen also complained that many Koreans believed that the U.S. Government was at fault for the Kwangju incident because of misinformation that had been broadcast. Chun responded that the U.S. should not worry about anti-Americanism in Korea because there were only a few who were using the issue for their own purposes.

69. Again, under instruction from Secretary of State Muskie, Gleysteen met with Chun Doo Hwan on July 8 to emphasize to him the Secretary's view that Chun had "abused" the U.S.-ROK security relationship. Gleysteen stressed to Chun that the long-term security relationship between the U.S. and Korea required that the Korean government have the support of the majority of its people.

Distortions of the U.S. Position

70. The U.S. policy of aloofness and public displeasure with the Chun takeover was known to the world, but not to the Korean people. The Chun regime used its control over the media under total martial law to distort the U.S. position, portraying it not as condemnation but as support. The distorted official radio reports of U.S. support for the actions of the Special Warfare forces in Kwangju and the authorities' reneging on their agreement to drop leaflets containing a U.S. statement supportive of a negotiated Kwangju settlement were only the first deceptions. On May 23, the Korean press distorted Ambas-

sador Gleysteen's remarks to National Assemblymen as "understanding" or "approval" of the events of May 17 (as noted Paras 54–55).

71. Immediately after the end of the Kwangju incident, Chun Doo Hwan gathered a group of Korean publishers and editors and told them that the United States had been informed in advance of the December 12 seizure of power, of his appointment at the KCIA, and of the declaration of full martial law on May 18. Ambassador Gleysteen sent the Embassy Press Attache to each of the media figures Chun had met with to set the record straight, but none reported the true U.S. position—nor, under martial law, could they. The Associated Press did quote the Embassy's denial which made explicit that Chun's statement "simply was not true and Chun knew it." The AP report, however, was not carried in the Korean media.

72. Under martial law, statements by U.S. officials on Korean developments were regularly ignored and distorted by the Korean media. Whenever a U.S. official mentioned support for the ROK-U.S. security arrangement, that statement was highlighted, but statements urging democratization and human rights were downplayed or not carried at all. On June 22, the U.S. Embassy took the highly unusual step of publishing its own compilation of statements by U.S. officials on Korea and mailing it out to over 3000 people in Korea. In response to Korean disinformation and to clarify U.S. policy, Deputy Assistant Secretary Michael Armacost appeared before a House Foreign Affairs Committee subcommittee on June 25 to discuss recent events and U.S. policy in Korea. On June 26, Gleysteen complained directly to Chun about misinformation on the U.S. role in Kwangju being broadcast.

73. Manipulation of the facts by the Korean media continued through the summer with the misquoting of President Jimmy Carter's strongly worded letter to Chun Doo Hwan upon his election to the Presidency on August 27, 1980. Carter said that political liberalization must resume in Korea, but the controlled media reported it differently. Korean newspaper headlines read: "Carter: Personal Message to President Chun Expresses Support for Korea's New Government" (*Donga Ilbo*) and "Security Commitment to Korea: The Major U.S. Policy" (*Joong-ang Ilbo*). A heavily censored wire service report of September 2 read (deleted material in parentheses):

> "President Carter said today that South Korea's new president, Chun Doo Hwan, should move quickly to restore democracy (and complete freedom of expression) to his country. Mr. Carter urged the liberalization of South Korea's political life when he answered a question at a town meeting held as he campaigned for re-election in November. (He said he believed the South Korean government should move faster toward complete freedom of expression and of the news media and should eliminate imprisonment of political opponents.) "Mr. Carter said his views were clear and were well-known to President Chun. (He said he would continue to use his influence to persuade South Korea to move towards a democracy.) At the same time, reconfirming U.S. security commitments to South Korea, Mr. Carter said . . . "

The Kim Dae Jung Trial and Human Rights Issues

74. The United States was deeply concerned about the fate of Kim Dae Jung and others who had been arrested. On May 18, the day after Kim's arrest, it protested to the Korean authorities on his behalf. President Carter had met Kim a year earlier and took a personal interest in his case. Although ROK authorities were displeased, they acceded to strong Embassy demands that a U.S. official be allowed to attend Kim's trial. The U.S. went on record after the trial that the charges against Kim were "far-fetched" (a statement not carried by the controlled Korean media). These efforts helped to focus international attention on Kim's case. Some months after Kim Dae Jung had been condemned to death, the Chun Government made it clear to the U.S. that it linked Kim's fate to some degree of normalization in the frigid political relations between the two governments. After extensive discussions with Chun, Kim's death sentence was lifted, and Chun visited the United States early in the Reagan Administration.

Conclusion

75. As outlined in this statement, the United States Government at the highest levels was extremely concerned at events in Korea from December 12, 1979 through the May, 1980 declaration of Full Martial Law and the ensuing Kwangju tragedy, and beyond, as military rule was consolidated and prospects for democracy receded. It is also apparent that despite persistent, strong remonstrances by both military and civilian officials, the United States' efforts had only a marginal impact on events. Human rights and civil liberties issues, nonetheless, remained significant areas of dispute between the U.S. and the Chun Government throughout the fifth republic. The record reveals that the U.S. Government exerted its best efforts for Korean democratization and for restraint of ROK military actions against civilians during this troubled period. The U.S. Government only regrets that U.S. objectives were not achieved at the time: consolidation of civilian, constitutional rule and resumption of the democratization process.

Appendix to United States Government Statement on the Events in Kwangju, Republic of Korea, in May 1980

Thile Appendix contains the written questions addressed to the United States Government by the Chairman of the Special Committee on Investigation of the May 18th Kwangju Democratization Movement. The Department of State received the questions on March 17, 1989 from the Embassy of the Republic of Korea in Washington, D.C. Each question is accompanied by reference to the appropriate paragraph or paragraphs in the United States Government Statement on the Events in Kwangju, Republic of Korea, in May 1980 (hereinafter referred to as the Statement). Some questions are also accompanied by clarifying comment.

It should be recalled that in agreeing to respond to written questions on December 2, 1988 the U.S. Government stated:

"Recognizing that the May 18th Kwangju Movement for Democracy is a matter of great concern to the Assembly and to the people of Korea, and therefore wishing to cooperate as fully as possible with the Committee, the Department is prepared to respond to written questions from the Committee. The Department's response would of course fully incorporate the facts as known by Ambassador Gleysteen and by General Wickham, as well as information provided by other cognizant persons and in relevant documents."

"We would expect such questions to focus on the matter before the Committee, that is, the May 18th Democratization Movement and relevant events. This exchange should also be public."

The furnishing of the Statement and Appendix does not constitute a waiver of applicable privileges and immunities of the United States Government, its officials, or its former officials under international law.

Committee Questions, References To Pertinent Statement Paragraphs And Clarifying Comments

A. Questions About the December 12 Incident of 1979

A.1. It appears that the Kwangju tragedy of 1980 grew out of the so-called "12/12 Incident" of 1979. Did the United States have prior knowledge of the December 12, 1979 incident

involving the arrest of Army Chief of Staff Cheong Sung Hwa by a group of soldiers including then DSC Commander Chun Doo Hwan?
- See Statement, paras 5–6.

A.2. General Sennewald has said that "prior to 1980 reconnaissance aircraft were active over Korea. Inside Korea they could even catch the movements of a single baby ant." That the movement of the troops during the "12/12 Incident," including the movement of the 9th Division which was under Combined Forces Command (CFC) operational control, was not known cannot be understood. From this point of view, to let those Korean units that were guarding the front line move to Seoul during December 12, disregarding their duty, is the responsibility of the CFC Commander, and going one step further, the responsibility of the U.S. What is your opinion of this?
- See Statement paras 5–10.
- General Sennewald made no such statement. Furthermore, no such information gathering capability existed then or now. Elements of the Ninth Division moved into Seoul without the knowledge of U.S. authorities.

A.3. When did the U.S. first come to know of the "12/12 Incident" (from whom), when, and of (sic) the U.S. actions on the matter?
- See Statement, paras 1, 5–12.

A.4. After the "12/12 Incident" you said that you expressed your strong protest and dissatisfaction with the violation of CFC rules by the Korean military. What measures has the U.S. taken to ensure that such a disgraceful event does not happen again?
- See Statement paras 1, 5–12.
- In addition to the strong U.S. action after the "12/12 Incident," the U.S. has continued to work closely with ROK authorities to ensure compliance with CFC procedures. Steadfast U.S. support for democracy in Korea contributes to a stable civilian government and the growth and institutionalization of democratic structures.

A.5. What are the details of the steps taken by the U.S. in regard to the demands made by Defense Minister Ro Che Hyon who had escaped onto the compound of the Eighth U.S. Army?
- See Statement, paras 5–12.
- ROK Minister of Defense Ro Jae Hyun arrived at the bunker command post on Yongsan garrison during the evening of December 12, accompanied by General Kim Chong Hwan, Chairman of the Joint Chiefs of Staff, and several other Korean officers. According to the senior American officials present, Ro and his ROK military colleagues knew little. Ro attempted to contact various ROK officers to persuade them to remain loyal to the government. He left the bunker later that night after receiving what he believed to be a guarantee of personal safety from the Vice Minister of Defense and the insurgent officers. He did this despite Ambassador Gleysteen's and General Wickham's advice to remain in the bunker. On arrival at the Defense Ministry, General Ro was ar-

rested and taken to President Choi's house where documents were signed which authorized actions relating to the arrest of Martial Law Commander General Chung Sung Hwa. Ro was subsequently released.

A.6. Is it true that in early 1980 Chief of Staff Cheong Sung Hwa's direct subordinates sounded out the U.S. side on their plan to remove the officers who were the main culprits in December 12? If so, who did so? It is said that the U.S. refused. If so, why?
- See Statement, paras 13–24.
- There were many rumors of possible military moves against the December 12 insurgent officers in the ensuing months. The U.S. position, well known to all, strongly opposed any extralegal action by any group within the Korean military.

A.7. As the Special Committee's hearings have revealed to a certain degree, Chun doo Hwan, Roh Tae Woo and the generals who grabbed military power through the December 12 incident were the center of administrative power. In the period after December 12 and before May 17, 1980 it is known that the U.S. consulted with this newly emerging military power, the so–called "strongman" group. Who was the channel for this consultation, and what discussions were held?
- See Statement, paras 13–29.

B. Questions Regarding the Expansion of Martial Law on May 17

B.1. What advanced information did the U.S. receive regarding the expansion of martial law in Korea on May 17 and the creation of the Emergency Measures Committee for National Security?
- See Statement paras 21–33.

B.2. There are differing opinions regarding the security situation in Korea during the spring of 1980, that is before the expansion of martial law on May 17. At the time, how did the U.S. analyze and assess the Korean security situation in light of North-South relations?
- See Statement, paras 13–14, 26–27.
- Throughout this troubled period, the U.S. remained alert to the possibility that heavily armed, unpredictable North Korea could perceive an opportunity to exploit the situation and order its massive military forces to attack. The U.S. issued repeated public warnings to forestall any possible misjudgements in Pyongyang and deployed air and naval units to the area. Gen. Wickham spent considerable time in early 1980 visiting front line units and talking with tactical commanders to focus attention on the continuing threat and the need to maintain readiness. However, no indications of an imminent North Korean attack were ever received, and the U.S. never perceived the ongoing military threat from the North as justification for measures taken by the authorities in power in Seoul. As the Statement makes clear, the precise contrary is the case. The U.S. position was repeatedly distorted by the government-controlled media.

B.3. In the Spring of 1980 did the U.S. authorities feel that whatever the student demonstrations, both on campus and in the streets, the danger justified the dissolution of the National Assembly through the expansion to nation-wide Martial Law?
- See Statement, paras 16–38.
- The U.S. consistently held that the situation never justified measures such as dissolution of the National Assembly, expansion of Martial Law, or the arrest of opposition politicians.

B.4. It is known that both before and after 5/17 U.S. authorities were frequently in contact with the leading forces of 5/17. Are you willing to publicly announce the list of those involved in the dialogue and their contents?
- See Statement, entire text.

B.5. In particular, could you not release the, contents of the mid-May meeting between President Reagan's Advisor Richard Allen and Chun Doo Hwan?
- Mr. Richard Allen did not visit Korea in May 1980 nor at any time during that year. Ronald Reagan was not President of the United States in May 1980.

B.6. Also, the consultations on May 9 between Defense Minister Choo Young Bok and General Wiener (Warner), the Commander of the U.S. Readiness Command, who was then in Korea on an inspection tour? What was discussed?
- Meetings and consultations between U.S. and Korean officials which had no bearing on U.S. policy or actions regarding the events within the purview of the Statement are not pertinent. Gen. Warner's visit to Korea was of this nature. Gen. Wickham participated in Gen. Warner's meetings, which dealt with professional U.S. military matters and also involved a number of courtesy meetings with ROK officers.

B.7. What were the contents of the May 10, 1980 discussions between the U.S. Embassy and Mrs. Colbert, the Deputy Assistant Secretary for East Asian and Pacific Affairs of the State Department?
- Mrs. Colbert's discussions in Seoul had no bearing on issues within the purview of the statement.

B.8. What were the contents of the discussion that took place on May 17–18, 1980, when the Ambassador to the U.S., Kim Young Sik called on Assistant Secretary for East Asian and Pacific Affairs Holbrooke at the State Department?
- See Statement, para 35.

B.9. What were the contents of the discussions between Ambassador Gleysteen and Foreign Minister Park Tong Chin on May 19–20, 1980?
- See Statement, para 46.
- All available channels were utilized to urge moderation and patience, including contacts with the Ministry of Foreign Affairs. We have no record of the above cited discussions.

B.10. Did presidential candidate Reagan's Advisor for Foreign Affairs, Retired General Singlaub, visit Korea in mid-May 1980? What was the purpose of his visit and who did he meet?

- During May 1980, Retired General Singlaub was a private U.S. citizen holding no U.S. Government position and did not represent the USG in any capacity. He engaged in no activity that is pertinent to the issues within the purview of the Statement.

B.11. Is it true that in a May 21, 1980 interview with American reporters at the U.S. Embassy you said that "I hope that the political agenda promised by President Choi Kyu Ha will be observed," and that "the U.S. understands the background and the inevitability for the measures to expand Martial Law on May 17?" If so, what do you think was the background and the inevitability?

- No transcript of the interview or alleged remarks can be located. However, as the Statement makes clear, at no time did the U.S. Government or Ambassador Gleysteen indicate that the expansion of Martial Law was appropriate, much less "inevitable." U.S. officials consistently urged a return to civilian rule and the implementation of a timetable for democratization.

B.12. In an interview for the August 1985 edition of *Shin Dong-A* you said that "since we could not know at the time that the situation was developing and because we tried to achieve a peaceful solution we have no reason to apologize." You also said that "reports offered by a USIA officer, Korean employees, Korean journalists, U.S. reporters, the U.S. Air Force Base, etc." were received. Given the fact that the documentaries of those days, which are available now, are all of them photographed by foreign journalists, we cannot understand how the U.S. Embassy, the 8th Army, or CFC could not know these facts. We wish you would please explain.

- See Statement, paras 30–51.

B.13. Before the declaration of the expansion of Martial Law on May 17, 1980 did you request of Kim Dae Jung (currently President of the Party for Peace and Democracy), Kim Young Sam (currently President of the Reunification Democratic Party), or dissident leaders a statement calling for restraint of student demonstrations? If so, what is the reason this was never announced in newspapers or on TV or radio?

- See Statement, para 28.
- Statement, paras 53, 55, 70–73 also document the difficulties encountered in disseminating the American view of events.

B.14. What information on North Korean military activities did the U.S. have during the period from after the December 12 incident in 1979 till May 1980, particularly what were the North Korean front line activities prior to the May 17 expansion of Martial Law in the South? Did you provide the information on North Korea to the Korean military authorities or government? If so, what was reported?

- See Statement, paras 2, 6–8, 10, 11, 13–14, 17, 24, 26–27, 52–54.

B.15. What was the content of discussions between General John Wickham and MND Minister Chu Yong-Bok on May 13, 1980?
- See Statement, paras 24 and 28.
- The record reveals a meeting on May 9 between General Wickham and Defense Minister Chu during which General Wickham warned of the dangers of escalation if troops were used against civilians.
- Also see Statement, Para 26, which records a meeting on May 13 between General Wickham and General Chun Doo Hwan. At the May 13 meeting, General Wickham told Gen. Chun that there was no sign of an imminent North Korean invasion, that political liberalization would bring stability and that stability was the principal means of deterring the North.

B.16. On May 14, 1980, General Wickham returned to the U.S. on official duties. At that time, the mass media reported that the purpose of the visit was for consultation with the Washington authorities on Korea's domestic situation as well as the situation on the Korean peninsula. Was it not to consult (with Washington) on those items that General Wickham had already agreed with the Chun Doo Hwan military group prior to the May 17 expansion of Martial Law?
- See Statement, paras 21–32.
- General Wickham returned to the U.S. for scheduled consultations and to attend his son's graduation from Wake Forest University. He had no discussion with General Chun concerning expansion of Martial Law; to the contrary, as the Statement paras 25–32 makes clear, American authorities including General Wickham did not believe that either the domestic situation or the threat from the North justified repressive measures.

B.17. What did General Wickham discuss with the U.S. authorities at that time, and what was decided? What relation was there between this and the meeting General Wickham had on May 13 with MND Minister Chu Yong-Bok?
- See Comment on Questions B.15. and B.16. above.
- Also see Statement, paras 25–29, which reflect U.S. officials' views and discussions. Gen. Wickham's discussions and reports were a part of this process.

B.18. What are the details of the U.S. Defense Department Announcement saying that on May 12, 1980 at 2230 Hours there was a small scale shooting engagement in an area South of the Joint Security Area in the DMZ?
- Such incidents occurred periodically along the DMZ. No special significance attached to activity along the DMZ during this period. Nothing occurred which would indicate that North Korea intended to attack.

B.19. On May 19, in answering questions by reporters at a briefing, a U.S. State Department Spokesman said that (the U.S.) has not detected any movement indicative of North Korean military provocation. On the other hand, the Korean military side maintained that

"The danger of North Korean military invasion was very serious." Is it possible for Korea and the U.S. to have conflicting assessments of this situation? To what extent was the CFC's intelligence assessment utilized by Korea in its assessment of North Korea?

- See Statement, paras 26–27, 52–53.
- Also see comment on Question B.18. above.
- Although information is freely shared between the US and ROK military authorities, each has an independent assessment capability. It is of course possible that such assessments may differ.
- Questions about ROK military intelligence assessments during this period should be addressed to the ROK military authorities.

C. Questions About the Korean Special Forces

C.1. In an interview for the August 1985 Edition of *Shin Dong-A* you said that "since the Korean Special Forces do not come under the CFC, the U.S. could not know that they were thrown in." What is the reason that the Korean Special Forces do not come under the operational control of the CFC?

- See Statement, para 1.
- Under the CFC arrangements, many combat units of the ROK military are not placed under CFC OPCON at the usual defense alert condition on the peninsula. This was the case with Korean Special Warfare Units in May 1980. They are to be committed to CFC OPCON as the alert status increases, which did not occur in May 1980. It is a sovereign decision for each nation as to which national forces are placed under CFC OPCON.
- During the period under review, the disposition of the Korean Special Warfare forces was not related to external defense, but rather was a domestic matter wholly within the sovereign authority of the Government of the Republic of Korea. Furthermore, the mutual defense treaty permits either party to develop appropriate individual means to deter armed attack.

C.2. When you consider it in light of Article 2 of the Mutual Defense Treaty's "spirit of consultation and agreement," even if the Korean Special Forces do not come under operational control of the Combined Forces Command, wasn't it necessary before they were committed to consult with or seek the cooperation of the U.S.?

- See Statement, para 1, and comment to question C.1. above and D.5. below.
- Article 2 of the 1954 mutual defense treaty provides that the parties will consult whenever either believes that its own or the other party's political independence or security is threatened by "external armed attack," that the parties will develop appropriate means to deter such attack, and that they "will take suitable measures in consultation and agreement to implement the treaty and to further its purposes." It does not provide for consultation on all military or defense matters.
- There was no requirement for ROK authorities to consult with the U.S. before moving Special Warfare units, and they did not consult or inform us before moving them to Kwangju.

C.3. According to Article 2 of the Korean-American Mutual Defense Treaty: ". . . the signatory parties acting singly or together, through unilateral or mutual assistance will take appropriate measures to strengthen themselves to block an armed attack. . ." This implies that an attack on North Korea is impossible without a prior consultation or coordination between the U.S. and Korea. Then isn't the existence of Korean Special Forces, trained primarily for anti-North Korean assault missions such as intelligence gathering in North Korea, harassing the rear, kidnaping and assassination, destruction, etc. a violation of the basic spirit of the Mutual Defense Treaty?

- See Statement, para 1, and comments to Questions C.1. and C.2. above.
- The existence of the Korean Special Warfare forces does not violate the treaty, nor its "spirit."
- ROK Special Warfare Command forces are tasked in the CFC defense plan, although these forces do not become OPCON to CFC until a higher state of readiness alert is declared than obtained in May, 1980.

C.4. In an interview for the August 1985 Edition of the *Shin Dong-A*, Ambassador Gleysteen said, "Korean Special Forces were not under CFC Command and the U.S. could not know of their deployment." What is the reason and background for not including under the operational control of Korean-American CFC the Special Forces Units, which excel beyond all other ROK military units in combat capability and mobility and whose mission is to attack North Korea?

- See Statement, para 1, and comments on Questions C.1. and C.2. above.

C.5. Nevertheless, General Wickham routinely received reports or notifications on the movements of these units and assented to their request for cooperation, why?

- See Statement, para 1, and comments on Questions C.1., C.2., C.3., and C.4. above.
- General Wickham, as CFC Commander, under normal circumstances was advised of the disposition of all U.S. or ROK combat forces on the Peninsula, whether or not under CFC OPCON. However, in May 1980 the ROK authorities were not required to and did not see fit to advise the CINC/CFC of the Special Warfare units' deployment to Kwangju.
- Gen. Wickham tried to keep open all available channels of communication, but he could not ensure that some information would not be withheld from him.
- Questions as to why this was not done should be addressed to the appropriate ROK authorities.

C.6. Ambassador Gleysteen's remarks that "the U.S. could not know the deployment of the Korean Special Forces," is very much different from what General Sennewald had said earlier. Do you agree with what Ambassador Gleysteen said?

- See Statement, para 1, and comments on Question A.2., C.1., C.2., C.3., C.4., and C.5. above.
- Ambassador Gleysteen's observation is accurate.

C.7. What is the basis for assigning the task of "executing the Chung-jong operation," the task of suppressing a popular uprising, to the Special Forces units whose primary mission is to carry out an assault mission against North Korea?

- This question should be addressed to the Korean authorities who made that decision.

D. Approval of the Move of the 20th Division

D.1. In an interview for the July 1988 issue of the *Wolgan Chosen*, Ambassador Lilley said that "the sole obligation of Korean military authorities towards the Combined Forces Command when it withdraws a division is to notify CFC." "According to the CFC Agreement he (Gleysteen) did not have the authority to approve or disapprove the movement of the 20th." Do you think that Ambassador Lilley was correct?

- See Statement, paras 1, 33–51.
- Ambassador Lilley's observation is accurate.

D.2. According to *The New York Times* of May 23, 1980, "The Defense Department has reported that the Korean government has requested the withdrawal from CFC operational control of several ground units to be used for demonstration suppression and security tasks, and the Commander of CFC, General John A. Wickham, has accepted this request." Are the contents of this article factual? If as Ambassador Lilley said the sole obligation was to inform, then was not this request unnecessary and the seeking of advance approval even more unnecessary?

- See Statement, paras 1, 31, 40, 47–51 and comments on Questions C.1., C.2., C.3., C.4., C.5., and C.6. above.
- The ROKG was under no obligation to notify or inform the CFC of movement of elements of the 20th Division to Kwangju, as that move took place after the Division was removed from CFC OPCON by Korean military authorities.
- As the Statement makes clear, after U.S. authorities learned of the serious situation in Kwangju and that the Special Warfare units had inflicted many civilian casualties, both Ambassador Gleysteen and General Wickham concluded that the Special Warfare units had clashed violently with the Kwangju populace. When the Korean authorities asserted that the 20th Division would be perceived by the people of Kwangju as less confrontational than the SWC troops then in the city, Ambassador Gleysteen and General Wickham, after consulting with their superiors in Washington, reluctantly accepted that the use of 20th Division units (which had some training in riot control) would be preferable to the SWC if negotiations failed. Gen. Wickham specifically urged ROK CJCS Lew to use restraint should military force be applied.
- As to why the Korean military authorities acted as they did in regard to the 20th Division, that question should be addressed to the Korean authorities involved.

D.3. According to Ambassador Lilley and the organizational chart of the Korean-American Combined Forces Command, the issue of approving the request for release of the 20th Division from CFC operational control was different than at the time of the 10/26, 1979 incident in that it required a very important decision involving the Kwangju suppression.

Isn't it true that both General Wickham and Ambassador Gleysteen at that time lacked actual power to make the decision on their own?
* See Statement, paras 1, 3, 31, 40, 47–51.
* The legal framework and the authority for removal of the 20th Division from CFC OPCON were the same in October 1979 and in May 1980.

D.4. One regiment of the 20th's Division (the 61st Regiment) began to move to Kwangju at 2230 Hours on May 20. When was the request to remove the unit from CFC operational control received, and when was assent given? And what was the process of deciding on the release of the 20th Division from operational control?
* See Statement, paras 1, 3, 31, 40, 47–51 and comments on Questions C.1., C.2., C.3., C.4., C.5., and C.6. above.

D.5. Under the guidelines of the Korean-American Mutual Defense Treaty, which provision allowed for operational control to be transferred?
* See Statement, para 1, and comment on Question C.1. above.
* No provision in the 1954 ROK-U.S. mutual defense treaty deals specifically with the Combined Forces Command or the issue of CFC OPCON; the establishment of the CFC, and the procedures relating to CFC OPCON, are measures taken under the authority of the treaty.
* The Combined Forces Command (CFC) was established in 1978, by agreement between the Governments of the United States and the Republic of Korea. Pursuant to that Agreement, the Terms of Reference (TOR) for the U.S.-ROK military committee and the U.S.-ROK Combined Forces Command (CFC) provide that the, Commander-In-Chief of the CFC (CINC/CFC) will exercise operational control of combat forces of the U.S. and the ROK that are assigned or attached to the CFC. Both the U.S. and the ROK Governments retain their sovereign right of command over their military forces at all times. They also retain their sovereign right to assert operational control (OPCON) over their forces at any time, and may thus assign such forces to or remove them from CINC/CFC OPCON without the consent of the other party. Only the commander with OPCON can, consistent with CFC procedures, order forces to undertake any movements or military action. Notification to CINC/CFC of removal of forces from the operational control of the CINC/CFC is required as a practical matter in order that CINC/CFC may be aware of the extent of forces under his operational control at any time, to enable him to make appropriate adjustments in force deployments as well as in defense plans.
* At the same time, the U.S. and ROK have recognized the desirability of consultation prior to removal of their forces from CINC/CFC OPCON, for the purpose of ensuring that such removal does not jeopardize the ability to respond to external armed attack. Such consultation furthers the CFC goal of deterring and defending the ROK against external aggression and is consistent with the provision in Article 2 of the 1954 Mutual Defense Treaty that the parties will consult whenever, in the opinion of either, the political independence or territorial integrity of either is threatened by external attack.

D.6. Did you have a prior consultation on the replacement of the Special Forces troops which were deployed to Kwangju with the 20th Division?

- See Statement, paras 1, 31, 40, 47–51, and comments on Questions C.1., C.2., C.3., C.4., C.5., C.6., and D.2. above.
- There was no requirement for consultation regarding movement of the Special Warfare units or of the 20th Division, after it was removed from CFC OPCON.
- Discussion between U.S. and ROK officials of the 20th Division's move did take place, and is described above, in the referenced paras of the Statement and in comments on the Questions noted.

D.7. After the 20th Division was deployed to Kwangju the Special Forces continued their violent actions for a certain period of time. In particular, very early in the morning of the 27th the Special Forces carried out the suppressive action against the provincial government building. What do you think of the assertion that the 20th Division was not sent to Kwangju to replace the Special Forces troops but to reinforce them?

- See Statement, paras 56–63.

D.8. On December 21, 1988 at the Kwangju hearing the then Commander of the 20th Division, Park Joon Byong, testified that "operational control over the 20th Division was received from CFC on October 27, 1979. Is this true?

A. If it is true, then at that time, too, were the procedures of the Korean side making a request and the CFC consenting observed?

B. Under CFC rules, after permission is received to withdraw a unit from CFC operational control, when and under what circumstances is it supposed to be given back to CFC?

C. Has there ever been a case where you were notified of the recovery of operational control?

D. At such time, were you notified that the entire division was recovered at the same time?

- See Statement, paras 1, 3, 31, 40, 47–51.
- Procedures for notifying withdrawal of the 20th Division from CFC OPCON on October 27, 1979 were observed. Return to CFC OPCON is routinely notified, although there are no written provisions for either withdrawal or return of units. Removal of OPCON normally involves either written or electronic means if time permits or verbal notification if the matter is more time critical.
- CFC rules do not address the issue of when and under what circumstances return of troops to CFC OPCON is to occur.

D.9. Is it true that on May 23, 1980 you approved the request for the removal from operational control of one battalion of the 33rd Division to restore order in the Kwangju area?

A. If it is true, on what basis and for what goal did you give your assent?

B. What was the reason for subsequently canceling that decision in such an abrupt manner?

- See Statement, paras 40, 47–63.
- We are unaware of any involvement of the 33rd Division in any Kwangju or Kwangju-related event. In 1980, the 33rd Division was stationed on the Kimpo Peninsula and was under CFC OPCON.

D.10. In an interview for the July 1987 edition of *Shin Dong-A* you revealed in substance that "the Korean military requested and permission was granted for the 20ᵗʰ Division which was deployed in Seoul to move to Kwangju." On November 18, 1988 while appearing before a hearing of the Ad Hoc Kwangju Committee, Lee Hee Sung, then Army Chief of Staff, commented on this, testifying that "it seems that Gleysteen's thinking was illusory." Would you please once again state your position clearly in regard to this?
- See Statement, paras 1, 31, 40, 47–51, and comment on Question D.2. above.

E. Questions About the Suppression of the Kwangju Struggle

E.1. Testifying at a hearing of the Kwangju Committee of the National Assembly, Lee Hee Song, the ex-Martial Law Commander said that when the then Commander of the 2ⁿᵈ Army, Chin Chong Che, proposed the operation to suppress Kwangju he said "because it is subject of Korean-U.S. consultations, let's put it off until the 24ᵗʰ of May." After that, on the afternoon of May 26 at 1640 Hours General Robert Sennewald held consultations with General Kim Che Myong. Is this all true? If so, what was the content of the discussion?
- See Statement, paras 52–61.
- Throughout this period, General Wickham and his staff (General Sennewald was Director for Operations) had frequent contact with their ROK military counterparts. American officials at all levels persistently urged caution and restraint. The U.S. Government did not wish military force to be employed to reoccupy Kwangju; it urged negotiated settlement. If military force were to be employed, the U.S. urged utmost care to limit casualties. American officials were not at any point involved in decision making, which was the sovereign responsibility of the ROK Government.
- Only the ROK military officers directly involved could explain the rationale for the General's reported statement. It is possible he was referring to these repeated contacts with U.S. military officers during which the latter urged caution and a negotiated settlement.

E.2. What was the final process of consultation, and what were the points of instruction made by the U.S.?
- See Statement, paras 52–63 and comment on Question E.1. above.

E.3. Although the United States said through a variety of channels before, during and after the Kwangju struggle, that "there is no indication for North Korean military activities," on or about May 27, when the suppression operation against the provincial government building was carried out, U.S. Early Warning Aircraft were dispatched, and the *USS Coral Sea* was moved to a point off of Pusan. What was the goal of these military moves? Who demanded them? Who made the decisions? Also, what was the background?
- See Statement, para 52, and comment on Questions B.2., B.3., B.14., B.18., and B.19.
- Although there were no indications during this period that North Korea was preparing to attack, the presence of massive North Korean forces normally deployed far forward along the DMZ in an offensive posture, plus the belligerent and unpredictable record of the North Korean leadership, gave rise to concern lest they perceive an opportunity

to try to take advantage of the unsettled situation in the South. This led the U.S. to warn the North against provocations and, in coordination with Korean authorities, to deploy air and naval forces to give substance and credibility to that warning.

E.4. Is it possible to send reconnaissance aircraft over Korean airspace or ships into Korean waters without consultations with the Korean side? What is the basis for this?
- No. The U.S. does not enter another country's airspace or territorial waters without appropriate coordination. This applies equally to Korea.

E.5. In the May 26, 1980 edition of *The New York Times* it was reported that "this afternoon (the 24th or the 25th Korean time) student leaders of the Kwangju uprising requested of the U.S. that Ambassador Gleysteen use his good offices to bring about a "cease fire" so as to be able to put an end to the blood-shed." Did you refuse this for the reason that you could not interfere in internal Korean affairs?
- See Statement, para 61.
- Ambassador Gleysteen concluded that the suggested use of good offices was not appropriate under the circumstances for the U.S. Ambassador and would not be accepted by the ROK authorities.

E.6. In an interview for the August 1985 Edition of *Shin Dong-A* you said that "the reason for the breakdown of negotiations between the Korean military and the demonstrators was, in the last instance, the refusal of the radicals to return their arms."
A. Does the Korean military have no responsibility for the breakdown of negotiations?
B. Also, why do you think the radicals refused to surrender their arms?
- See Statement, paras 39–63.
- Questions relating to negotiations between ROK authorities and the insurgent leaders in Kwangju should be addressed to those directly involved.

E.7. During the Kwangju struggle it is said that the U.S. side made an agreement with the Korean authorities for a statement addressed to the citizens of Kwangju to be dropped by helicopter and also broadcast on TV and radio. What was the reason for the Korean authorities breaking their promise? Also, what was the contents of that statement?
- See Statement, paras 53, 70–73.

F. Questions Regarding the Weapons Used to Suppress the Kwangju Struggle

F.1. We know that aside from our own weapons the Korean military uses weapons received via Military Aid Plan (MAR), Foreign Military Sales (FMS) purchase, the Surplus Arms Sales Plan (EDA), and through joint production with the U.S.; and that there are agreements so that these arms cannot be used to massacre citizens of the country. Did you approve the use by troops deployed to Kwangju of helicopters (UH–lH, 500MD, AH–1H, O–1), tanks, APC's, etc.?

- The Arms Export Control Act states that the United States Government may sell or lease defense articles or services to friendly countries under the Foreign Military Sales and Excess Defense Equipment programs solely for internal security, legitimate self-defense, participation in collective arrangements consistent with the U.N. Charter, or economic and social development. These limitations on use are reflected in documents exchanged in each case. Similar restrictions are applied to equipment provided under the Military Assistance Program, as well as co-produced defense articles. Although the term "internal security," as used in the Arms Export Control Act, does not include routine law enforcement activities, it does include the preservation of internal order against armed uprisings and other serious disturbances. In some instances, although not in the case of Korea, statutory provisions or bilateral agreements impose additional limitations upon the uses to which certain defense articles may be put. The United States Government does not typically require its consent to the use in particular instances by a foreign government of defense articles of U.S. origin (unless the use is for a purpose other than that authorized by the U.S. Government).

- In the case of Kwangju, the U.S. Government did not approve, or disapprove in advance the use of any such articles by the ROK armed forces. Based on the information available at the time to the U.S. Government on the magnitude and nature of the situation in Kwangju, U.S. officials did not believe the use of U.S.-provided equipment to restore order would violate the terms of their transfer to the ROK Government. U.S. officials did, however, convey to responsible ROK officials on a variety of occasions concern over the behavior of certain ROK military units and urged against the use of military force to reoccupy the city and for a negotiated settlement. If negotiations failed and troops were sent into the city, U.S. officials urged utmost restraint on ROK military officers to limit casualties.

F.2. If they were used without U.S. approval, this is a violation of the agreements. Has the U.S. ever censured Chun Doo Hwan and his government for this violation? If not, does not this confer tacit approval or ratification?

- See Statement, paras 64–69, and comment on Question F.1. above.

G. Questions About the U.S. Attitude Towards the Kwangju Struggle

G.1. On May 22, 1980 (U.S. time) State Department Spokesman Hodding Carter announced that "the U.S. is very worried abut [sic] the popular strife that has developed in Kwangju in the southern part of Korea. We urge that all sides use the greatest self-restraint, and that a peaceful means for ending this conflict be found through negotiations. Should there be any foreign attempt to use the current situation in Korea, the United States will respond fully under the provisions of the Korean-U.S. Mutual Defense Treaty." What is the reason that this, coming 4 days after the start of the Kwangju incident, was the first public U.S. response?

- See Statement, paras 30–51.

- The U.S. Government spoke out forcefully and repeatedly as soon as it knew about the situation in Kwangju.

G.2. This was already after a large number of citizens had been killed in cold blood by the Special Forces troops. What was the reason that, in spite of this was there no warning or censure against such atrocities and only mention of the security situation on the Korean peninsula?
- See Statement, paras 30–51, 70–73.
- Throughout this period U.S. official statements were repeatedly distorted and censored by the Korean media, which was strongly influenced by the Korean military authorities at that time.

G.3. Isn't it because the Carter Administration, at the same time it was announcing its policy of supporting human rights, thought that the U.S. national interest (the strategic importance of the Korean peninsula against the Soviet Union) was more important than democratization in Korea so that it gave tacit approval to the use of violence (the coup d´ etat) by the military authorities?
- See statement, all paras and comments on Questions G.1. and G.2. above.
- The Carter Administration, like prior and successor U.S. administrations, consistently held that true stability and security can be achieved only by governments which enjoy broad support from the people. This conviction guided the actions of the Carter Administration during the period under review.

G.4. Was it not because of the worry that if there was the slightest mistake in the use of the U.S. direct and physical power of influence that Korea, which had until then been the most anti-Communist and the most-pro-U.S. country in the world, might become a second Iran or Vietnam?
- See Statement, all paras and comments on Questions G.1., G.2., and G.3. above.
- This question is based on totally erroneous assumptions.

G.5. Since 1980 the tide of anti-American sentiment and the anti-American movement have gradually risen in Korea. Why do you think this has happened?
- It is clear that one cause of increased anti-Americanism in Korea in the 1980's is the false impression held by many Koreans that the U.S. was directly involved in and significantly responsible for the Kwangju tragedy—a misperception in part fostered by the deceptions of the Korean authorities at the time, and in part by the restrictions on the dissemination of facts about the Kwangju May 18th Democratization Movement throughout the Fifth Republic.

G.6. It is said that after the Kwangju struggle the U.S. Embassy wanted the creation of a civilian government through fair elections while the UN Command wanted a military government to be created for the sake of Korean security. Is this true? Did General Wickham help Chun Doo Hwan consolidate his power. If so, why?

- Those rumors and allegations are unfounded and untrue.
- The Statement and Appendix clearly demonstrate that throughout this period, the U.S. Government was united in its advocacy of democratization and in opposition to repressive military rule. General Wickham and his staff played a key role along with Ambassador Gleysteen in pursuit of those objectives.

Korean Personalities

Cha Chi-chul. Chief of the Presidential bodyguard and rival of Kim Jae-kyu, chief of KCIA. Cha favored repressive responses to increasing student demonstrations, while Kim favored restraint. Believing that Cha had poisoned President Park's attitude toward him, and fearful that he was about to be replaced, Kim assassinated both Cha and Park.

Choi Kyu-ha. Premier of the ROK under President Park Chung-hee. Appointed as acting president following the assassination. Named Major General Chun Doo-hwan, director of DSC, as lead investigator after Park's assassination. Elected president in December 1979. Coerced during the "12/12 Incident" to sign a document agreeing to General Chung's arrest after the fact. His government, in a relatively weak position, was unable to control the efforts of Chun Doo-hwan to consolidate power. Government concessions to university students led to demonstrations that sparked the military repression in Kwangju during May 1980. Resigned in August 1980.

Chu Yong-bok. A retired ROK Air Force chief of staff at the time of the "12/12 Incident," Chu immediately replaced Rho Jae-hyun as minister of defense.

Chun Doo-hwan. One of the "Taegu Seven Stars," members of Korean Military Academy Class 11 who received early promotions to flag rank. Protege of President Park Chung-hee. Director of DSC and a major general when Park was assassinated. Charged by Choi to investigate the assassination. Believed that a conspiracy to assassinate the president existed between KCIA director Kim Jae-kyu, Blue House Chief Secretary Kim Kye-won, and ROK army Chief of Staff Chung Sung-hwa. Used his position to overthrow the military leadership under the guise of arresting Chung. Appointed director of KCIA and also promoted to the rank of general. Elected president and later arrested on charges of mutiny, treason, and corruption in connection with the "12/12 Incident" and Kwangju massacre. Convicted in August 1996, sentenced to death and a fine of $132 million. Pardoned in December 1997.

Chung Sung-hwa. ROK Army Chief of Staff, was nearby when Kim Jae-kyu, KCIA chief, assassinated Park. Chung supported the appointment of Premier Choi Kyu-ha as acting president. Chung was later arrested (under the pretext of being connected with Park's assassination) by DSC agents on the orders of Major General Chun Doo-hwan, beginning the coup known as the "12/12 Incident." Sentenced to life imprisonment, his sentence was reduced after Chun became president and he was later cleared of involvement in the assassination.

Kim Dae-jung. One of the "three Kims" and a major political opponent of Presidents Park Chung-hee, Choi Kyu-ha, Chun Doo-hwan, and Roh Tae-woo. The government under Choi Kyu-ha and the military under Chun Doo-hwan falsely accused Kim of fomenting the student demonstrations in Kwangju that led to the use of military force to regain control of the city. Kim was convicted of sedition and sentenced to death. His sentence was commuted by President Chun. Elected president in 1997, joined in pardoning Chun and Roh. Inaugurated in February 1998.

Kim Il-sung. First president of the Democratic People's Republic of Korea (DPRK) which was established in Soviet-controlled northern Korea in September 1948. Brutally repressive, launched the invasion of South Korea in 1950. Following the cease-fire agreement in 1953 he continued to provoke incidents involving UN, U.S., and ROK forces. Began military modernization and buildup in 1972, doubling the size of his forces in just three years. Forward deployed offensive-oriented combat forces along DMZ and maintained pressure on South Korean defenses by sending numerous infiltrators across the demilitarized zone. Died in 1994.

Kim Jae-kyu. Director of KCIA, long-time friend of Park Chung-hee, and rival of Cha Chi-chul, chief of the presidential bodyguard detail. Kim favored restraint in response to increasing student demonstrations, while Cha favored repressive measures. Believing that Cha had been conspiring against him, and fearful he would be replaced, Kim assassinated both Cha and Park in October 1979. Hanged in May 1980.

Kim Jong-pil. One of the "three Kims" and a major political opponent of Presidents Park Chung-hee, Choi Kyu-ha, and Chun Doo-hwan. As a ROK army lieutenant colonel, led a military coup from which Major General Park Chung-hee emerged in control. Served under Park's leadership until political differences led him to form an opposition party.

Kim Kye-won. Blue House chief secretary (chief of staff) under Park. Present when Kim Jae-kyu assassinated President Park Chung-hee. Because he escaped unharmed, and did not immediately identify the assassin, DSC under Major General Chun Doo-hwan charged him with complicity. He was convicted and sentenced to life imprisonment. President Chun later reduced his sentence to 20 years imprisonment.

Kim Young-sam. One of the "three Kims" and a major political opponent of Presidents Park Chung-hee, Choi Kyu-ha, Chun Doo-hwan, and Roh Tae-woo. Park had Kim expelled from the National Assembly, which caused other opposition party members to walk out. The president's treatment of Kim sparked student protests over which security chief Cha Chi-chul and KCIA director Kim Jae-kyu disagreed, leading to the presidential assassination. Repressed during Chun Doo-hwan's rise to power, Kim Young-sam eventually succeeded Roh Tae-woo as president.

Lee Hee-sung. Following President Park Chung-hee's assassination, this former ROK army vice chief of staff was appointed KCIA head. After the "12/12 Incident" he was named army chief of staff, a position in which he was also martial law commander.

Mun Hyong-tae. Chairman of the National Assembly Defense Committee, Mun was a retired general and former chairman of the Joint Chiefs of Staff.

Park Chung-hee. Ruled South Korea for 18 years. A major general who assumed power in 1961 through a military coup, assumed the rank of full general, and eventually replaced President Yoon Bo-sun, who resigned. Assassinated in October 1979.

Rhee Syngman (also known as Syngman Rhee). First president of South Korea, inaugurated in 1948. Ousted from office in 1960, after fraudulent elections led to a demonstration in which the police killed 142 students.

Rho Jae-hyun. Minister of Defense under President Park. Coerced, after the fact, during the "12/12 Incident" to sign a document agreeing to General Chung's arrest and the replacement and retirement of several senior military officers. Forced to resign in December 1979.

Rhu Byong-hyun (also known as Lew Byong-Hion). Deputy CINC CFC under Generals John Vessey and John Wickham. After the "12/12 Incident," appointed chairman of Joint Chiefs of Staff and later served as ambassador to the United States.

Roh Tae-woo. One of the "Taegu Seven Stars" of Korean Military Academy Class 11 and a classmate of Chun Doo-hwan. A major general in 1979, he commanded the 9th Infantry Division, under CFC OPCON. Moved elements of his division to Seoul from defensive positions near the DMZ to support the "12/12 Incident." Following the Kwangju massacre, promoted to lieutenant general and appointed chief of the DSC. Succeeded Chun Doo-hwan as president (1988–1993). Arrested on charges of mutiny, treason, and corruption in 1995 in connection with the coup and the Kwangju massacre. Convicted in August 1996, he was sentenced to 22½ years in prison and a fine of $158 million. Pardoned in December 1997.

Glossary

AWACS airborne warning and control system
CIA Central Intelligence Agency
CFA Combined Field Army
CFC Combined Forces Command
CINC commander in chief
CINCPAC Commander in Chief of U.S. Pacific Command
CJCS Chairman of the Joint Chiefs of Staff
DCM deputy chief of mission
DEFCON defense condition (alert status)
DMZ demilitarized zone
DPRK Democratic People's Republic of Korea (North Korea)
DSC Defense Security Command
EUSA Eighth United States Army
FEBA forward edge of the battle area
FROKA First ROK Army
JSA Joint Security Area, surrounds Panmunjom in DMZ
KCIA Korean Central Intelligence Agency
KMA Korean Military Academy
MND Ministry of National Defense
OPCON operational control
PACOM U.S. Pacific Command
PRC People's Republic of China
ROK Republic of Korea (South Korea)
SCM Security Consultative Meetings
SROKA Second ROK Army
TROKA Third ROK Army
USFK United States Forces, Korea
UNC United Nations Command

Index

About the Author

General John Adams Wickham, Jr., served as the thirtieth Chief of Staff of the U.S. Army. Born in Dobbs Ferry, New York, he was graduated from the U.S. Military Academy. In 37 years of active duty he was Vice Chief of Staff of the U.S. Army; Commander in Chief of United Nations Command and Combined Forces Command and Commander of United States Forces, Korea, and Eighth United States Army; Director of the Joint Staff; and Commander, 101st Airborne Division (Air Assault). He led the 5th Battalion, 7th Cavalry, 1st Cavalry Division (Airmobile) in the Republic of Vietnam and served as the Deputy Chief and U.S. Representative to the Four-Party Joint Military Commission in Vietnam. General Wickham's awards include the Silver Star, Bronze Star (with "V" device), and Purple Heart. After retiring he became the President and CEO of the Armed Forces Communications and Electronics Association and served on the board of the Cooper Institute for Aerobic Research, Honeywell Federal Systems. He and his wife, the former Ann Lindsley Prior, now live in Tucson, Arizona.